Looking for Jimmy

Also by Peter Quinn

Banished Children of Eve

Dry Bones

Hour of the Cat

The Man Who Never Returned

Looking for Jimmy

A SEARCH FOR IRISH AMERICA

PETER QUINN

An imprint of Fordham University Press

New York · 2022

Visit us online at https://www.fordhampress.com/new-york-relit/.

Library of Congress Cataloging-in-Publication Data available online at https://
catalog.loc.gov.

Printed in the United States of America
24 23 22   5 4 3 2 1
First Fordham University Press edition, 2022

Overleaf: Patrick F. Quinn (the author's grandfather), president of the Central
Federated Union, leads the New York City Labor Day parade on September 5, 1904.
The horse was rented for the occasion.

For Thomas More Quinn,
twin, teacher, fellow traveler:
go raibh míle maith agat.

Contents

IV. SILENCE AND HISTORY

CONCLUSION

Looking for Jimmy

Foreword

I often vacillated about whether Jack's life was tragic, comic, or a bit of both, or merely a pathetic muddle. I admit the muddle theory moved me most at this point.
                                            —WILLIAM KENNEDY, *Legs*

A MIX OF REVERIE, REFLECTION, AND HISTORY, *Looking for Jimmy: A Search for Irish America* springs in part from a childhood fascination with relatives and elders who were dismissive of the past. The attitude they handed on, which I've come to reject, was that the specifics of the past are unimportant and, in instances controversial, embarrassing, hurtful, or bloody, are best left to rest in peace—undisturbed and undiscussed.

Fathers and mothers, forgive me. I know what I'm doing, and am doing it anyway.

This is a work in progress, a collection of previously unpublished pieces and, more often than not, articles and reviews substantially rewritten since they first appeared in print. "The Skillins," which recounts a trip to Ireland in the early 1980s, was published in *The Recorder: The Journal of the American Irish Historical Society.* "The Bronx Is Burning," an account of my short career as a court officer, has never before been published. "The Perils of Pat" expands on an article in *Irish America*

Magazine. The focus varies from particulars of family history to the larger historical context, but the same process of exploration and investigation is at work throughout.

While my purpose with this volume isn't to provide definitive, one-size-fits-all answers, I've tried (and will keep trying) not to avoid some basic questions. For example:

Q. Do you have a theory of history?

A. Doesn't everybody?

Q. Can you be more specific?

A. Could I be less?

Q. Then you have no theory?

A. If I did—and I'm not saying I do—it would be close to William Kennedy's take on Jack "Legs" Diamond: the muddle theory. Whether in myth, story, or history, human beings will always be driven to make sense of the past. (And by the way, history is a late entry in that quest, arriving with Herodotus and the Greeks, the day before yesterday, relatively speaking.) Marxists and free marketers view history through the solitary lens of economics. Creationists and believers see the clear workings of a divine plan. Evolutionists and geneticists equate human behavior with biology. On and on.

Neat, simple explanations beckon from left and right. Yet it seems to me that the deeper we dig into the microcosm, the farther out we push into the macrocosm, the subtler our analyses, the harder we delve into the morass of experience, the more we explore the interplay of heredity, history, and serendipity, then the more elusive the answer(s), the more ineffable the muddle. I've tried to get at this in my novels, *Banished Children of Eve* and *Hour of the Cat.*

Q. Did you ever find Jimmy?

A. Those seeking to discover the whereabouts of any Jimmy living or dead—including Jimmy Hoffa—should ask for their money back. My Jimmy isn't an individual but an Irish-American attitude/essence/distillation.

Q. Are you true to history?

A. In my fashion. *Looking for Jimmy* is tentative, subjective and personal. The views and values it reflects were formed in the Bronx-based religious schools I attended from kindergarten through graduate school. A full account of the Irish in America would include the Protestant Scotch-Irish and the many Catholics who settled outside cities. As worthy as their stories are, they are not part of my tale. The Irish America of my search is the one into which I was born— a cohesive urban Catholic community constructed from a peasantry fragmented, transplanted, transformed and defined by the Great Famine and its consequences.

The formative impact of the Famine, it seems to me, was paid little more than lip service, usually in the form of ritualized indictments of British treachery. It's always easier to assign blame for causes, I suppose, than to trace the profound, ordinary and subastral ways in which effects insinuate themselves into institutions and families, playing out across generations. If I beat this drum insistently, well, it's because, through the decade of research and reflection that resulted in my first novel, I came to believe the beating was long overdue.

In youthful innocence, I aspired to academic accreditation as a historian. My intent was to learn Irish (only later did I add Irish-American) history and achieve if not peace with the past, then perspective. I proceeded to the last stages of a Ph.D. in history at Fordham University, where I was a graduate assistant to Professor Maurice O'Connell, great-grandson of nineteenth-century Irish parliamentarian and political chieftain Daniel O'Connell, "The Liberator," who achieved Catholic emancipation but failed in his attempt to repeal the union with Great Britain.

I was fortunate to study under Maurice. Though we banged heads over his decidedly conservative interpretations of Irish history (he was a descendant of Irish landlords, I of Irish peasants), he was a mentor and friend. Along with Professor Frederick Schweitzer at

Manhattan College, whose erudition and Catholic humanism profoundly affected my life, Maurice did his best to cultivate in me a pref-
erence for favoring facts over preconceptions and putting truth ahead
of tribe. I treasure the words of approval that both these mentors
bestowed on *Banished Children of Eve.*

Sadly, as a profession, history proved a bust for me. It turned out
that the demographic wave I surfed into post-graduate study—the
cresting swell of baby boomers now poised to crash on the ineluctable
shore of universal mortality—had already washed over academia, leaving in its wake beached and flopping schools of aspiring professors.

History let me down, but luck proved a lady. In 1979, just as I was
beginning my dissertation, I published an article in the Jesuit weekly
America entitled "An American-Irish St. Patrick's Day." As well as being
my earliest public attempt to reflect on my background, the article led
to me being hired as a speech writer for Governor Hugh Carey of New
York, and to a quarter-century career as a political and corporate prose
monger.

I made a good living mining words for mouths not my own, for
which my family and I are grateful. But my heart was always elsewhere.
The day job was just that. Pre- and post-work, my enduring/consuming
interest remained history, a passion I pursued with fanatical regularity,
rising early each morning to spend two hours at my own labors before
turning to my income-producing responsibilities.

Thanks to that regimen, in addition to my novels, I was able to
produce a steady stream of nonfiction pieces that appeared in, among
other places, *American Heritage, Commonweal, Eiré-Ireland, America,
World of Hibernia,* et al. From 1986 to 1993, at the request of Dr.
Kevin Cahill, another mentor, I was editor of *The Recorder,* a labor of
love that allowed me to stay on top of developments in Irish/Irish-
American historiography and writing. This book draws from that work.
I take sole responsibility for its opinions, assertions, contradictions,
and guesses.

My good fortune as a writer has left me in debt to a large number
of people whose long-term support and encouragement (and, when
necessary, patience and tolerance) has meant everything to me. The
demands of simple gratitude require that I recognize a few: Al Silverman,

the late Tom Flanagan, Terry Golway, Bill Hanlon, William Kennedy, George Hunt, S.J., Dan Barry, Pat Harty, the late Helen Ross, Sandy Teller, Debbie Quinn, Jeff Casper, Mary Gargan, Bob Sullivan, Joan Nicholais, Robert Murphy, Fred Wistow, Bob Rackleff, Reneé Topper, Brendan Loonam, Mike Tuberty, Robin Straus, Peter Mayer, Sheila McGayhey, Ed Adler, and, of course, Kathy, Genevieve, and Daniel.

Q. Are you done looking for Jimmy?

A. I've only begun to muddle.

Q. How long will you continue?

A. As long as I can.

Q. How long is that?

A. That's unknowable. But my mother taught me to hope for the best. It's always been a helpful corrective to the Irish part of me, which tends to expect the worst. Given where Irish America in general and my family in particular began and where they are today, it strikes me as credible advice.

Top of the world, Ma!

—Peter Quinn

Hastings-on-Hudson
September 2006

I. FAMILY AND MEMORY

*Peter A. Quinn (the author's father) on his First Communion.
St. Brigid's Church, New York's Lower East Side (1911)*

Looking for Jimmy

Tell us, doctors of philosophy, what are the needs of a man.
At least a man needs to be notjailed notafraid nothungry . . .
not a worker for a power he has never seen . . . that cares
nothing for the uses and needs of a man . . .
—JOHN DOS PASSOS, *The Big Money*

THE PHOTOGRAPH OF THE ELEVEN IRONWORKERS perched nonchalantly on an I-beam suspended over Midtown Manhattan may not enjoy the same celebrity as Dorothea Lange's Dust Bowl madonna, her handsome face plowed under by want and worry, or Alfred Eisenstadt's sailor kissing the nurse in Times Square on V-J Day, a serendipitous recapturing of Ulysses's return to Penelope, but it is famous enough. Several years ago, I purchased a copy outside the Time & Life Building from a street vendor, who told me it was his best-selling print.

I was drawn to the picture by what a cultural historian might call its "iconic significance." Like those photos by Lange and Eisenstadt, it seems to hold in frozen permanence not just a single moment, but a whole era. It is one of those images that a historical novelist studies for long periods, scanning faces, clothes, gestures, searching foreground and background, in the hope of slipping away from the dead certainties of facts and dates to touch the kinetic intensity of a once living, now departed moment. The novelist's impossible dream isn't merely to distill the subtle particulars, but to unfreeze the entire scene and melt into it, much like the main character in Jack Finney's novel *Time and*

Again, who actually succeeds in transporting himself back to gaslight New York with the help of such visual aids.

I had the print of the ironworkers framed and hung it on a wall in my office. Although I have spent more working hours gazing at it than I care either to count or admit, I have never achieved the long-sought sensation of transtemporal transport.

The discoveries I have made have been more prosaic, the result of a casual mix of research and reverie. According to Phil McCombs, a reporter for the *Washington Post* who investigated the photo's provenance several years ago, the image was taken as part of a shoot done in 1932 by Hamilton Wright, Jr., a professional photographer and pioneer in the practice of public relations. Wright was involved in promoting the construction of Rockefeller Center and snapped this photo as part of that assignment.

McCombs tracked down Wright's son, who told him that either his father "took it personally, or one of his guys." Whichever the case, the man behind the camera caught—or arranged—his subjects in a breathtaking tableau that juxtaposes the run-of-the-mill New York sight of construction workers enjoying a time out with a setting that would turn most inhabitants of terra firma into jelly. The ironworkers appear utterly oblivious to where they are. Aligned not unlike the figures in Da Vinci's *The Last Supper*, they seem as at ease on their steel aerie as the disciples with Jesus in the cenacle.

On the left, a worker lights the cigarette of the man next to him. You can see the muscles in his biceps as he crooks his arm to offer the light. Three men in the middle are having a conversation. Several have what look like rolled-up newspapers in their hands. Four hold what appear to be cardboard lunch boxes. One is shirtless. The man at the extreme right provides the only exception to the subjects' unawareness of being photographed. He holds a flask and stares directly at the camera with a look of grumpy disdain, as though intent on puncturing the illusion of workers on an ordinary break who didn't know a photographer had them in his sights. To me, he has always seemed ready to lift his right hand with middle finger extended, a traditional New York gesture of disapprobation.

* * *

Several years ago, on a book-tour stop in Austin, Texas, I dropped in to a soi-disant New York-style deli that had a poster-size version of the photo framed behind the counter. Usually, I concentrated my focus on the men. My routine was to start with the second figure on the right. He has his cap pulled down over his eyes, but his sharply chiseled profile remind me of my mother's oldest brother, a World War I veteran and roustabout/bartender who died in 1933, fourteen years before I was born, and who I knew only from photographs. This time, however, perhaps because I was seeing it in an entirely new venue, my eyes didn't settle on my uncle's doppelganger, but on the buildings beneath the men's dangling feet, especially the distant dome of the Mecca Temple. (Described in the 1939 *WPA Guide* as "the largest Masonic Shrine in the city," the temple now operates as the City Center.)

Judging by the position of the Mecca Temple, I suddenly realized that the building under construction was the R.C.A. Building (now the G.E. Building), the main tower of the Rockefeller Center complex. I suppose this should have been obvious before, but obvious or not, it hadn't made an impression. Every working day for several years I had been looking out of my office in the Time Warner Building at the very site where the photograph was taken without giving it a thought. This perception of missing the obvious drew me in even deeper. I wondered what else I had overlooked in my years of gazing at the faces mounted on my wall.

The year the picture was taken, 1932, the Dow-Jones Industrial Average, which had reached an all-time high of 381 in September 1929, bottomed out at 41. The American economic slump no longer had the feel of a cruel interlude but of a permanently altered reality in which the collapse or overthrow of capitalism was eminently possible. However, there is no hint of that crisis anywhere in the photograph. In fact, the combination contained in Wright's photo—the obvious brawn and casual daredevilry of the men on the beam, the soaring height of the edifice they are raising, the engineering and financial know-how implied, the sprawling city in the background, and the pall of auto exhaust and factory smoke obscuring Central Park and the Hudson River—all speak of a strength more elemental and enduring than the economic paralysis that was dragging the country to its knees.

The central show of confidence emanates from the men themselves. They are lean and wiry, their toughness of an old-fashioned kind, before Nautilus machines and steroids made the pretentious deltoids of Sylvester Stallone and Arnold Schwarzenegger an archetype of masculinity. These men didn't work at staying in shape. Life saw to it. They all look as though they could handle themselves in a fight, and probably had. They are union workers, men with steady jobs (at least as long as Rockefeller Center was under construction) in a period when millions were just scraping by or standing in breadlines. There is nothing sorrowful about them, no uncertainty or fear in their faces, least of all of heights. It seems the talk going on among them would be natural and relaxed. Their everyday interaction is part of the magic of the scene, a surreal contrast of everyday behavior and extraordinary setting.

In all the years I have studied the faces in the photo, I have found in them a familiarity that goes beyond resemblance to a single uncle of mine. These are faces I knew firsthand in my childhood in the Bronx, faces of relatives, teachers, priests, Christian Brothers, cops, firemen, fathers and brothers of friends, my own father's political associates; Irish faces that, in my mind, have no connection to the fields or boreens of Cork and Tipperary, but are natural to the concrete precincts of New York, to its streets, bars, and parish halls. Looking at them, I am always struck by the thought that what they are sitting upon is more than merely a beam. It is the hyphen between Irish-American, and they are straddling it in perfect equipoise.

Six decades before Wright produced his photograph, the cartoonist Thomas Nast drew a scene with two figures sitting on metal pans, their feet dangling in space. The pans are suspended from the beam of a weighing scale. From the side of the beam labeled "South" hangs the pan holding Sambo, the barefoot, thick-lipped, bug-eyed stereotype of the ignorant Negro ex-slave whose recent elevation to citizenship supposedly threatened to subjugate defeated but chivalrous whites to the rule of "pickaninnies" and scalawags. From the other, labeled "North," hangs Paddy, a grotesquerie that Nast borrowed from contemporary English newspapers and journals and regularly employed as a

December 9, 1876

The Ignorant Vote—Honors Are Easy.

pug-nosed, half-simian representation of Irish ignorance and savagery.
The pans of Nast's scale are in balance: Sambo and Paddy embody the
equal burdens of rural blacks and urban Irish, underclasses that weigh
down the future of America's recently reunited Anglo-Saxon republic.
(The sardonic solution to this dilemma was offered by the British
historian Edward Freeman, who wrote that America might one day be
a great nation "if only every Irishman would kill a Negro, and be hanged
for it.")

The view of Irish Catholics that reigned in Anglo-Saxon America through the later half of the nineteenth century is well described in Harold Fredric's 1896 novel, *The Damnation of Theron Ware*. Frederic's story of the loss of faith by Ware, a Methodist minister in the fictional town of Octavia, New York, is built upon his close encounter with the town's Irish Catholics—"this curiously alien race." Having served only rural congregations, Ware has no previous acquaintance with the Irish. This hasn't stopped him from acquiring a stark and disturbing impression:

> . . . the Irish had been to him only a name . . . But what a sinister and repellent name! His views on the general subject were merely those common to his communion and his environment. He took it for granted, for example, that in the large cities most of the poverty and all of the drunkenness, crime, and political corruption were due to the perverse qualities of this foreign people . . . The foundations upon which its dark bulk reared were ignorance, squalor, brutality, and vice. Pigs wallowed in the mire before its base . . . Above were sculptured rows of lowering ape-like faces from Nast's and Keppler's cartoons, and out of these spring into the vague upper gloom—on the one side, lamp-posts from which Negroes hung by the neck, and on the other, gibbets for dyna-miters and Molly Maguires, and between the two glowed a spectral picture of some black-robed tonsured men, with leering satanic masks, making a bonfire of the Bible in the public school.

The historian and musicologist William H. Williams has done an exhaustive study of the Paddy stereotype as it played out in popular music. In *'Twas Only an Irishman's Dream: The Image of Ireland and the Irish in American Popular Song Lyrics, 1800–1920*, he makes the case that the massive immigration of Famine-era Irish Catholics inundated the cities of the Northeast with Europe's poorest, most unskilled peas-antry, a population with no experience of English-style village life, never mind of rapidly industrializing urban centers. The utter unfamil-iarity of the Irish with the routines and demands of city life, and the absence of any previous immigrant group to blaze a path, or at least offer some hint of how to act or what to do, put the Irish at a distinct disadvantage. They would spend a long time climbing out of what Williams describes as "the worst slums in American history." Yet Williams perceives that their unfamiliarity with cities also gave them an advantage:

> In spite of their peasant origins, they had none of the Jeffersonian suspicion of, or disdain for, the city. Having no place else to go, the Irish burrowed into American cities and came to understand them better than many Yankees, as they turned politics into a profession, instead of a nose-holding duty, a function of upperclass noblesse oblige.

Williams makes clear that Thomas Nast wasn't alone in equating Irish and blacks. (Indeed, one popular mid-century term for blacks was "smoked Irishmen.") On stage, Paddy and Sambo were both childlike buffoons, lazy, superstitious, given to doubletalk, inflated rhetoric, and comic misuse of proper English. Unlike Sambo, Paddy was highly temperamental and always ready to fight, but this easy irascibility didn't diminish their shared status "as an endless source of fun." For both groups, the stereotype became so ingrained in popular attitudes and perceptions that it passed from being regarded as a theatrical parody to being a predeterminant of group behavior. "An Irishman," writes Williams, "taking a drink, getting into a fight, or just generally having a high old time, was not like other men who might drink, fight, or celebrate. He was acting an elaborately scripted role. He was fulfilling a grimly comic prophesy. He was playing the stereotype of himself."

The difference was that, although they lived on the periphery of American society, the Irish were not barred by law as well as custom from trades and professions, or routinely denied their civil rights. The mere fact that they could vote gave them a wedge, which they used forcefully. Starting far behind America's "old-stock" Protestant whites, despised for their religion and clannishness, and burdened by poverty and social dislocation, they were at least allowed to compete. In terms of the theater, the rise of Irish-Americans to prominent places as actors, performers, and songwriters allowed them not merely to suffer the Paddy stereotype, but to change it to their own purposes. In the hands of a writer and producer like Ned Harrigan, whose "Mulligan

Guard" plays were so popular that he had his own theater to house them, the stage Irishman was transformed from goonish Paddy to good-natured, hard-working, decent Pat.

Pat retained elements of the old Paddy caricature. He was volatile and a born brawler. But whereas Paddy had echoed Theron Ware's nightmare vision of Molly Maguires and their wild-eyed cousins who tried to incinerate New York City during the Draft Riots, Pat's combative instincts were tamed and Americanized. Instead of being a term of opprobrium, "Fighting Irish" became the moniker of the 69th Regiment and the University of Notre Dame football team. By the time of World War II, the association of Irish and fighting, once so basic to Paddy's disruptive image, had become a rallying cry for American patriotism. The 1944 movie *The Fighting Sullivans* portrayed a brood of five brawling Irish-American brothers, all lost on the same ship, as the apotheosis of loyalty and sacrifice. In the 1941 movie *Yankee Doodle Dandy*, which celebrated the life and music of the Irish-American actor and songwriter George M. Cohan, the actor playing President Roosevelt says to Cohan (played by Jimmy Cagney), "I like the way you Irish-Americans wear your patriotism on your sleeve." Gone were the days when Paddy was told to not even apply. Now Pat was assured that he was "in like Flynn."

Irish progress from Paddies to Pats was gradual and incremental. It both reflected and hastened the diminishment of anti-Irish prejudice. But it would be misleading to lump the ironworkers in Wright's photograph in either category: as the bog-trotting ape-men of Thomas Nast's imagination, or as suburban-bound Pats about to springboard on the G.I. Bill right into the middle of the American mainstream. These men are of another type. For them, rural Ireland is barely a memory, the never-never land of Tin Pan Alley productions such as *When Irish Eyes Are Smiling* or *A Little Bit of Heaven*. Suburbia is still a white-collar, Protestant place. Their home is the city. It is the context that defines them, and which, in their hard-edged, streetwise style, in their slang and their gait, in the way they hang a cigarette out of their mouths or wear their caps or ogle a girl, they helped define. They are no longer a living part of urban America, but they remain a major ingredient in its genetic composition.

*　*　*

By the time the Depression struck, the urban Irish community that had been created willy-nilly in the aftermath of the Famine no longer ruled New York the way it once had. Along with making the Catholic Irish seem less threatening to America's Protestant majority, the waves of immigrants from Italy and Eastern Europe dwarfed the size and significance of Irish neighborhoods. The reflexive link between urban and Irish, which was forged in the 1840s and '50s and which at one point was so strong in popular music that, as William Williams summarizes it, "an Irish name conjured up the American urban scene," was no longer as all-embracing or surefire as it once had been. Italians came to provide much of the city's rude, unskilled labor. Jews became dominant in entertainment. The African-American migration from the South was adding a dynamic new element to the city's mix.

The relations of the Irish with these groups has mostly been framed in terms of conflict and struggle. Jews have frequently written about the pugnacious belligerence with which the Irish harassed and bullied them. Italians, though nominally sharing the same Catholic religion, found little welcome among the Irish. Black and Irish relations have long seemed synonymous with ethnic bitterness and strife. This was never the whole story, however. With the Jews, for instance, Tammany Hall had early on recognized the potency of their vote, and while many progressives were agonizing over the introduction of a Semitic strain to Christian America, Tammany was working hard to win and keep their loyalty.

Their shared religion might not have produced brotherly love between the Italians and Irish, but it did increasingly lead to inter-marriage. *Coitus vincit omnia.* The parish school I attended in the East Bronx was made up of both Irish and Italians, so that by the 1940s, in addition to classmates named Caesar Di Pasquale and Dennis O'Shaughnessy, there was the Italo-Hibernian Salvatore Monaghan.

The outcome of the Irish-black struggle, which began as a contest over which group would find itself relegated to permanent status as impoverished and oppressed outsiders (a position the Irish peasantry had occupied for centuries), wasn't simply a case of Irish success in using their white skin as a trump card. Upper- and lower-class white

Protestants continued to see Irish-Catholics through much the same lens as Theron Ware. The revival of the Ku Klux Klan in the 1920s was more directed at up-and-coming immigrant Catholics than at segregated and disenfranchised blacks. The Irish presence in Ivy League schools and on corporate boards was tiny.

The gulf that separated urban Irish-Catholics from their white Protestant countrymen was portrayed in a revealing incident that occurred in Camp Mills on Long Island, soon after the entry of the U.S. into World War I. The 69th New York, composed mostly of Irish-Americans, was quartered near the 4th Alabama, a white southern regiment. Relations were bad from the start. Albert Ettinger, a member of the 69th, remembered fistfights breaking out between the two regiments "at the taverns in Hempstead." Tensions mounted further when the 15th New York, "comprised of Negro troops," arrived in camp. In his memoir, *A Doughboy with the Fighting 69th*, Ettinger described what happened next:

> Our boys from the 69th received those of the 15th New York as buddies. Not so the Alabamians. They resented blacks coming into camp. Hell, they resented us! The first thing you know fights erupted all over the place, and the 69th guys actually stood up for the 15th men and fought alongside them against the Alabamians.

The camp commander required the men of the 15th New York— but not the Alabamians—to surrender their ammunition. Ettinger and others of the 69th "thought this was unfair" and slipped ammunition "to our fellow New Yorkers." The black New Yorkers, wrote Ettinger, "never forgot that, and once, when I visited a unit of the 15th in France, some of the fellows thanked me for it."

To the half-Irish, half-German Ettinger, the essential characteristic of the soldiers of the 69th New York was their identification as New Yorkers. Their "whiteness" created no instant camaraderie with "crackers" from the South. They were mightily impressed by the 15th New York in part "because their music was simply out of this world." Led by the famous black musician James Reece Europe, the 15th paraded into Camp Mills with a rhythmic swagger that made them "a sight to behold."

The Negro troops knew how to move. They had style, and what mattered most to profane, sarcastic New York Irish recruits like Joe Hennessy ("a con artist and wiseacre" whom Ettinger summarizes in three sentences: "'Fuck you. If you got any sisters, fuck them too.' That was Hennessy.") was the act of self-assertion, the distinctive way a man carried himself, the unmistakable impression he made. Perhaps because they were off their own turf, in unfamiliar circumstances, Hennessy and company could, at least this once, look past skin color and see in their black counterparts some reflection of themselves.

I suppose it would be possible to compare the roster of the 69th in 1917 with the payroll list (should it still exist) of ironworkers employed in building Rockefeller Center. Given the heavy presence of Irish-Americans in both, it is feasible that a number of the same names would appear. In my free-form contemplation of Hamilton Wright's photo, I have come to imagine that Private Joe Hennessy is the man on the extreme right. Hennessy isn't about to allow himself to appear as if he is swinging over the void with no idea it's all part of a publicity stunt. *Sorry, pal, that's something a cracker might do. But it's not my style.* The sarcasm etched in his face says it: *You know what you can go do, and if you got any sisters, they can go do it too.*

In *Call It Sleep*, Henry Roth's classic novel about his turn-of-the-century Jewish childhood, the boy protagonist scouts out a saloon on Avenue D, not far from my grandfather's real-life saloon on Drydock Street (now Szold Place) between Avenues C and D. To a Jewish child, it seemed a foreign, exotic place:

> In the blue, smoky light of Callahan's beer-saloon, Callahan, the pale fattish bar-keep, jammed the dripping beer-taps closed and leaned over the bar and snickered. Husky O'Toole—he, the broad-shouldered one with the sky-blue eyes—dominated those before the bar (among them, a hunchback on crutches with a surly crimp to his mouth, and a weazened coal-heaver with a sooty face and bright eyeballs) and dwarfed them. While he spoke they listened, grinning avidly. Now he threw down

the last finger of whiskey, nodded to the bartender, tinned his lips and looked about.

Roth identifies Husky O'Toole as an ironworker, just like Hennessy and the others on that beam. A blue-eyed, brawny mick with none of the straight-faced attitudes of Irish-Catholic aspirants to middle-class respectability, O'Toole is regaling his bar mates with tales of his sexual prowess. Boasting that he "doesn't have to buy his gash," he spouts, in classic New Yorkese, a lusty, crude monologue that is as easy to imagine coming out of Hennessy's mouth as his own:

Shet up, down 'ere, yuh bull-faced harps, I says, wait'll I'm troo! Cunt, I says, hot er snotty 'zuh same t'me. Dis gets 'em hot. Dis gets 'em hot I sez. One look at me, I says, an yuh c'n put dat rivet in yer ice-box . . . didja ever see dat new tawch boinin' troo a goider er a flange er any fuck'n' hunka iron . . . de spa'ks wot goes shootin' down. Didja? Will dat's de way I comes.

The Irish working-class types like Hennessy were never of much interest to social scientists. By the 1920s, when urban studies were becoming a formal discipline, the Irish were largely regarded as part of a dying political order or subsumed into faceless categories. The intricate and far-flung parish infrastructure they had built, which created a unique network of schools, hospitals, and charities that paralleled those of secular society went largely unexamined. Hennessy also lacked a full-time literary chronicler. F. Scott Fitzgerald and John O'Hara, who shared Hennessy's ethnic background, were seeking to escape an Irish identity, not draw attention to it. James T. Farrell's Studs Lonigan novels capture some of the nuances of Irish working-class life in Chicago, but often seem (at least to me) one-dimensional.

Yet, if there was little sociological examination of the urban Irish and no poetic witness to do for their quotidian existence what James Joyce did for their Dublin counterparts—to the dense complexity of lives that the privileged often saw as bereft of subtlety or depth—they are not so remote that it is impossible to venture any generalities about the way they were.

The smirk worn by that ironworker on the far right—the one I have identified as Hennessy—was widely applied. One on one, Hennessy would almost certainly be respectful of his parish priest. Together, in a bar, the urban Irish were derisive of everyone in authority, priests included. Sarcasm was embedded in their speech and attitudes. It was used for offense and defense. It was a weapon to cut down anyone in the community who might think or act like he was better than his peers, a pretension that, both in Ireland and America, was most often associated with those trying to gain entry to the realms of WASP culture. Such ambition was regarded as a form of treason. Sarcasm was equally a means for dismissing those realms as the preserve of frauds and pompous lightweights, whose philanthropic interest in the working class was forever motivated by the urge to control and remake them. Sarcasm was a form of subversion, a defense mechanism of colonized people like the Irish.

Boisterously patriotic, the urban Irish had at best a suspicious view of the country's political structure. They generally regarded the country's capitalist economy as a rigged game in which a workingman's best hope was sticking by his union and holding off any outside interference, whether from bosses interested in breaking up the unions or from radicals seeking to make them open to everyone, thus destroying what the Irish regarded as their own best guarantee against immiseration.

The genus Hennessy and his coworkers belonged to was best delineated by those two Jimmies—Walker and Cagney—who personified Paddy's transmogrification from mud-splattered, simpleminded, shillelagh-wielding spalpeen into skeptical, fast-talking urbanite who could never be mistaken for a greenhorn or rube. In his book *The City in Slang: New York Life and Popular Speech*, Irving Lewis Allen recounts how by the middle of the nineteenth century "Irishman's sidewalk" was used as slang for a city street. The implication was that, rather than the sidewalk, "the street was a more suitable place for the hated Irish to walk, or that perhaps they were too dumb to know the difference." Gradually, however, the Irish turned their association with the city streets from a slur into a strength.

In tandem, debonair Jimmy Walker, songwriter and politician, and Jimmy Cagney, the actor-hoofer with the looks of a handsome prizefighter lucky enough never to have had his face smashed in, expressed the style of the urban Irish in its definitive form. These Jimmies had the blend of musicality and menace, of nattiness and charm, of verbal agility and ironic sensibility, of what is known today as "street smarts," that the Irish, as New York's first immigrant outsiders, had developed.

In their desire to belong, the Irish had created a behavior and bearing that was adapted to the pace and demands of the metropolis, a way of life totally different from what they had known in rural Ireland.

Jimmy had his own style of walking and talking that proclaimed his natural place on the sidewalks of New York. You can see it in the newsreels of Walker and in Cagney's films, in their gait, fast and loose, halfway between a stroll and a dance step, an evanescent strut, an electric edginess, as if they find it difficult to stand still, their ears permanently cocked to the syncopation of the streets. They move with the fluidity of tap dancers, a bastardized dance form that, in William H. Williams's analysis, mixes Irish, Lancashire, and African-American steps. When the African-American men of the 15th New York paraded into Camp Mills, they had a high-voltage version of that urban walk, which, as their cheering made clear, the Irish-Americans of the 69th instantly recognized.

Fundamental to Jimmy's style was the presumption that the border between legal and illegal was a question of convenience rather than morality. The unforgivable offense was to be boring or colorless, to surrender to the tedious anonymity of the factory or the tenement. Long before Ronald Reagan obliterated the distinction, Tammany began erasing the line between entertainment and politics. Tammany was woven into the fabric of the city's wards, into the saloons and sporting clubs they were often home to, into the gangs and unions. Tammany was a regular provider of picnics, boat trips, and clambakes, as well as municipal jobs. Tammany's leaders usually made a name for themselves in the social orbit of the saloons before they began a career in politics. Richard Croker, the greediest of all Tammany bosses, began as the leader of a street gang; Charles Francis Murphy, the smartest, was an outstanding baseball player; Al Smith, Murphy's protégé, was an actor and singer.

Nowadays, a public recitation of Tammany sachem George Washington Plunkitt's attack on educated men in politics ("the dudes who part their names in the middle") would be greeted with laughter. But Plunkitt was serious. What did academics have to do with finding men jobs or bringing color and excitement into the monotony of gray streets? How did college equip a man to convey the style and strength that would cause, say, a gang of ironworkers to fall in and follow his lead? Didn't a good shortstop know more about teamwork and facing the opposition than a gaggle of sociology professors?

Jimmy never had time for the theories of educated men. Jimmy belonged to the concrete, to what won the respect of his peers and made him stand out. The urban Irish passion for nicknames—"Mugs," "Red," "Knocko"—evidenced their ceaseless pursuit of an identity that allowed them to stand out, to be a person who didn't sink under the mass sameness the industrial city constantly threatened to impose. From the days of the "Bowery b'hoys" in the 1840s—when a distinct urban street type first appeared—through the flashy, flip, fashionable mayoralty of Jimmy Walker, the Irish were makers and molders of the qualities that set city people apart. In the earliest phase, as immigrant Paddies, the very language used to describe the rough and tumble of the streets became replete with their presence—"hooligans," "shenanigans," "Micky Finns," and "paddy wagons."

Later on, as Jimmies, they pioneered the pose of cool detachment, of sangfroid, on which city dwellers, especially New Yorkers, pride themselves. Perhaps even today, after nearly seven decades, there is no better representation of that pose than the eleven ironworkers casually sitting on an I-beam suspended above midtown. High on their steel perch, their feet dangling in the air like a line of hoofers in mid-jump, the Jimmies of Hamilton Wright's photo continue to embody some part of the bravado of city life, the determination to take everything in stride, never to be caught off balance, always to appear in control.

Verbal agility was another important part of Jimmy's modus operandi. It is estimated that a third of the 1.5 million Irish who fled to America because of the potato famine were native Irish speakers. English was, at best, a second tongue. Like their ancestors had done for centuries, the Irish in America maintained a cavalier attitude toward the English language. They never regarded it as a sacred inheritance, its rules incised in stone, but as a device with which to negotiate their way in an unfamiliar world, to soften their massive dislocation and assert their own identity. English was pliable and elastic, an instrument that could be adapted for purposes apart from grammatical purity.

In Jimmy's hands, one of the irradicable characteristics of urban speech became its glibness; a fast, smooth, non-stop flow that duplicated the pace of metropolitan life and was instantly recognizable as "city talk." The origin of the very word "glib" is uncertain, but one possible source is the forelock that the Irish wore in Elizabethan times and that they tugged on incessantly in their conversations with the English conquistadors. In English eyes, the pulling on the glib and the accompanying torrent of words were pieces of the same sly tactic, a stratagem to distract them from their work of conquest and settlement. The stereotype of Paddy preserved that perception. Paddy, writes Williams, was characterized by "volubility and loquaciousness."

In *Terrible Honesty*, a study of the intense and fecund mongrelization that took place in Manhattan in the 1920s, Ann Douglas traces the evolution of modern urban speech. Although she has little to say about the Irish, it is impossible to scan the pedigree she describes without perceiving the presence of Paddy and Jimmy:

> Just as ragtime developed into the freer and more self-sufficient jazz form, comic Negro and ethnic dialect led to the use of Black English and white self-consciously modern urban slang. The two vernacular branches of the language, Negro and white, had much in common.

Essential to that vernacular, beneath its playfulness, was a hard core of indignation, a pervasive resentment of the subtle and not-so-subtle barriers meant to keep the lower classes in their place. Slang was an implicitly subversive assault on proper grammar and usage, a bastion of social distinction. Irish, Jews, and African-Americans, the three groups most responsible for the formation of urban slang, had long histories as outsiders. In each case, they cultivated a comic style designed to mock the pretensions of the well-to-do and cut the powerful down to size.

Sometimes the underlying resentment was too raw to be cloaked in humor. Ettinger recounts that during his service in France with the 69th he was unjustly thrown into the stockade. When he was released, finally, and returned to the regiment, he started "to blubber like a baby." The chaplain of the regiment, Fr. Francis Duffy (his statue stands in the middle of Times Square), put his arms around Ettinger and helped him express "the irreverence toward secular authority in general so characteristic of the Irish-American Doughboy."

"'All right Albert,' Duffy told him, 'forget about what has happened, just forget it. Repeat after me: TO HELL WITH THEM ALL!'

"'To hell with them all!'

"'Fine! That's the spirit. Say it again louder: TO HELL WITH THEM ALL!'"

It was an old Irish imprecation. The Irish were a people who never "knew their place," or, rather, knew the place that others intended for them but refused to accept it. At least since the sixteenth century, Irish-Catholics had been resisting the laws and customs that assigned them to be "hewers of wood and drawers of water." Their chronic resistance and restiveness led some English observers to detect a racial bent toward querulous insubordination. In America, during his tour of the antebellum South, Frederick Law Olmsted was told by a plantation owner that although the temporary hire of Irish labor was a less expensive alternative to the purchase of slaves, he didn't employ the Irish because they were "dishonest, would not obey explicit directives about their work, and required more personal supervision than negroes."

By the time Hamilton Wright trained his camera on an Irish-American construction crew in 1932, the notion of ethnic and/or racial inferiority, of different groups having a "natural place in the social order," had been clothed in the authoritative-sounding pseudoscientific gibberish of eugenics. Tom Buchanan's outburst in *The Great Gatsby* that "It's up to us who are the dominant race to watch out or these other races will have control of things" echoed the widespread conviction that there was a moral threat to America's Anglo-Saxon genetic stock, the source of the country's greatness, from the growing numbers of immigrants and "colored." (The book cited by Buchanan as "*The Rise of the Colored Empires* by this man Goddard" was in fact by the eugenicist Lothrop Stoddard and was prominently advertised in the debut issue of *Time* in 1923.)

Eugenics had a pervasive influence on American medicine and underlay the widespread sterilization of the "feeble-minded." It also provided scientific rationale for a 1923 revision of U.S. immigration laws, intended to end the influx of southern and eastern Europeans in general, and Jews and Italians in particular. By the 1920s, some eugenicists seemed ready to admit the Irish, or "Celts," to a racial status close to that of Anglo-Saxons. But not all. In *The Passing of the Great Race* (1916), a widely read and highly influential attack on "racial mongrelization," the eugenicist Madison Grant waffled about where the Irish stood.

Grant observed that a physical change had occurred among the Irish in America. The "Neanderthal physical characteristics of the native Irish—the great upper lip, bridgeless nose, beetling brow with low growing hair, and wild and savage aspect"—had largely disappeared. The Irish ape-men of Nast's cartoons had evolved into a more human form. Yet, with the Irish, in Grant's view, looks could be deceiving. When it came to intellectual and moral traits, "the mental and cultural traits of the aborigines have proved to be exceedingly persistent and appear in the unstable temperament and the lack of coordinating and reasoning power, so often found among the Irish."

For many, the irrefutable proof of this unstable and unreasonable temperament was the tie between Irish-Americans and alcohol. The crime and corruption that besieged American cities in the wake of large-scale immigration was believed by many to grow out of the saloon, a putrescent institution joined at the hip with its Siamese twin, the Irish political machine. Prohibition was aimed at extinguishing the whole of saloon culture, which so offended the piety, propriety, and moral sensibility of mainline Anglo-Saxon Protestants.

Had it been attempted a generation or two earlier, Prohibition may have enjoyed a greater chance of success. At least there might have been more of a willingness to put Paddy in his place once and forever. But by the time Prohibition became law, on the eve of the "Roaring Twenties," Paddy had been replaced by Jimmy, and where Paddy had been a hairy, beetling-browed alien, with a "wild and savage aspect," Jimmy was slick, smooth, an evolutionary adaptation to the American scene who not only looked and acted like he belonged, but at some level seemed to embody what urban life was all about.

In the description Ann Douglas gives of Jimmy Walker, she makes clear his emblematic status as a rebel against the country's old code of behavior as well as the newer notion of a genetically predestined upper class:

> The debonair Walker came from working-class Irish stock; however dilatory and scant his reform impulses might be, his sympathies were with the people and they knew it . . . He showed little prejudice against blacks or ethnic minorities; he lifted the restriction against the hiring of black doctors at Harlem Hospital, and he was among the few public officials who greeted Charles Lindbergh in 1927 after his transatlantic flight and found no need for references to Lindbergh's Nordic lineage.

There is a passage in John O'Hara's *From the Terrace* that describes the WASP resentment against the Jimmy-type, the Irish-American who didn't know his place, who thought he could charm his way in, all the time wearing the subversive grin that said, "TO HELL WITH YOU ALL." Though barely removed from his working-class origins, this Jimmy-type knows what to drink and how to dress. He seeks to insinuate himself among the privileged not because he admires their morals or envies their genes but because theirs is the power and the glory and the wealth and the beautiful, sophisticated women. In O'Hara's novel, the WASP protagonist is warned to watch out for a character named Duffy, who is assiduously trying to elbow his way into the smart set:

> . . . there's a difference between a Catholic and a Mick, and Duffy is a Mick. Sharp, shrewd, brilliant, dresses well, good manners and all that. But when I meet an Irishman and I get that instinctive feeling that I

can't trust him, I know he's a Mick. I've had it with grooms and I've had
to fire them . . .

On the screen, the gangsters and hard men Jimmy Cagney
played were powered by a mainspring of Mickness, a tightly wound
inner coil of charm and resentment that could unwind into laughter,
song, or a grapefruit in the face. It was rumored that Cagney's portrayal
of Tom Powers, a street kid on the make, in *The Public Enemy* (1931)
was modeled on Legs Diamond, a Mick from the slums of Philadelphia.
Whether consciously derived from Diamond or not, Cagney caught
the stylish surface and inner ferocity with which the tabloids made
Legs synonymous. As William Kennedy described him in the novel
Legs, Diamond was "one of the truly new American Irishmen of his
day: Horatio Alger out of Finn McCool and Jesse James, shaping the
dream that you could grow up in America and shoot your way to glory
and riches."

Legs in the tabloids and Cagney in the movies raised the urban
Irish hoodlum, a character of long standing in America's cities, to, in
Kennedy's words, a "paradigm for modern urban political gangsters,
upon whom his pioneering and his example were obviously not lost."
Legs was an exaggerated version of Jimmy. Jimmy over the line. Legs
was a vicious gangster, and yet many Americans saw in him something
quintessential to life in the big city. In the case of Italian-American
gangsters like Bugsy Moran and Frank Costello, their adoption of Irish
surnames was more than an attempt to take on less foreign-sounding
monikers. They wanted the aura the Jimmy mobster had, the wiry
Mick in the expensive suit who knew how to handle himself wherever
he went, the docks, the track, the streets, a hoity-toity night club, or a
jail cell. Per Cagney and Hollywood, Jimmy became a celluloid role
model for future generations of non-Irish gangsters.

Because he didn't "know his place," the Jimmy-type was invariably a Mick, and a Mick was naturally at home *in urbe* since this was
the one space in which the very idea of knowing or having a place was
forever in question. The odds are that when they took off their work
clothes some of those eleven ironworkers (young, single, good-looking,
with a steady paycheck) slicked back their hair, put on a jacket and tie,

and hit the clubs and speakeasies on 52nd Street, a stone's throw from where they worked. These watering holes were themselves well known for their casual mélange of clientele that blurred old lines of class and ethnicity, sometimes even of race.

Jimmy traveled around under the impression that he was as good as anyone else, that it all came down to the wad of bills in your pocket. Had he ever heard Fitzgerald's observation that the rich are different from the rest of us, Jimmy would tell you that if you gave him enough simoleons, he would be different too. Class rested on cash, not character, and Jimmy never regarded the pretensions of the upper classes to higher morals or loftier values as anything but that. In many cases, this conviction had been passed down to him by aunts, uncles, and grandparents, the maids and grooms who had lived behind the façades of the Big Houses, in America as well as Ireland, and washed and ironed wardrobes filled with the emperor's clothes.

The career of James Forrestal, the country's first secretary of defense, who committed suicide in 1949, provides a revealing look at the Jimmy-type. A descendant of Famine immigrants, James grew up in the Hudson River town of Beacon, New York. He left as fast as he could, a Mick who shook from his feet the dust of working-class Irish sandlots and headed off for the courtyards of Princeton, the executive suites of Wall Street, and the lush lawns of the North Shore. He knew where he wanted to go and was ready to do what it took to get there. He cut off his relatives, left the Catholic Church, married a WASP, and eventually pushed his way into the inner circles of the Anglo-Saxonry at the moment when the Old Boys were at the top of their game, not only running the country, but thanks to America's pivotal role in World War II, running the planet.

High as he went, however, at base James Forrestal stayed a Jimmy. First there was the face, a classic Irish mug, aptly punctuated by a broken nose. (Put a cap on Forrestal and a pair of work pants and he would make a perfect twelfth on that I-beam.) And then there was the attitude. Though he succeeded in becoming a player, Forrestal could never hide his belief that the game was rigged. He had Walker's cynicism about the eugenic delusion that society's distribution of wealth and privilege was rooted in biology. In the most recent biography of

Forrestal, *Driven Patriot,* Townsend Hooper and Douglas Brinkley write that he had "a detached and sardonic humor, as though commenting on the scene from outside it." One acquaintance wrote that his stance of ironic detachment made him seem "the non-Jewish equivalent of the wandering Jew." According to his son, Forrestal's financial success as a bond trader didn't deter his conviction that "the whole Wall Street apparatus was, in major respects, a discreet conspiracy to protect the already rich."

Forrestal threw himself out a window of the naval hospital in Bethesda, Maryland, in May 1949. He was a burnt-out case, exhausted from his years in Washington. Earlier on, his biographers tell us, Forrestal had perceived "it was better to be rich than poor, white than black, Protestant than Catholic," and aware of the degree to which his background reeked of the lesser essences, he expunged them. Yet, no matter how far he rose into the WASP empyrean, he couldn't rid himself of "the mental and cultural traits of the aborigines." A millionaire and power broker, he lived in a world that he never felt part of, a groom in Brooks Brothers clothing. He was left with a sense of being utterly alone. Perhaps in an attempt to reconnect himself to the world he had abandoned as a young man, Forrestal asked the chief psychiatrist at Bethesda to be allowed to see a Catholic priest. The psychiatrist turned him down because, Hooper and Brinkley speculate, "a Catholic confessional might risk disclosing sensitive national security information." (A wildly anti-Catholic conjecture that, if it truly describes the doctor's reasoning, couldn't have done much to lessen Forrestal's agonized feeling of isolation.)

Forrestal may have traveled too far, too fast, and suffered a case of the psychic bends, but he wasn't alone in his journey. Joe Kennedy was another Mick on the make. Raised in Irish Boston, married to the Irish-American mayor's daughter, Kennedy had no real hope of slinking unnoticed into the ranks of the social elite. He stormed the WASP citadels—Harvard, Wall Street, and the sanctum sanctorum, the Court of St. James—and though he often felt snubbed and out of place, he couldn't be deterred. Early on, he groomed his sons to shove through the breech he made and take hold of the very center of power, the White House itself.

Moving in tandem with the Kennedys was the bulk of Irish America. The social revolution brought about by the New Deal and the G.I. Bill, a revolution the urban Irish political machines endorsed and supported, paved the highways (real and metaphorical) that carried the Irish on the final leg of their journey, from immigrant spalpeens to urban insiders to suburban homeowners and whatever lies beyond. JFK's election was less a last hurrah than the political icing on a socio-economic cake that a great many Irish-Americans were already consuming.

Like Paddy, Jimmy is history. The hard edges of the Irish-American urban experience—the struggle against prejudice, sickness, poverty, the conflicts with other racial and ethnic groups—have been softened by the sepia tint of nostalgia and selective memory. There are still Irish construction workers, cops, and bartenders around, but most commute in and out of the city. The era that Jimmy was part of is dead and buried. Heroic capitalism has been replaced by digital-global-designer capitalism. Magazines no longer run pictures of the type Hamilton Wright took. If he were alive today, Wright would most likely be photographing cyber-geeks at computer terminals.

.   Jimmy's legacy is in the physical infrastructure he helped build —tunnels, bridges, skyscrapers. This is the tangible part. The intangible part requires more searching. Jimmy never stepped foot in the intellectual and cultural inner circles of cosmopolitan New York. (A recent history of the city's intellectual life doesn't even have a reference to Irish or Irish-American in its index.) Jimmy's influence was in the streets, in his understanding that a city is a theater and the street a stage. First off the boat, expelled from the most backward agricultural society in western Europe, totally unfamiliar and unprepared for urban life, Jimmy's ancestors were bereft of a usable past. Yet, though instantly saddled with the Paddy stereotype, they came to see that they had the power to change their role. In the city, whoever the streets belong to gets to define what it takes to belong. Paddy learned that. Jimmy lived it.

Today, you won't find Jimmy where Hamilton Wright did, out on a steel limb. Don't bother looking in any of those phony Irish pubs that make a living selling five-dollar bottles of beer to tourists and money managers. Look instead in the places where attention is paid to all the profound superficialities of the street/stage, how to walk, move, strut, dance. Look where there are no pretty illusions about what it takes to survive or succeed, where everybody knows the odds and appreciates how luck and connections can make the difference between a job and a jail cell, and where you never, no matter what, let on to being impressed or lost or afraid.

Yo, Jimmy.

In Search of the
Banished Children

ⓢⓖ

That's what makes it so hard—for all of us. We can't forget.
—EUGENE O'NEILL, *Long Day's Journey into Night*

MEMORY IS UNIQUE TO EACH ONE OF US, and it is familial, tribal, communal, the seepage into our minds of other memories, an intravenous inheritance, the past in our bloodstream, elixir, narcotic, stimulant, poison, antidote.

I was raised in a family that asked few questions about the past. We lived in a world whose boundaries seemed solid and settled. We knew who we were, took it for granted as naturally and unthinkingly as gender or eye color. We were conscious of being Irish to the degree that almost everyone in the Bronx of the 1950s was conscious of an identity rooted outside New York and America. But our Irishness was largely synonymous with Catholicism and the Democratic Party. It didn't involve much, if any, awareness of Irish history or literature. I never heard my parents mention Yeats or Synge or Joyce. As far as I knew, Brian Boru was a bar on Kingsbridge Road.

The event that first brought my family to America, the Great Famine of the 1840s, was barely part of my family's conscious memory. My father's maternal grandfather, Michael Manning, left Ireland in

1847. He lived into the first decade of the twentieth century and died in a tenement (so the building is described on his death certificate) on New York's Lower East Side. Born in 1904, my father remembered Michael as a blind old man, kindly and attentive.

Michael was born in the 1820s and left Ireland in one of the worst years of a sorrowful decade in which a million people died and over two million, a quarter of the population, took their leave. "The scale of that flight," as David Fitzpatrick has written, "was unprecedented in the history of international migration." Beyond this, I know little of Michael Manning's life. I suppose he was a tenant farmer, part of the mass of Irish peasants who worked holdings of less than five acres and lived in "fourth-class" accommodations—one-room cabins built of turf or loose stone. Two-fifths of Ireland's pre-Famine population existed under such conditions.

There was never any family lore about what Michael Manning did or the specific place where he lived. Just as there were no heirlooms handed down to us from Ireland, not a trunk or dish or stick of furniture, there were no stories or reminiscences rooted in some particular corner of the countryside.

Michael's wife, my great-grandmother, was Eileen Purcell. Perhaps Michael met Eileen on the journey over or perhaps they were already married and left together. I'm unsure. Soon after they arrived in America, Michael and Eileen came to the village of Fordham, then a part of Westchester County, in which, I was told, relatives of Eileen had already settled. Michael worked a farm he owned, or more likely leased, across the road from the College of St. John, which Archbishop John Hughes had recently entrusted to the Jesuits, and supposedly earned extra money by cobbling the boots of the reverend fathers. My grandmother, Margaret Manning, was born on that farm, in what is now the Central Bronx, in 1868.

Eventually, Michael ended up back in Manhattan, drawn perhaps by the prospect of a job. By the time she was in her teens, his daughter, my grandmother, was working as a seamstress. Michael eventually came to live with her and her husband. He seems to have spent his life as a man of no property and little luck.

My father, who was more interested in the past than my mother, or at least more willing to talk about it (she militantly disliked and discouraged such activity), sometimes seemed to weave his stories from the twin spools of truth and fancy.

Michael Manning, for instance, had a brother Robert who sailed to Galveston, Texas, in the same year that Michael left for New York. (According to my father, Robert had only the vaguest notion of his destination and how far away he would be from New York.) Although there is no surviving picture of Michael, there is a faded daguerreotype of Robert taken in New Orleans in the 1870s. In a spidery, hesitant scrawl, it is inscribed on the back, "To my dear brother Michael." Robert died in a cholera epidemic in 1876.

My father, however, was fond of recounting a tale in which Michael and Robert were almost reunited during the Civil War. Michael, the story went, worked as a hand on the boats that ferried Confederate prisoners from Newport News, Virginia, to imprisonment on Blackwell's Island, in the East River, and Robert, who had joined the famous "Louisiana Tigers," was one of those prisoners. Neither brother was aware of how close they had come to meeting one another until the war ended and they resumed their correspondence.

It is possible that there is truth in this story. Working on a prison boat may well have been one of the many jobs Michael Manning held throughout his life. Robert perhaps served in the Confederate army. Yet the neat recapitulation of the Civil War's fratricidal tragedy is so transparent that I regard it as a romantic embellishment on the otherwise unadorned lives of these two men.

At one point, in pursuit of an Irish passport, I did some research into the life of my mother's mother, Catherine Murphy (née Riordan), who listed her place and time of birth as Blarney, County Cork, in November 1868. I could find no person of that name born in Blarney within two years—plus or minus—of that date. A friend of mine, a priest in Ireland, undertook an exhaustive search for me and turned up the 1858 marriage certificate of Catherine's parents, Patrick Riordan and Mary Looney (both listed "labourer" as their occupations; Mary, at age 18, is described as a "spinster"). He also found the baptismal records of four infants from this marriage who apparently died soon after their births. The trail grew cold after this. I still don't know where and when Catherine was born.

The immigrant past I inherited was more generic than specific, a shared sense of the "No Irish Need Apply" prejudices that our forebears had faced and overcome. I knew Catherine Riordan worked as a maid, and detested the job, but I have no idea where she was employed or by whom. There were no individual lives offered to us as examples, Horatio Alger-style, of how to get ahead, no family lore minted into a coinage that was to be treasured and reinvested, a moral patrimony passed from one generation to the next, emblazoned with the hortatory motto, "Go thou and do likewise."

The only real record of their lives that I have is from their self-described "betters," the social critics and reformers whose well-intentioned interest in the "other half" was almost always tinged with condescension, if not outright contempt, an attitude which, in the case of the Irish, drew on old and enduring stereotypes that were common to Anglo-Saxon culture on both sides of the Atlantic.

Writing about the New York slums in 1890, Jacob Riis remarked on the inability of segments of the population to pull themselves up and move on to something better. He found the Irish in particular, who had arrived en masse in the 1840s, susceptible to this inertia: "The result is a sediment, the product of more than a generation in the city's slums that, as distinguished from the larger body of this class, justly ranks at the foot of tenement dwellers, the so-called 'low Irish.'" (Today we call these second- and third-generation slum dwellers "the under class" and blame their condition on government programs.)

In the view of Riis—a view that had been shared by Charles Loring Brace and other early philanthropists—the Roman Catholicism of the Irish and their romantic Celtic temperaments hobbled their progress and made them lag behind admirably ambitious immigrants like the Germans and Scandinavians.

"Down in the streets," Riis wrote, "the saloon, always bright and gay, gathering to itself all the cheer of the block, beckons the boys." In many such blocks the census-taker found men, women, and children who called the saloons home:

> This picture is faithful enough to stand for its class wherever along both rivers the Irish brogue is heard. As already said, the Celt falls most read-

ily victim to tenement influences since shanty-town and its original free-soilers have become things of the past. If he be thrifty and shrewd his progress henceforward is along the plane of the tenement, of which he assumes to manage without improving things.

The prevailing angle from which we get our view of how the great mass of poor and working people lived (and most often they were not the "other half" but the other three-quarters or nine-tenths) has been from above, with all the inevitable distortions and omissions this implies. As given to us, these lives seem flat, gray, undifferentiated, an existence without density or subtlety, without the emotional complexity that marks every human community, wherever it is found.

For their part, the poor have traditionally lacked not only the education and time to record their lives, but also lacked the interest. The stories the poor carried with them were rarely about their own particular travails and tragedies. These events weren't remarkable or exceptional, but the everyday context of life itself. For people steeped in rural existence, or only recently in transition from it, the storytelling they were familiar with was communal rather than individual. It offered mythic explanations of evil, death, failed crops, cures, curses, the feared or welcomed interventions of heroes, fairies, angels, saints, or God Himself.

On arriving in the cities of America, these stories quickly shrivelled in meaning and significance. The old may have continued to tell them, and the young pretended to listen, but the landscape and mindscape that nourished them were lost forever. Besides, there were new fables to take their place, new tales and incantations, the mass-manufactured entertainments of vaudeville and Tin Pan Alley, dime novels, newspapers, sheet music, variety shows.

Even if the opportunity had presented itself for the Famine Irish to make a full accounting of their story, it is questionable how many would have done so. In their day, the assertion of victimhood—of subjection, mass poverty, starvation, flight—was not a way to gain attention or claim a voice in the country's political conversation.

American triumphalism was at full tide. Irish self-assertion usually tried to mirror the arguments made in favor of Anglo-Saxon exceptionalism. The emphasis was on Irish virtue, on the purity of their religion, the antiquity of their origins, and the bravery of their soldiery. Like England, Ireland had long been a nation of stouthearted peasants and high-minded noblemen. Ireland, however, had been undone by treachery and by superiority of numbers, so the story went. Even John Mitchel's famous howl of protest was short on individual examples of what the Famine did, on the class aspects of the suffering and want among the poor, and long on English perfidy.

Of all the New York Irish families I know who can trace their American origins back to the Famine migration, not one possesses a single artifact or memory from that time. Yet over a million Irish crossed South Street into America in that single decade. Given the sheer volume of this passage as well as its nature—described by historian Robert James Scally as bearing "more resemblance to the slave trade or the boxcars of the Holocaust than to the routine crossings of a later age"—and the immense disaster in Ireland that caused the most horrific spectacles of civilian suffering in nineteenth-century Europe and drove most of them to leave, the silence around these events seems at first hard to explain.

Here again, I think, this silence in part describes the plight of the poor throughout history. Out of all the millions who have endured deprivation and brutalizing poverty, out of all the families pulverized by punishing degrees of want, how many memoirs are there? How many detailed renderings of the conditions of the destitute—of broken hopes, lives, communities—do we have from the hands of those who suffered these events? Hasn't it been the experience of every group to let the dead bury the dead, to get on with the business of survival and hide or romanticize a record of degradation that might be embarrassing as well as painful?

It is not hard to imagine why many of the Famine immigrants chose not to instill in their progeny a vivid recollection of what was left behind in Ireland or encountered in America. "My mother was left, a stranger in a strange land, with four small children," James Tyrone tells his son in Eugene O'Neill's *Long Day's Journey into Night*. "There was no damned romance in our poverty."

The Famine migrants suffered not only physical want and deprivation, a lack of food, the debilitating rigors of living on the road, of a journey across the Irish Sea or the Atlantic, often under brutal and dangerous conditions, but deeper scars as well. The effects of their own powerlessness, of humiliating dependency on landlords and government officials, were imprinted on their minds and souls, on their communal character. "The Famine," as one Wicklow farmer put it, "left the survivors so sad in themselves," and "made many a one hard, too."

Dead children are not such stuff as dreams are made of. Or mass graves. Or tuberculosis, cholera, and typhoid. Or illiteracy and rude physical labor. Or alcoholism. The memory of the streets of New York during the Draft Riots of 1863—of the pent-up rage of the Famine Irish, of firing from rooftops at Federal troops, of looting, arson, and lynchings—was never likely to be cherished and passed down.

The saga of the Famine Irish is studded with reminders of the bitterness these people carried with them. It is there in the story of the Irish deserters from the American army who went over to the Mexicans and formed their own brigade, the San Patricios. Preferring to fight with the Catholic Mexicans against the Protestant Americans, the San Patricios were the only group of deserters in American history to band together in the service of a foreign enemy. Those who were caught were hanged en masse by the Americans.

The Famine echoes loudly in the court-martial of Michael Corcoran, the commander of the 69th New York Militia. Corcoran served in the treasury police in Ireland during the Famine and resigned in protest against the policies of Her Majesty's Government. After arriving in New York, he became a founding member of the Fenian Brotherhood, the secret revolutionary society built upon the Famine's legacy.

In October 1860, the Prince of Wales (the future Edward VII) made the first visit of a member of the Royal Family to the United States. His arrival in New York created a high degree of excitement, except among the Irish, to whom His Royal Highness was known as the "Famine Prince." As part of the official welcome, Governor Edwin Morgan ordered the militia to march in the Prince's honor, but Corcoran refused, and the regiment stood by him. In perhaps the only instance of such an ethnic mutiny in American history, Corcoran accepted a court-martial rather than obey.

* * *

The Famine immigration changed the American ethnic equation. The rural Catholic culture of the Irish, the beliefs and mores of peasants accustomed to living in tight-knit, pre-capitalist communities with little experience of the yeoman individualism of English or American farmers and few of the entrepreneurial skills of other immigrants, introduced a new element of confusion and conflict. White America would never have the same degree of homogeneity that it did before the Famine.

Beginning in the 1840s, New York and other cities entered a period of rioting and public violence that wouldn't be repeated for another century. In addition to the week-long horror of the Draft Riots, the city witnessed one of the bloodiest incidents in American urban history, the Orangeman's Day Riot of 1871, when the militia opened fire on a crowd protesting at a Protestant parade through a Catholic area, shooting a hundred people and killing more than forty.

As a result of the swelling numbers of Papist foreigners being washed up on the East Coast, the largest third-party movement in American history took wing. Though subsequently overshadowed by the slavery question, the anti-Catholic, anti-Irish, anti-foreign impetus this movement embodied remained strong and could be easily stirred. In the aftermath of the Famine, controls were put on immigration that hadn't existed before.

The great wave of immigration set off by the Famine swept over America and changed the face of the country. In terms of sheer brawn and sweat, the Irish would provide much of the cheap labor that built America's infrastructure of canals and railways. The work was brutal and unremitting. Tensions between American bosses and Irish laborers often ran high. In the coal fields of Pennsylvania, the Molly Maguires became synonymous with labor radicalism and terrorism, and the mass hanging of twenty of them in the 1870s, most of whom were from Donegal, was intended as both punishment and warning.

The summary description that Peter Way gives of Irish canal workers in the pre-Famine period might as easily be applied to a large number of the Irish who arrived in its wake:

They were paid poor wages, toiled under severe conditions, and regularly found themselves without work. As a result, they and their families were drawn into a marginal existence along public work lines, lucky to live at a subsistence level and wholly exposed to the vagaries of the market . . . [T]hey served the essential function of feeding industry's fluctuating need for labour. They were the miners and sappers of capitalism, sent in to undermine the old order and to lay the foundations of the new, dispensed with when the war was won. Few made it up through the ranks, or even out of the trenches, regardless of which industrial army conscripted them.

As the century wore on, the panicked, desperate nature of the Famine years receded. The three million people who formed the broad base of Ireland's social pyramid—those cottiers and laborers who lived at a subsistence level—had either died or left. The new immigrants from Ireland were more likely to have some experience farming besides potato cultivation. A growing number would head west to try their hand at homesteading.

In the cities, the Irish created their own neighborhoods and a tightly-woven network of parishes, unions, and social and political organizations. In a single generation the Irish went from the most rural people in western Europe to the most urbanized in North America. As Kevin Whelan has pointed out, "the cities of the Irish were in America, not in Ireland." Here, they began the process of recovering from the shattering experience of the Famine, of unbending from the defensive crouch it had forced them into, of building a new identity in America that preserved their deep sense of being Irish as it prepared them to compete in a country in which the hostility they faced was interwoven with possibilities for advancement that had never existed before.

The political, religious and labor organizations formed by the Famine immigrants became the basic infrastructure of Irish-American life for the next one hundred twenty years. A century after my great-grandfather Michael Manning landed in New York, I attended Catholic grammar school, high school, and college in the Bronx, in institutions all founded in the 1840s by the Famine generation. I did my graduate studies across the street from the fields Michael Manning had worked, and was taught by men whose predecessors' boots he had repaired and shined. My education was paid for by my father's political career, in the Bronx organization run by Ed Flynn, and my father in his turn had been pushed ahead by his father, a union organizer. Though rarely remembered or discussed, the inheritance of the Famine surrounded us.

The cohesiveness of the Irish was often remarked upon. Their own culture put an emphasis on communalism and sociability, and the entrenched antipathy of many Americans to all things Irish and Catholic helped to turn those traits into necessities. But the Famine also set in motion what one historian has called "a vagabond proletariat" that went wherever there were jobs which required little more than muscle and a shovel. Sometimes these migrants stayed together. Not infrequently, I think, they wandered off, or their children did, their descendants rapidly losing any conscious sense of an Irish past or identity.

I was reminded of these Irish vagabonds by Don Graham's 1989 biography of Audie Murphy, *No Name on the Bullet.* The most decorated American soldier in the Second World War, Murphy grew up in North Central Texas. On his mother's side, Audie descended from old southern stock. His father, Emmett Murphy—or Pat, as his friends called him—had a decidedly different pedigree. Pat's father, George Washington Murphy (oh, how the Irish loved that name! The way it rang with the notion of the British Empire turned upside down!) came to Texas from Louisiana in 1872.

The original Murphys, George Washington's parents, arrived in New Orleans as part of the Famine migration. Perhaps, like my own great-granduncle Robert Manning, they had landed in Galveston and then traveled to New Orleans to rejoin a substantial Irish community. In any event, about the same time Robert died from cholera, George Washington Murphy traveled to Texas in search of an American future that turned out to have a lot in common with the Irish past. As Graham tells us, the Murphys were decidedly unsuccessful, and Audie's father was a tenant farmer remembered by many for what seemed feckless inertia:

> Emmett Murphy wasn't a very good provider. He might have worked hard in his life—there were neighbors who said he was a good worker

(but many more who said he wasn't)—but what he did never seemed to amount to much in the long run. Or the short run, for that matter. He liked to go to town and play dominoes, and he didn't mind gambling a little bit if he had any walk-around money, which most of the time he didn't. After the war, Audie wrote that his father "was not lazy, but he had a genius for not considering the future."

It is possible to find in Emmett Murphy's life Irish continuities that don't exist. Maybe Emmett was just another poor white tenant farmer scraping out a hardscrabble existence. But it requires no historical sleight of hand to discover in the description of Emmett—in the man's love for music and for company, in his poverty, drinking, and resignation to life's failures and futilities, in the disapprobation of his more earnest, determined neighbors—the tendrils of the Irish past, of the Famine and its pain.

The Irish Famine of the 1840s and the Jewish Holocaust of the 1940s are very different events and should not be confused or equated. Neither a passing pogrom nor a sudden outburst of ethnic violence nor a wartime atrocity nor, as in the case of the Famine, the turning of a natural catastrophe to the brutal purposes of social engineering, the Holocaust was a death sentence leveled against every Jewish man, woman, and child under German rule. No exceptions. None. The full force and organizational power of the modern industrialized state were dedicated to bringing about the total eradication of the Jews. As terrible and as traumatic as the Famine was, as formative of all that followed in Irish and Irish-American history, it was not that.

In the underlying justification of official policies and in the attitudes of those who survived, however, there are similarities. By the time the potato blight struck, the fixed and time-honored image of the Irish in the mind of the British public was a people whose main role in the United Kingdom was as problem, scourge, infection, perpetual nuisance, and source of national weakness and unrest.

The *London Times* was expressing a widely shared view when, in 1847, at the height of the Famine, it editorialized that "by the inscrutable but invariable laws of nature, the Celt is less energetic, less independent, less industrious than the Saxon. This is the archaic condition of his race . . ." Within a century, buttressed by the bogus medical and scientific logic of eugenics and racial biology, the National Socialists had codified nature's "invariable laws" into the state's and, in applying them against the Jews, taken the underlying logic to its psychotic conclusion.

Among the survivors of both events what is at once strikingly similar is their silence. Each group had watched its world be shattered in such a way that demolished the comforting illusion of Providence having set a limit to human suffering. The survivors of the Holocaust resisted looking back. It would take the rigorous proddings of a new generation of historians and documentary filmmakers to piece together the record of astounding cruelty and unparalleled depravity which had been inflicted on the Jews of Europe, a process driven in part by the attempt of Nazi apologists to deny the Holocaust had ever happened.

Such a challenge was never made against the Famine. There were few if any arguments about the scope or impact of the disaster that had befallen Ireland. Nationalists and government officials, Protestant missionaries and Catholic bishops, relief workers and journalists, all agreed on the epochal nature of what had taken place. Though the responsibility for the magnitude of the suffering and dislocation might be argued, the dimensions of the event provoked little debate.

Asenath Nicholson, a widowed American temperance crusader and Protestant evangelist who arrived from New York on the eve of the Famine to distribute Bibles among the Catholic poor and stayed to become a one-woman relief expedition, left behind a vivid record of what she had witnessed:

> The work of death now commenced; the volcano, over which I felt Ireland was walking, had burst, though its appearance was wholly different from anything I had conceived; a famine was always in Ireland, in a certain degree; and so common were the beggars, and so many were always but just struggling for life, that not until thousands were reduced to the like condition . . . did those, who had never begged, make their wants known. They picked over and picked out their blackened potatoes, and even ate the decayed ones, till many were made sick, before the real state of the country was made known; and when it fell, it fell

like an avalanche, sweeping at once the entire land . . . [T]he wave rolled on; the slain were multiplied; the dead by the way-side, and the more revolting sights of families found in the darkest corner of a cabin, in one putrid mass, where, in many cases, the cabin was tumbled upon them to give them a decent burial, was somewhat convincing, even to those who had doubted much from the beginning.

Somewhere in the mass of statistics compiled on the Famine—bowls of soup distributed, evictions, deaths from fever, departures, etc.—are my ancestors. Over the years, as I poked at the fringes of those lives, as I tried to piece together some coherent record of the long day's journey of my family from Famine Ireland to the Bronx of my childhood, I came to realize that in their particularity, in their individuality, these people were beyond my knowing. They had been swallowed by the anti-romance of history, immigrant ships, cholera sheds, tenement houses. They had dissolved into genetic influence, pigment of skin, size of feet, shape of nose, into unconscious inheritance, presumptions, fears, ambitions, into thin air: the exhalation of the past that shapes the present, like the glassblower's breath in the bubble of hot, melted sand.

Even amnesia, the absence of remembrance, cannot erase the imprint of the past. Recalled or unrecalled, memory is embedded in the way we love, hope, believe. Tamed, sublimated, suppressed, it will not disappear. It pulls on us like the moon's elemental urgings on the sea. Full, gibbous, eclipsed, obscured by clouds, or enthroned as regent of the sun, memory has its sway, a distant, immediate, irresistible direction: neap and spring tides.

Memory is more than a recollection of discrete events, battles, inaugurations, assassinations. It is more than history proper. Memory is a reel of endless, haunted gossip, a montage of snippets, remnants, patches, whispers, wisps, the way our parents held us, the acceptance or reluctance in their arms, shadows on the nursery wall, the smell of cut grass, chalk dust, mother's breath.

Eventually, in my search for my family's past, I turned away from history. I tried to reach beyond the quantifiable, factual material of the historian to explore the territory that belongs to imagination alone: the ordinary moments of ordinary, unrecorded lives.

I set out to write a novel. At an early stage in the process, I visited Ireland and traveled to my sister-in-law's relatives outside Skibbereen, in County Cork. I stayed with her uncle, who brought me to meet a relative of his, Bernard O'Regan, then in his nineties, who as a boy had known some of the people who had lived through the Famine which had devastated the area around Skibbereen.

Sometime after the turn of the century, when he was a small boy, Bernard remembered watching an old man of strange and tortured gait struggling up the boreen to the O'Regan house.

Bernard had heard his parents talk of the man and of the reason for his twisted legs and awkward stride. As a child during the Famine, the man had collapsed from hunger and been taken for dead. Rather than see him consigned to a mass grave, the boy's mother consented to his legs being broken so he could be fitted into the only coffin that was available. When his legs were snapped the pain forced out a deep moan that saved him from being buried alive.

That old man is in my head. He walks the lanes of Ireland and the streets of New York. He is at home in both places. He has the face of Robert Manning in the photograph. He is glad to be alive. Though his sticklike legs are bent and there is a queer swivel to his hips, he has no pain, and when he dances, it is impossible to tell his legs were ever broken at all.

The Skillins

—A nation? says Bloom. A nation is the
same people living in the same place.
                    —JAMES JOYCE, *Ulysses*

"THIS," SAYS FRANKIE O'DRISCOLL, pointing at me, "is my cousin
from America." Invariably, this is how Frankie introduces me
to the friends and neighbors who come into his kitchen to discuss a broken fence or a lost cow or the state of the world, and to examine the stranger—his American identity written all over him—who got
off the bus by Ita Fitzgerald's house and walked down past Minahan's
Pub to Frankie's.

Some of them I've met before. Yet, on a spring morning in the
early 1980s, in this small cluster of farms outside Skibbereen, County
Cork, the arrival of visitors is still observed with careful ceremony. I sit
in a corner, and the conversation rattles on until there's a pause.
Frankie turns and goes to the stove and puts on a pot of tea, and the
neighbor, looking around for a chair, says, "Do you find things more
expensive here in Ireland than in the States?"

Frankie doesn't give me a chance to answer. "The only thing more
expensive here than anywhere else is sex," he says. He roars with
laughter at his own joke. Frankie is my only relative in Ireland. Actually,

he is a relative only in the most extended sense: the uncle of my brother's wife. But by mutual agreement we refer to each other as cousins. Frankie welcomes the idea of having another cousin in America, and I have always wanted a flesh-and-blood connection to Ireland, someone to embody the vague yet deeply sensed ties that were part of my Irish-American childhood.

I go to Ireland every few years for vacation. Occasionally, my roles as a writer and member of the staff of New York's governor have taken me to Northern Ireland to gather facts. In the North the facts have never been hard to find. The place is afflicted with facts, hard and bloody facts—religion, class, nation, martyrs, rebellions, assassinations, plantations, executions—Catholic facts, Protestant facts, Irish facts, Loyalist facts. Facts that explode and kill.

Whether it is business or pleasure that takes me to Ireland, I always manage to make the time to spend a few days with Frankie. He never asks about the North. If I bring it up, he says, "They're all mad, but you're madder still for going there." Mostly we talk about New York and Skibbereen.

Frankie is convinced that there isn't a great deal of difference between the two places. He imagines New York is five or six times larger than Skibbereen—a farming and resort town of about 3,000 people—and that their problems differ in quantity, not quality.

"The people of this area," he explains, "are the laziest people on earth. That's a good thing and a bad thing. It means most people are poor when they don't have to be. But if they had any energy they'd only be up to no good, anyway."

Recently, someone stole one of Frankie's calves, and although he was as angry as I've ever seen him, he seemed to take satisfaction in proving to me once and for all that for sheer criminality, Skibbereen was New York's equal. "I don't know," he said, "but I don't see how New York could be worse than Skibbereen." For Frankie, romantic Ireland is a non-starter.

Frankie is a bachelor. But even at fifty-two he is not beyond the age when many Irish farmers marry. He is strong, in the solid, thick way that farmers are strong—no toning of muscles, no hint of body-building, Nautilus machines, jogging. But his strength is at first hidden by the loose-fitting, mud-spattered black suit jacket he wears everywhere except to church, and by his boyishness: a gentle, credulous inquisitiveness and a high voice made even more pronounced by the singsong cadence—the rhythm of Gaelic, I think—in his speech.

Despite his jeremiads on Skibbereen's declining mores and morals, the area has the ould-sod loveliness that the Irish Tourist Board uses on its posters to lure Americans: wild, wind-torn landscape; rugged coast; cloud-riddled Atlantic sky; small, neat farmhouses—everything in Aer Lingus order.

For as long as anyone can remember, Frankie's family has fished these waters and lived on these lands. Until this century they were unable to speak English—cut off from Europe, existing in their own world, observing their own customs, keeping their own myths, a people apart. Sir Edmund Spenser, the English poet and courtier, wrote *The Faerie Queene* not far from here (to the north, at Kilcoman, nearer to Macroom where my own grandfather was from). Spenser described the Irish natives as "stubborn and untamed," willfully ignorant and treacherous, delighting in "licentious barbarism." The Irish in the area left no written opinion of Sir Edmund, but in 1598 they burned down his house, killing his infant child, and drove out his retainers. Woodcuts from the sixteenth century by Albrecht Dürer depict these "wilde Irish;" a shaggy-haired people, barefoot, their bodies wrapped in great woolen mantles, exotic and ferocious, as foreign to Renaissance Europe as the Hottentots or the American Indians.

Whenever I picture my Irish-American relatives in these outfits, I laugh. Even Frankie—red-cheeked, wild-haired, iron-muscled Frankie—comes out looking sheepish, as if wrapped in an enormous bathrobe. I have thought of mentioning this to Frankie, but he always looks at me a little strangely when I start mentioning names like Spenser and Dürer and go on about history.

History for Frankie is a specific place and a specific people. It is the land, his mother, his farm; people he knew, faces and events tied to family names; drownings and deaths and uprisings told in stories and songs that have been repeated over and over again. My litany of disembodied names and facts—Parnell, O'Connell, Chief Secretaries, Lord Lieutenants, parliaments, Orangemen—baffles him.

"Spencer?" he will say to me. "We had a Spencer here, Spencer Tuttrell, an evil bastard. He set his dog on my mother one day because she was walking across his land without permission, the bastard. I wish he was alive so I could break him in half."

During the Great Famine of the 1840s, when large parts of rural Ireland dissolved in chaos and starvation, Skibbereen was the scene of some of the country's worst suffering. In a letter to the *London Times*, in December 1846, Mr. Nicholas Cummins, a Cork magistrate, wrote of "scenes of frightful hunger" around Skibbereen, and described "ghastly skeletons" barely able to move:

> Suffice it to say, that in a few minutes I was surrounded by at least 200 such phantoms, such frightful spectres as no words can describe, either from famine or fever. Their demoniac yells are still ringing in my ears, and their horrible images are fixed upon my brain.

Here, almost one hundred forty years later, there is little or no trace of that suffering. There are a few local monuments to the Famine victims. (Indeed, there are few such monuments anywhere in Ireland. One of the only public references to the Famine I have seen is an advertisement for a restaurant, which reads: "Established 1847—the year of the Great Famine. Adjoining the car park is a Famine mass graveyard.")

In 1980, one of Skibbereen's last links with the era of the Famine was broken. Dick McKenna, the last of Skibbereen's "spalpeens," died. Though in his late seventies (Dick was never exactly certain of his age), he worked as a hired man, a spalpeen, traveling from farm to farm, renting out his labor. Once there were thousands around Skibbereen who made their living this way, men without land or a house. The Famine fell heaviest on them and their families. It swept them away; to Australia, to America; to graves, undivided, beside a car park.

"Dick had more brains than the ones that come out of university nowadays," Frankie said to me. "He was never in a school, except to piss, but he knew all about the world and he knew his history, the history of the world and of Skibbereen.

"Once when he was near starving to death, I took him in to live with me. I offered to hire him permanently. But permanent was a word made him nervous. Yerra, though, he was grateful. 'Frankie O'Driscoll' says Dick, 'we haven't seen your like since the men who went to fight the wars of Troy.'"

Frankie wasn't born in Skibbereen. He comes from the Skillins, a tiny archipelago that sweeps south, from the coast of Cork out into the Atlantic. If you walk out the back door of his farmhouse, up the meadow to the crest of the hillock, you can see the Skillins. They are small, rugged islands, treeless, with tiny beaches and angular, sandy cliffs. Behind them, far in the distance, is the much larger Cape Clear Island, which looks green, almost tropical. Beyond Cape Clear, out of sight, is the Fastnet Rock and its famous lighthouse.

The largest island in the Skillins is St. Killain, the island of Frankie's birth. Skillins is in fact a corruption of St. Killain, named for the Irish monk who came there in the sixth century to escape the world. His community flourished until the ninth century, when the Vikings sacked the monastic settlement and drove the survivors to the mainland. The ruins of a church—three low walls on a small cliff—are the only reminder of the monks' presence.

Frankie's family rented St. Killain sometime after the Famine— he's not sure exactly when—from the Tuttrells, the Anglo-Irish landlords who owned most of the land in this area. The Tuttrells left the area in the 1920s, during "the Troubles" (the generic name the Irish give to their revolutions and civil wars), and with the help of the government, Frankie's parents were able to buy the island.

Their life was brutally difficult. They had to tear a living from between the island's stones, planting potatoes in small patches of earth, lugging seaweed up from the beach to use as fertilizer, rowing back and forth the two miles to the mainland, often in the midst of storms. When he wasn't farming, Frankie's father fished, going out into the Atlantic in an open boat for days at a time. His parents died early. "Sheer exhaustion," says Frankie. Some of his seven brothers and sisters went to England, others to America. Frankie stayed. Finally, in 1956, he sold the island.

It has passed through several hands since then. The present owner is a lawyer from England who uses it as a summer home. He has joined the old one-story stone house to the small stone barn next to it and let the weather wear away the whitewash that once covered the stones. "It looks more natural that way," he told Frankie. Or so Frankie claims—if he quotes the lawyer, it is only to let the man condemn himself.

After citing some incriminating inanity, Frankie usually drops the conversation, falling silent—his signal to change the subject. I press him for more facts on the island, saying that it is a matter of history and that it is his responsibility to preserve what he knows. "History, my arse," Frankie answers.

The first several times I visited him, Frankie refused to take me out to St. Killain. "There's nothing out there," he kept saying. It was easy enough to see that Frankie despised the lawyer. But it wasn't a case of Irish animosity for the English. Frankie would have resented anyone who could own that island without working it, who didn't break his back to hold on to it.

One winter afternoon as we stood behind his house, he stared over at the island and pointed out a small cove. "That," he said—as much to himself as to me—"is where they keep their speed boat." He spit out the last two words. "And they swim there in the summer," he added.

When Frankie speaks of the sea, he speaks of work: fishing, lobstering, rowing. He knows the sea as a source of food, a road, sometimes a grave. Raised on an island, he can't swim. Death in the sea is more merciful that way, if you don't struggle against it, alone in the bone-numbing swells around the Fastnet. The sea is to be respected, feared, never trifled with.

He fell silent. We changed the subject.

The last time I was with Frankie, I didn't mention going out to St. Killain. The weather was very wet, mist changing to rain, rain changing to mist. On Sunday, my last day there, we went to an early Mass. When we came out of church, the mist was lifting, the sun burning through. The day tasted like spring. "It's a miracle," I said to Frankie. "In your honor," Frankie laughed. "We will go out to St. Killain," he added; "it will be a fine day for it." He didn't offer any more of an explanation, and I didn't ask for one. Frankie has his own reasons for things—reasons that are often a mystery to me. "Another miracle," I said. "Praise be to St. Killain."

We rowed out to the island. Rather, he rowed, with hard, even strokes. I didn't offer a hand. And Frankie, recognizing in me the physical characteristics of an English lawyer—soft hands, unweathered face, a narrow body—didn't ask me to row. With his face flushed from rowing and the salt air, his white hair tousled by the wind, Frankie looked like a postcard vision of an Irish peasant. I liked that picture, liked being in it, liked feeling his acceptance of me as a relative, liked sharing his boat and his island. As we neared St. Killain, I pointed to a great flock of sea gulls near the shore. "See," I said, "wild geese in disguise. They're here to welcome me home."

Frankie gave me a small smile. I had once told him how my father used to insist that my family was descended from the "Wild Geese," the Irish soldiers and aristocrats who fled Ireland in the 17th and 18th centuries and rose to positions of prominence in Austria, Spain, France. We weren't, of course. We were the descendants of Cork peasants, impoverished and uneducated, who left Ireland only once, to come to New York. "But maybe the description fits," I had said to Frankie. "A goose: halfway between a duck and swan. Sometimes I think that's what I am."

Frankie hadn't asked me to explain any further. He had seemed to like the imagery. "Well," he said, "if you're a goose, you're a silly goose; and I'm the ugly duckling."

The closer we got to the island, the grayer both Frankie and the day got. When we landed, he walked ahead of me, grayer still. We went up a narrow path that curled its way up the cliff. At the top, about twenty yards in front of us, was the lawyer's house, Frankie's old home, nestled into the roll of the land. Frankie stood several feet away from me. He looked toward the far end of the island, a quarter of a mile off, where the ruined church was.

I walked over to the shuttered windows and lifted the wooden latches. Frankie wouldn't allow me to think he had the slightest interest in the house. "All he did was muck the place up," he yelled over to me. "Connecting the house to the barn—I suppose that's more natural, too."

I looked through the window into the great middle room that occupied almost a third of the house. The room was lovely in its simplicity: a slate floor covered in the middle by a mottled woolen rug, rich strands of gold and red woven through it; a heavy oak dining table and sideboard, old and beaten but beautifully polished; a dark green couch drawn up in front of an enormous fireplace. Irish peasant life according to Harrods.

Frankie walked away from me, toward the beach. I thought about the ironic turn of events that was making this corner of Ireland, so long a place of poverty and deprivation from which so many women and men had emigrated, into a growing destination for vacationers. I kept the thought to myself. I caught up with Frankie and we walked together in silence. "Well, at least he's preserved the buildings," I said finally. He didn't answer.

We walked on and I realized Frankie had never mentioned the lawyer's name. It had always been simply "him," or "himself," or "your man," or "the lawyer."

"What's his name?" I asked.

"Whose name?"

"The lawyer."

"Barrett," Frankie answered, "Michael Barrett."

"But that's an Irish name," I said.

"Oh, Jesus," said Frankie, "two or three generations back, I suppose so, or so your man would like to think. He's always walking around in his Aran sweater, trying to get old Florrie Fitzgerald to tell him some of the old stories. He brought a tape recorder one time. Florrie fixed him. He told him 'The Three Little Pigs' in Irish and your man sits there like he's hearing Holy Gospel for the first time.

"He's even learned a little Irish and now he walks around trying to say hello in Irish to farmers who don't know what he's talking about, thinking to himself, 'Well, now and sure, aren't I the real Irishman himself, with me tweed cap and wee cottage.'"

I laughed at Frankie's imitation of an Irish peasant; I laughed at Barrett, too. Yet I knew that I deserved the same scorn, and if I weren't a relative, Frankie would give it to me. "And there he was," Frankie would tell his friends at Minahan's Pub, "Brian Boru himself, come over from New York to tell us all about ourselves."

Frankie could laugh, I knew. He was right. This past belonged to him. This island, too. They always would. Barrett could never hold them the way Frankie did. But the attempt to belong, to possess something forever out of reach, was only partly ridiculous. It was also a bit sad, a final footnote to that chapter of Irish history that still echoed in the North but ended here with Dick McKenna, the last of the spalpeens: exile, loss, the flight of the Silly Geese.

I imagined Michael Barrett tall and thin, elegantly dressed—the best of Savile Row—with elegant silver hair. Michael, the grandchild of immigrants. Michael, still unsure of where he belonged. He would never be anything more to Frankie and his neighbors than an English visitor, quietly despised. I tried to imagine my imaginary Michael in a great woolen mantle, shaggy-haired and barefoot.

I laughed again.

"I'm glad you can't stop laughing" said Frankie. "But you don't have to see him walking around here like St. Killain himself risen from the dead."

We were on the beach now, and to the right was a small scarp, about eight feet high, topped by the ruined walls of St. Killain Church. At high tide the sea ate into the embankment, in and out, remorselessly completing the work of the Vikings.

Frankie made the sign of the cross. He explained to me that in penal times, when Catholicism was proscribed, people from the mainland brought their dead out here and buried them around the church, in sacred ground. As a child, he used to find bones and skulls strewn across the beach. Once, on a dare, he picked up a skull and kicked it as if it were an Irish football.

"I was only nine," said Frankie. "My older brother dared me to do it. I can still see the thing—the skull all brown, and the empty eye sockets—as my foot crashed into it. It broke in two neat pieces; broke and came down in the water—*splash, splash.*

"God forgive me. Every night for two years I went to bed afraid the skeleton would come to find the boy that done the terrible thing to its head."

I listened and at the same time dug my hand into the wet, soft earth of the embankment. One big clump fell away. In front of me, imbedded in the earth, was a leg bone, its skeletal foot distinct, white, awful in its whiteness. I had never seen death this way, this near, the closed-earth, cleaned-bone fact; a bloodless, fleshless, disembodied finality. For one hideous moment I thought that somehow I might have known this person. Then, standing there in silence, I realized this was someone long dead: a spalpeen, an acquaintance of Spenser's, a Viking, a monk. Someone long at peace in the Skillins.

"God's mercy on him," Frankie said.

He started to walk away from me, back toward the boat. It was a wintry day now, the sun gone, the sea rising, the gulls screeching and soaring with the wind.

"Come on," Frankie said, "or we'll end up with your man here."

I was still shaken, staring at the exposed grave. "Frankie, but who do you think it was?"

"Yerra," he said, "if he's one of mine he can thank St. Killain he left before the lawyer got here."

(All the events in this chapter are true. The names have been slightly altered to protect the intensely private people it describes and the places they hold dear.)

The Perils of Pat

Cast your mind on other days
That we in coming days may be
Still the indomitable Irishry.
                    —W.B. YEATS, "Under Ben Bulben"

THE MAN ON THE HORSE is my paternal grandfather, Patrick Francis Quinn. The date is September 5, 1904. Pat is about to take his place as Grand Marshal of the New York City Labor Day Parade. The horse was rented for the occasion. I have the sash he is wearing in the photograph framed and under glass. Pat's name and title are embroidered in gold lettering on the faded blue silk:

P.F. QUINN—PRESIDENT—CENTRAL FEDERATED UNION

The photograph was taken near the old Fifth Avenue Hotel, which stood at the corner of 23rd Street across from Madison Square Park. Somewhere out of view, my grandmother tended her three children: Gertie, John, and my father, Peter, born the previous May.

Pat was just short of his forty-fifth birthday. According to his obituary, which ran in the *Bronx Home News* on October 10, 1941, he was born in Thurles, in County Tipperary, Ireland, September 27, 1859. Barely a decade before, Colonel Douglas, in charge of local relief efforts during the Famine years, had despaired of describing the widespread suffering. "Nobody who has not personally seen the state of matters in this country can form to himself any idea," he wrote.

Money sent by relatives who left for America in the late 1840s paid for the Quinns' one-way passage to New York. They arrived in 1873, when Pat was fourteen, and settled on the Lower East Side. Pat drew a curtain over his childhood in Ireland. In later years, though a sympathizer with the Irish Republican Brotherhood, he had no use for romantic reminiscences of Ireland. He dismissed all those who pined for the old country with the same curt comment: "If you liked it so much, you should have stayed."

In New York, he went right to work, first in menial jobs, then in the better-paying but exhausting position of stoking furnaces in an iron foundry. After several years of the same routine, he and his brother John decided to pack up and head west. When they left, how they traveled, and where they arrived is uncertain. The obituary in the *Bronx Home News* states that Pat "worked on the Santa Fe and Southern Pacific Railroad as a fireman and engineer, and took part in frequent encounters with the bands of Apache Indians who were on the warpath along the border."

In my father's telling of the story, fully amplified by his skills as a public speaker and raconteur, Pat wasn't merely one of the army of laborers, Irish and otherwise, stoking furnaces on the hundreds of trains that crisscrossed the Southwest and were harassed with rapidly decreasing frequency by increasingly desperate Indians. Pat was a coal-shoveling version of John Henry, "a hard drivin' man," and his train was regularly pursued through the wildest of the Wild West by the most ferocious bands of Apache warriors.

The irony of an Irishman helping drive forward the same process of colonization that had gotten underway in Ireland several centuries previously was lost on me, and I doubt Pat ever gave it any thought. It says in his obituary that "He was one of the train-crew who piloted the train that carried Geronimo, leader of the Apaches, into captivity." Pat was a man of his time. He had his contradictions. What was, in my childish mind, an adventure tale was, for him, a quest for survival. *See Pat. See Pat run. See Pat leave behind the squalor of Tipperary and the tight quarters of New York's tenements for broader horizons.*

He didn't find them out west. Or maybe, as with other Irishmen and women, the range was too *big* to feel at home on, the empty space and isolated settlements making him feel lost, adrift. His brother John stayed and eventually opened a dry goods store in Bisbee, Arizona, but didn't have much success. He died there sometime early in the twentieth century. There's no record of him marrying or having children. His place of burial is unknown to anyone in the family. Pat drifted back east, riding the rails, making money as a boxer, a skill he prided himself on and tried, unsuccessfully, to pass on to my father.

When Pat returned to New York, he was able to apprentice himself to a coppersmith in an East River shipyard. Along with picking up a trade, he became involved with the labor movement, joining the Knights of Labor, which was founded by Terence Powderly, another Irish immigrant. He became a professional labor organizer, spending a part of each year traveling around the country to encourage the spread of new unions.

Labor militancy fit Pat's temperament. He told my father that "I know what it's like to be hungry, and that changes a man." Pat had a chip on his shoulder—several, in fact: against inherited privilege and snobbery; against the Catholic hierarchy, most of whom he regarded as allies of the rich (which never stopped him from being a practicing Catholic); and against bosses, bullies, and lackeys. The last two he despised most of all. "There are only three types of men," he warned my father. "Bullies, lackeys, and them who refuse to be either." Eventually, he said, "every man has to decide which he'll be."

It's easy to write about Pat's exploits, easier still to dress them up as heroic or filled with excitement. It's harder to imagine the hard-scrabble, hard-knock existence of an uneducated Paddy kicking around stockyards and rail junctions, making a living with his fists or a shovel, the only marketable skills he possessed, and unsure where his next meal was coming from. He had a lot of company, no doubt, especially when the economy went bust.

As a union organizer, he faced different dangers. In 1894, he traveled to Chicago to lend support to the workers on strike against the Pullman Company, the manufacturer of railway sleeping cars. The strike took place in the middle of an economic depression and generated nationwide sympathy from other workers. Pat was met in Chicago by two Pinkerton detectives hired by the Pullman Company to help isolate the strikers. They followed him out of the station. One offered him a cigar. The other poked a gun in his ribs, stuck a return ticket in his pocket, and told him to be on the next train back to New York.

Pat reboarded, traveled east for an hour, and then headed back to Chicago. He kept up this peripatetic existence throughout the 1890s. More than once, he was set upon by goons or had his life threatened. In the late 1890s he went to Cuba. In the version I was told as a child, he went to prospect for gold. The truth was more personal and tragic, but I wouldn't learn that until I was an adult.

His obituary (the sources of which are unknown but my father must have been one of them) doesn't give a reason: "Just prior to the outbreak of the Spanish-American War, Quinn was master coppersmith of the U.S. Naval Yard in Key West, but he left his post and went to Cuba where he joined the Cuban Insurrectionists and fought against Spain as a cavalry man in the Cuban Irregular Army. With the arrival of U.S. troops he attached himself to the Eighth Tennessee Regiment as a scout and farrier, although he never formally enlisted."

There were a number of stories about Pat's exploits while with the Cuban rebels. At one point, he was on the run, trying to elude the Spanish. He met up at last with American troops who stopped the train on which he was a passenger. Tanned, mustachioed, dark-haired, Pat startled them when he spoke English. They found his explanations of who he was and why he was in Cuba far-fetched. He was sure he was about to be taken off the train and shot as a spy when he noticed a sprig of green in a trooper's hat. He asked about it. What else should an Irishman have in his hat on St. Patrick's Day? the trooper replied. It turned out he was a fellow Tipperary man. Pat was convinced for the rest of his life that it was his namesake, St. Patrick, who saved his life.

One story in particular fascinated me. While he was with the Insurrectionists, Pat was staying in a village that was raided by the Spanish. He was in a cabin with a Cuban woman and her infant. She had him squeeze himself into a space in the wall. When the soldiers came in, she discreetly pinched the baby, making it fuss and cry, and pleaded with them to bring a doctor because the baby was sick. They made a perfunctory reply and left quickly. Pat went undiscovered.

The sexual subtext stirred interest in my boy's mind (innuendoes my father would have been horrified to think he planted in my head). What was Pat doing in the cabin with that woman? He spent a year in Cuba before the U.S. arrived. Whose child did that woman have in her arms? Pat reported to my father that he thought Cubans were the handsomest people he had ever encountered. Was he living with one of them? Had he fathered a child?

There was always a hint of raffishness about Pat. My father's older sister, Gertie, a skeptic when it came to anything to do with her father, was unmoved by the religious piety he displayed at the end of his life. (The church-related activities listed in his obituary include the Knights of Columbus, the St. Vincent de Paul Society, the Holy Name Society, and the Catholic Layman's Retreat League.) "He'll be the last man out of Purgatory," she once commented, "if, God willing, he was lucky enough to get in."

Gertie was also the source of the less-than-heroic Pat stories, the ones my father didn't tell, devoid of Indians or Insurrectionists. Once, after they had moved from the Lower East Side to the Bronx, she met him on the elevated train on the way home from her nighttime job as a telephone operator. He was drunk. They got off together at West Farms. She attempted to help him down the stairs from the elevated station. He pulled away, telling her to mind her own business, turned, and tumbled down the steep flight of cast-iron steps to the street. Except for crushing his hat, he was unscathed. "Truly," Gertie said, "God watches over drunks and babies."

It wasn't until Pat was dying that my father learned that Gertie was his half-sister. Pat looked up from his bed on the last night of his life and said to my father, "You're a lawyer, so don't try to cheat Gertie out of what's coming to her because she's only your half-sister." My father was more stunned than hurt. For the first time, my father learned that before Pat had married my grandmother, he had been married to a woman named Delia Best, who died giving birth to Gertie.

Delia Best's death was the reason Pat had gone to Florida and then Cuba. He left the baby with his sister in 1897 and didn't return to New York until 1900, when he married Margaret Manning. None of this appeared in my grandfather's obituary. When and where Pat met Delia Best, where she was from or where she is buried, are mysteries. No one in my family seemed to have a clue about her life, at least not one they were willing to pass on. She remains a cipher. I never heard her name until Gertie's death, when my father told us that she was, in fact, his half-sister.

Whatever the different emphases in their stories, Gertie and my father were agreed that Pat was tough. He was particularly tough on my father, his youngest child. He took him at age five to Coney Island, walked him to the end of a pier and threw him off. For Pat, this was what it meant to teach your son to swim.

My father told that story to the end of his life. He told it dispassionately, with no apparent anger against his father but neither any bravado claim of yelling "Geronimo!" as he plunged toward the water. I always found the story amusing because it seemed a light moment, as though my father knew Pat would dive in to save him. But my father didn't, not at age five. Sometimes when he drank, he grew sad and withdrawn, as if the dark, green ocean water was covering him. His eyes filled with a sunken, abandoned feeling.

It's struck me all these years later that I never asked my father the outcome: Did he learn to swim in that moment or did Pat jump in to save him? My guess is that my father made it back to the dock on his own. The distance probably wasn't great, a yard of two, no matter how vast it might have seemed as measured by the panicked flailings of a small boy. Pat, I'm sure, was pleased: it was a lesson that had to be learned. The weak starve to death. They let themselves be pushed around. They never put up their fists. They give up and sink, unnoticed.

Union organizing kept Pat on the road a good part of the year. He worried my grandmother would undo the toughening he tried to do and turn my father into a "mama's boy." He started taking my father with him, a week here, a few days there. "He's smart enough he can miss some school," he told my grandmother. "It will do the boy good." And it did.

My father enjoyed traveling with Pat; their silent companionship on trains and boats, while my father read and Pat smoked and stared out the window; the thrill of watching Pat at a podium, stirring other men with his words. I'm sure in those days on the road together, my father felt closer to Pat than at any other time in his life.

My father remembered one time in particular, in the summer of 1916, when they traveled from a labor convention in Detroit for a day's outing in Toronto. It was at the time of the British offensive on the Somme, and the imperial patriotism of many Canadians was running high. Pat and my father were crossing a public square at dusk when a military band began to play "God Save the King." Silent, reverent men removed their hats as the Union Jack came down. My father went to take off his cap.

My grandfather stopped him. "That flag is a symbol of royalty and aristocracy," he said in a loud voice. "It stands for empire and greed. *Never* doff your hat to it."

There were shouts from the crowd, and threats. My father was scared but kept his eyes on Pat, who showed no sign of fear.

Pat stood there with my father at his side until the anthem was done, hats unremoved, heads unbowed. And that's how I like most to think of them: the Irish immigrant laborer and his son, together in that twilight, refusing to bend a knee before emperors or empires.

Stones of Memory

The annals of mankind have never been written; nor would it be within human capacity to read them if they were written. We have a leaf or two from the great books of human fate as it flutters in the storm winds ever sweeping across the earth. We decipher them as we best can with purblind eyes, and endeavour to learn their mystery as we float along to the abyss; but it is all confused babble, hieroglyphics of which the key is lost.

—JOHN LOTHROP MOTLEY

HISTORY STAYS WITH US, even when we don't want it to. Forgotten or unwritten, history shifts beneath our feet, one minute imperceptibly, the next tectonically, shaping nations, neighborhoods, and families. Sometimes what has disappeared is restored through the labors of historians. Robert Scally's masterful work, *The End of Hidden Ireland,* is a perfect example. In a brilliant exercise of investigative scholarship, Scally's book brings to life the long-forgotten fate of the inhabitants of a single Roscommon townland during the Great Famine.

More often than not, especially in America, we live oblivious of history, or with truncated, simplified versions having about as much to do with the actual past as the cute, sanitized, scaled-down turn-of-the-century town through which visitors pass on their way into Disney-world's Magic Kingdom. In fact, as Scally's singular achievement reminds us, history, as lived by ordinary people, wherever they may be, is rarely remembered or recorded.

Ignorance of history is understandable, if not advisable. History is a bloody mess, filled with such cruelty, folly, and mass homicide that it can lead a thinking person to despair. My mother was among those with an active dislike of history. An avid reader, she declined to touch any of the works of popular history I occasionally recommended. "Old news that's stale as well as bad," was how she once described history to me.

Unlike my deeply pessimistic father, who paid attention to history, Viola Murphy, my mother, was an optimist, which partly explains why she had no use for the past. She had enough personal experiences of bad history (a brother who returned from World War I unable to keep a job, a brother-in-law murdered by mobsters during Prohibition, her parents' life savings wiped out by the Depression) that she avoided immersing herself in the national or global variety.

She did her best to scour our family's history so that what was passed down to the next generation was suitable for children of the middle—and one day, with any luck, upper—class. Her blanket dismissals of my questions about the family's past were supplemented by an active program of destroying birth and death certificates, diaries, letters, newspaper clippings, and the like. "Excess baggage" was her unadorned explanation.

I think that the era in which my mother came of age influenced her low opinion of history. Like the 1960s, the 1920s was a time when the future had a better reputation than the past. Progress was as palpable as a radio dial, as exciting as talking films and sleek automobiles. New styles embodying new freedoms were everywhere. In 1922, which F. Scott Fitzgerald identified as "the peak year of the younger generation," my mother, a sophomore at Our Lady of Angels Academy in Fort Lee, New Jersey, bobbed her hair, cutting away her cascade of curls and causing consternation and disbelief among the nuns who taught her.

She met my father in 1928, on March 17th, at a St. Patrick's Day dance at Our Lady of Solace, my father's parish. Graduated in 1926 with a B.S. in civil engineering from Manhattan College, he was working on the construction of the IND subway and attending Fordham Law School at night. She was a junior at Mount St. Vincent College, majoring in classics. None of their parents had gone beyond grade school. The road ahead seemed wide and open, until the economy went flooey and history postponed their dreams.

The religious affinity between my parents was obvious and fundamental, but the immediate attraction was physical and intellectual. They were both thin and good-looking. (Even in old age, after two mastectomies and a general withering, the outline of my mother's beauty, her graceful form, was still intact.) They were wonderful dancers. They loved going to nightclubs and the theater, where they enjoyed everything from the Marx Brothers to Shakespeare. They shared a sharp sense of humor that could quickly edge into sarcasm and had a general skepticism about human nature that seems part of being Irish—"cynical humanism" is how William Kennedy describes it—a consequence, perhaps, of a deeply ingrained belief in original sin and a tribal history which until recently always seemed to end in disappointment and tragedy.

Of the two, my mother started out the more sophisticated, with a keener appreciation of the nuances of class. She taught my father the social graces, beginning with a Henry-Higginsish recasting of his speech so that he no longer pronounced oil as "earl" or boil as "berl," a dead giveaway of lower-class origins. She furnished their apartment with a decorator's eye, accumulating high-end furniture piece by piece, instead of rushing out to buy an entire set at a department store. She cooked with a finesse rare for her time.

My mother was "lace-curtain Irish," but with a flapper's heart. For the rest of her life, she reminisced about the night she met a Columbia University student at a college dance who helped pay tuition by working as a model for the Arrow Shirt and Collar Company. He asked her out on a date. But when the night arrived, she was laid up with measles. He never called again. "I don't know if I could have kept my self-control if he did," my mother said, laughingly, but with a flash of conviction in her eyes.

My mother's taste and style came from her mother, Catherine Murphy (née Riordan). There were no frills and few comforts in Catherine's upbringing. Her parents had emigrated from the countryside to Cork City during the Famine, seemingly unable to afford the fare to America. She came to New York alone as a teenager and went to work as a maid. It was an experience she rarely talked about, to the point that my mother suspected an unpleasant incident of some sort, maybe an employer's unsolicited sexual advance. But whatever happened (or didn't), living in the homes of New York's elite introduced Catherine to an entirely different way of living, none of which was lost on her.

Catherine had six children, but it was my mother, the last, who arrived when there was money enough to afford the tuition at a Catholic girl's academy and women's college (and before it disappeared again in the Depression). As well as being provided an education, my mother was showered with all the knowledge Catherine had soaked up in her years as a maid: how to dress, act, speak, furnish a home, set a table, hold a cup of tea. Catherine was determined that no one would ever mistake her daughter for a servant girl, or treat her as such.

In my family, stories like Catherine's never got the same attention as those of the men who went off to prospect for gold or fight wars. At some level, by dint of observation, I knew the central role women played in Irish-American life, but it wasn't until I read Hasia R. Diner's *Erin's Daughters in America* that I understood how uniquely feminine the Irish immigrant experience was.

"Irish women differed from most other immigrant women," Diner writes. "They were the only significant group of foreign-born women who outnumbered men; they were the only significant group of women who chose to migrate in primarily female cliques. They also accepted jobs that most other women turned down, and their rate of economic and social progress seems to have outdistanced that of the women of other ethnic groups."

The Famine—not Jansenism, a form of Catholic Puritanism imported from France—was the "great convincer," says Diner. It changed the conditions of marriage in rural Ireland, sweeping away the widespread practice of early marriage and large families sustained by ever smaller subdivision of the land. The Famine made late marriage the rule. It ended the practice of subdivision, putting the land in control of one son, giving him alone the option of marriage. The Famine and the new economic conditions it introduced, not the Church, molded and determined Irish attitudes toward the question of reproduction.

In a single generation the Irish countryside was transformed, and one of the biggest changes was the exodus of its women, most of them to America. They came, as Diner points out, in far greater numbers than their immigrant counterparts from Germany or Italy or eastern Europe, and they came with different attitudes about a woman's place in society as well.

The Irish family structure these immigrant women came out of was more a constitutional monarchy than a patriarchy, and if men held responsibility for the land, women enjoyed authority in the home and a say in the finances. The Famine increased gender segmentation and erased any cultural stigma that might have attached to women choosing not to marry at all.

In America, Irish rural customs took on a special significance because, Diner believes, they "continued to make economic sense." Irish women, accustomed to a certain independence, did not hesitate to take domestic jobs that required them to live apart from their families. Feeling no cultural pressure to marry, many of them remained single working women, and since Bridget was not as hateful to nativists as Paddy, she enjoyed an economic success far greater than Irish men.

Catherine spent nearly a decade as a domestic before she married my grandfather, James Murphy, a mechanic. I remember her as a woman in her eighties, exceedingly kind and attentive to me and all her grandchildren. She was significantly shorter than my mother, and there was a physical solidity to her—a thickness, a compact strength—that resulted from years of hard work, both as a servant and mother of six. The contrast with my mother was striking and, as described by John

O'Hara in *BUtterfield 8*, was another innovation enjoyed by those who came of age in the 1920s:

> The young girl who was about twenty years old in the latter half of the 1920s [my mother turned 20 in 1927] did conform to a size. She was about five-feet-five [my mother was several inches taller], she weighed about 110 [my mother's weight exactly]. She had a good body. There must have been a reason for the fact that so many girls fit that description, without regard to social classification. And the reason may well be that between 1905 and 1915 the medical profession used approximately the same system in treating pregnant women and in feeding and care of infants. Even the children of Sicilian and Ghetto parentage suddenly grew taller . . .

In contrast to my thoroughly modern mother, Catherine had an old-time aura about her. It permeated the formal, substantial comfort of her home, which seemed immune to the down-at-the-heels condition of the surrounding neighborhood in the blue-collar river town of Edgewater, New Jersey. I loved being in her house, which is where we celebrated major holidays. Yet, despite the popular notion of Irish grandmothers as repositories of folklore and music, she rarely spoke about Ireland in my presence. She wasn't much for history, but for reasons different from my mother's.

Catherine Riordan was one of the immigrant women Hasia Diner described: pragmatic, devout, hard-working, determined to see her children across the great divide between deprivation and a decent standard of living. Her interest wasn't in denying the past but in overcoming it. When she looked at my mother, her admiration and pride were obvious. She needed no poets or scholars to explain the course of history. All she needed or wanted to know was right there in front of her, in the shape of her lovely, well-formed, college-educated daughter.

Catherine came from out of the Irish peasantry. But she never expressed nostalgia for the land. Scarlett O'Hara notwithstanding, longing for the land was absent from my family and every other Irish-American family I knew. For my grandparents, the city was an escape from the accumulated misery and poverty of the Irish tenantry; for my parents, a place free from Prohibition, Fundamentalism, and small-town Republicanism. Where my grandparents were urban by choice and necessity, my parents were urban by nature. They reveled in the culture, company, and conviviality of the city.

By the end of the nineteenth century, there wasn't a trace of the old clod clinging to the spats of urban Irish sports, no more than to the stylish dresses of Irish maids like Catherine Riordan strolling through Central Park on an afternoon's holiday. As one nineteenth-century observer noted, "These girls had been brought up in the floorless mud cabins covered with thatch, and gone to Mass without shoes or stockings very likely, and now enjoy all the more their unaccustomed luxuries."

As Hasia Diner makes clear, the transition these immigrants made was often traumatic, and the high rates at which the Irish were sent off to jails and asylums is one measure of the dislocation they endured. But the Irish weren't simply crowded into the cities by poverty or the native population's prevailing hostility. Crowding was a part of who they were. The traditional Irish village, or clachán, that many came out of bore no resemblance to the classic European model of orderly streets, neat squares, tidy rows of shops and homes. The clachán was a clump of cabins that leaned on one another, a physical embodiment of the tight-knit community built on a communal method of land distribution called the Rundale system.

Outsiders often remarked on the intense conviviality of the clachán, the incessant emphasis on singing, dancing, and storytelling that wasn't merely *part* of Irish culture but its living heart, the vessel of its survival. Traveling through Ireland at the time of the Famine, when the clachán were being wiped out, Asenath Nicholson wrote of one such community that was owned by a well-intentioned landlord determined to introduce the British system of widely spaced cabins, with fields individually tenanted and tilled.

As described by Mrs. Nicholson, the inhabitants resisted the plan because they feared "it would thin out the crowds and break up the clanship too much." When they finally complied and tore down their homes, they did so in a way that asserted the very identity that was being called into question:

> The destruction of the Rundale system brought new difficulties to these people; it broke up their clusters of huts, and the facilities of assembling-nights, to tell and hear long stories; and they must tumble down their cabins, which were of loose stones; and the owner of a cabin hired a fiddler, which no sooner known, than the joyous Irish are on the spot: each takes a stone or stones upon his back (for women and children are there)—they dance at intervals—the fiddler animates them on while the day-light lasts, and then the night is finished by dancing.

Perhaps no force in human history is more persistent or less appreciated than the tenacious survival of traits, customs, and attitudes that embody a group's values and beliefs, and that resist almost every effort to uproot or pull them down. The cabins are razed. The people move on and are scattered. But quietly, without fanfare, beneath the radar of history, they carry the stones of memory and understanding with them, in their souls and minds, to some new place to be reassembled as the foundation of a new life.

Fifty years after Mrs. Nicholson's sojourn in Ireland, Jacob Riis, in his famous exposé of the tenement districts of New York, compared the lackadaisical Irish immigrant and his descendants to the industrious German, who, Riis wrote, "makes the most of his tenement . . . and as soon as he can save up money enough, he gets out and never crosses the threshold of one again." The Celt, in contrast, appeared attracted by the density and motion of tenement life: "The Irishman's genius runs to public affairs rather than domestic life; wherever he is mustered in force, the saloon is the gorgeous center of political activity."

Riis didn't approve of saloons. What reformers did? At best they saw them as a poor man's recreation, a sorry substitute for the parks and libraries the working classes should have access to; at worst, as a tentacle of the parasitic political machines that deceived and exploited the masses. The reformers weren't entirely wrong. Saloons weren't settlement houses. Yet the dyad of politics and the saloon wasn't a pernicious weed grown out of the noxious soil of slumdom, which choked the immigrant's ability to rise to something better. It was an urban inflores-

cence of what had long been basic to the Irish people's shadowland existence beneath the superstructure of Great Houses and colonial rule.

For the Irish, the saloon was no more restricted to drinking or the
business of vote mustering than the church was to the worship of
God and the salvation of souls. These activities or ambitions weren't
entirely absent. But the power of saloon and church were as corner-
stones of the urban clachán; sodalities for the shared performance of
the rituals of song, dance, and talk; labor exchanges and community
forums; intimate spaces in the urban vastness that reduced the bewilderment of the immigrants and allowed them to make sense of their
surroundings. At the end of the twentieth century, Irish-Americans in
New York or Chicago or Boston were still identifying their neighborhoods not by cross streets or avenues but by parishes or even pubs.

There is an incident from the "Long Strike" of 1872 in New York City
that is revelatory of the cultural strands spun forward from rural
Ireland into an urban web of mutual support and solidarity. At that
time, the closest the city ever came to a general strike, one hundred
thousand workers left their jobs to demand the eight-hour day. Unified
resistance by employers seemed to doom the strike. But John Roache,
an Irishman who was both a professional singer and an employee of
one of the city's largest foundries, organized a musical group. Roache
wrote songs about the workers' cause and went with his troupe from
saloons to labor halls, rallying the strikers. Though the walkout eventually failed, the resonance of Roache's appeal among the Irish helped
prolong the strike and left behind an organization to carry on the fight.

Out west, the Irish who went to the frontier often wrote of the
loneliness and disorientation they experienced amid the wide open
spaces other settlers seemed to thrive on. For better or for worse,
rugged individualism wasn't an Irish characteristic or aspiration. Back
east, weighing the success of Tammany Hall, the cultural elite thought
it detected among the Irish a natural proclivity to "bread and circuses."
The tendency was there, if by "bread" is meant the desire of the labor-
ing classes for work and some measure of security for themselves and
their families, and if by "circuses" is implied not idle spectacle but the

ceremonies of community—the rituals of clambakes, boat rides, Fourth of July picnics, election parades, etc.—that dispelled the drabness and alienation that so readily envelop the urban poor.

In 1975, the year after my father died, my mother announced she was planning a trip to Ireland. It struck me as odd, since no one from her family had ever expressed the slightest interest in paying the place a visit. But she was adamant. And she wasn't interested, she said, in a guided tour of the if-this-is-Tuesday-this-must-be-Dublin type. She wanted to take her time, exploring the countryside and visiting the places in County Cork that her parents had emigrated from in the 1880s

She brought along one of her sisters and her eldest granddaughter, and I served as driver. We left on the evening of March 16th, a date I'm sure my mother chose so that she wouldn't be without my father in New York on St. Patrick's Day for the first time in almost half a century. We stayed in upscale hotels and inns, where my mother made a point of engaging the maids in conversation and telling them about her mother.

March isn't the best month for touring Ireland. The weather was a seamless curtain of gray, chilly mizzle, occasionally graduating into a driving rain. We found the mill in which Catherine Riordan's father had worked. We lit a candle in the Franciscan church in Cork City in which Catherine had attended Mass as a girl. My mother picked up a thin paperback history of Ireland, which she finished quickly, without comment or acknowledgment of the novelty of her choice in reading.

On our next-to-last day, we found the village her father came from, a small forlorn crossroads outside Macroom, in what had been an Irish-speaking area until the early twentieth century. "Greatly shrunk in size and spirit from what it must have been a century ago" is how the parish priest described it to us. The old church had burned years before, and with it the parish records. There wasn't even a faded scrawl on a moldering baptismal registry to connect us to these empty, mist-shrouded fields.

My mother and I left the others on the church steps and walked together a short distance down an unpaved road. Nearby was a crumbling concrete barn with a rusted iron roof. There was a radio on. I looked at my mother. I knew she was still deeply grieved by my father's death, and I was afraid the utter absence of any trace of her own father, of a past gone and forever beyond reach, might bring her to tears.

The mist was once more changing to rain. "We should go back," I said.

"Listen," she said. I heard the quick fluctuations of fiddles coming from the radio, Irish sounds. "My father sang that tune."

She smiled and lifted her coat above her thin ankles and did a small, graceful jig, the soles of her American shoes gently slapping the ground. It was a step I'd never seen her do before.

II. POLITICS & PLACE

Peter A. Quinn, in 1936, the year he was
elected to the New York State Assembly.

Plunkitt of Tammany Hall

◎◎

When I consider how my life is spent,
I hardly ever repent.

—OGDEN NASH

"OF ALL OUR PASSIONS AND APPETITES," wrote Edward Gibbon, the famed chronicler of Rome's decline and fall, "the love of power is the most imperious and unsociable nature, since the pride of one man requires the submission of the multitude." It is a mystery what Gibbon would have made of George Washington Plunkitt, leader of the Fifteenth Assembly District, sachem of the Tammany Society, holder of assorted public offices (at one point four simultaneously), a man skilled at seeking power yet who shunned all imperiousness and proclaimed sociability as the first law of politics.

For his part, it seems fairly certain that Plunkitt neither knew nor had any desire to learn about Gibbon's theories on leadership or the role it played in the fate of imperial Rome. Had they been contemporaries and neighbors, Plunkitt might well have spent an afternoon conversing with Gibbon. But if *Plunkitt of Tammany Hall: A Series of Very Plain Talks on Very Practical Poltitics* is any guide, Plunkitt was more given to soliloquies than conversations. But there's no doubt that, as disinterested as he might have been in Roman history, he would have paid careful attention to the needs and concerns of a constituent. *And what brings ya here, Mr. Gibbon? Is it a job you're seekin'? Or is that boy of yours in trouble again? Not to worry, Mr. Gibbon, you've come to the right place.*

Plunkitt's collection of short disquisitions or lectures or rambling observations—in truth, a mixture of all three—is a unique document. Aside from a few newspaper interviews and the official transcripts of numerous investigatory bodies, it is our only written record of the thoughts, musings, and philosophy of the men who operated the most successful and long-running urban political machine in American history. (The near-total absence of documentation makes it likely that the most penetrating accounts of Tammany will be authored by novelists, rather than historians.)

The dislike of the Tammany leadership for public statements or speeches is legendary. It was raised to an art form by its greatest tactician and most taciturn chief, Charles Francis Murphy, whose longest written statement is, perhaps, the four-sentence tribute that he composed (or, more likely, commissioned) for Plunkitt's book. So famous was Murphy for his silences that when an observer once commented on the fact that the Boss was standing with his mouth shut during the singing of the national anthem, a Tammany brave replied that the Boss wasn't being unpatriotic. He just didn't want to commit himself in public.

There is no question that as well as being a unique American political document, Plunkitt's book is also among the most lively. This is a text free of convoluted theorizing, or impenetrable statistical analyses, or the mind-numbing language of the social sciences. It is politically incorrect in every sense, displaying equal contempt for "good government" reforms and for the conservative proponents of free enterprise as a solution for every social problem. "It's a grand idea," says Plunkitt, "the city ownin' the railroads, the gas works and all that. Just see how many thousands of new places there would be for the workers in Tammany!" Plunkitt makes little or no attempt to censor himself, even when it comes to offensive and despicable racial and ethnic epithets.

Plunkitt's formal schooling lasted, he tells us, "three winters when I was a boy." In spite of (or, more likely, because of) this, he is forceful and concise in expression and has a keen appreciation of the power of anecdote. Whatever readers might think of Plunkitt's low opinions of the civil service or the propriety of politicians wearing formal dress clothes, they will be hard put to forget the story of the young man driven by frustration with the civil service to fight with the Spanish at the battle of San Juan Hill, or of the young politico reduced to a hobo by his love of formal wear. Spun out a little longer, these are New York yarns worthy of O. Henry.

The pungent wit and concise effectiveness of each of Plunkitt's "plain talks on very practical politics" raises a question that isn't often asked but should be: How much is Plunkitt? And how much William L. Riordan, the newspaperman who listened to Plunkitt hold forth from his rostrum—the New York County Court House boot-black stand—and wrote it all down? Anyone who has transcribed an interview or conversation and then shaped it into readable prose knows the dimensions of the challenge. Often enough, the editor must do so much cutting, reorganizing, and filling in, he deserves status as coauthor of the piece.

What's more, there is an amazing affinity between the flesh-and-blood Plunkitt and the fictional Martin J. Dooley, the contemporaneous Chicago barkeep and nonpareil American political philosopher invented by another Irish-American newspaperman, Finley Peter Dunne. Like Plunkitt, Mr. Dooley went about armed with the sharp, bitter shiv of the Irish comic sensibility, an attitude so attuned to the presence of absurdity in human affairs that it finds it hard to take anything seriously. Here, for example, is Mr. Dooley on reformers, words that, if delivered in New Yorkese, might as easily have come from Plunkitt: "A man that'd expict to thrain lobsters to fly in a year is called a loonytic; but a man that thinks men can be tu-rrned into angels by an iliction is called a rayformer an' remains at large."

Though we will never know with certainty where Plunkitt ends and Riordan begins, it seems safe to say that whatever editing he did, Riordan captured the authentic man, wit, and wisdom, warts and all. Along with being richly larded with stories and anecdotes, these talks reek of a real-life professional utterly free of the grating tendency of modern-day politicians to apologize for taking up their trade.

Today, in our confessional age, it is common for those who enter politics to claim they are driven by a psychoneurotic impulse "to give something back" to the system. Once in office, elected officials as well as appointed ones begin plotting their eventual departure, paying careful and solicitous attention to the industry or business that will one day find their experience and connections attractive. With this lucrative prospect in mind, they regulate or legislate for the very firms or corporations they hope to be employed by. The game is wrapped inside the techno-jargon that the financial and service industries are so adept at creating, but it still comes down to the formula of George Washington Plunkitt: "I seen my opportunities, and I took 'em."

Plunkitt is compellingly honest about the true lure of politics— first and foremost, the desire to hold and wield power—and about the rewards those who take up such a calling might expect. According to Plunkitt, "when a man works in politics, he should get something out of it." In another place, Plunkitt defines that something as "honest graft," an oxymoron that has come to summarize for many the venality at the heart of Tammany.

Greed there was aplenty throughout the history of Tammany. It is estimated that William Magear Tweed and his ring stole in the vicinity of $50 million (multiply by ten to get today's equivalent) before they were caught. Boss Croker, an immigrant boy who apprenticed with the Fourth Avenue Tunnel gang and at an early point in his political career was tried for murder, made no secret that he was working for his own pocket "all the time." In conjunction with Police Chief Bill Devery, Big Tim Sullivan, a friend of Plunkitt's and district leader of the Lower East Side, ran a multimillion-dollar gambling syndicate. Plunkitt's obituary in the *New York Times* of November 23, 1924, estimates that "the Senator's estate will amount to considerably more than $1,000,000." Seven years after Plunkitt's death, in 1931, the inquiry led by Judge Samuel Seabury brought to light the magical tin box of Sheriff Farley and the massive peculations it was symbolic of, an exposé that ultimately forced the resignation of Mayor Jimmy Walker.

A detailed accounting of the thievery connected with Tammany would run to volumes. But while the plundering was often fearsome, it would be a mistake to imagine that Tammany enjoyed a corner on the corruption market, or that the long reign of the Organization was little more than a succession of comico-criminal Irish pols who had no concept of what to do with the power they held other than to line their pockets and employ their friends.

In America, bribery and influence-peddling have always been bipartisan affairs, and Tammany's appetite for ill-gotten gain was probably on a par with political machines throughout the rest of the country. It doesn't excuse the depredations of the Tweed ring, for example, to point out they were of a piece with the era—with the Whiskey ring, the Union Pacific ring, the Erie ring—expanding circles of corruption that occasionally overlapped. America was up for grabs. George Templeton Strong damned the entire New York State legislature as the "Sanhedrin of rascality," a title it more than lived up to during the struggle over the Erie Railroad, when men on both sides of the aisle openly sold their votes.

What was different in New York City was the size of the trough. In the second half of the nineteenth century, New York mushroomed from a fair-sized seaport to a sprawling metropolis, the money market of North America. Romancing the dollar was the city's passion and pastime. "All the world over," wrote one observer in 1872, "poverty is a misfortune. In New York it is a crime."

Plunkitt, whose life encompassed this transformation, was acutely aware of its implications. "It makes me tired," he complains, "to hear of old codgers back in the thirties or forties boastin' that they retired from politics without a dollar except what they earned in their profession or business. If they lived today, with all the existin' opportunities, they would be just the same as twentieth-century politicians."

By the turn of the century, when Plunkitt's words were taken down, the equation of Tammany with the Irish was ironclad. Plunkitt himself, overcoming any temptation to tribal self-effacement (a lapse that few if any of New York's ethnic groups have ever been accused of), declared that the "Irish was born to rule." This destiny, however, was decidedly unclear a half century before, and it is worth remembering that the vaunted machine ran on tracks set in place by old-stock Americans. The Irish were the rank-and-file majority for at least a generation before one of their own, Honest John Kelly, became the boss.

Tammany began as a red-blooded patriotic fraternity that took its name from a long-vanished Indian chief. Dedicated to keeping alive the ideals of the revolution and resisting any resurgence of Tory snobbery and aristocracy, its members paraded in Indian garb and addressed each other with titles appropriate to their costumes, like "brave," or "sachem," or "wiskinkie." At this stage, it could have evolved into a house tabby, as tame as the Shriners, instead of into the feared political tiger it became. Not until Aaron Burr took hold of the leash did Tammany's true stripes begin to show.

Although the symbol of the ferocious Bengal tiger wasn't attached to Tammany until Boss Tweed (it had been the logo of the volunteer fire company he headed), it was Burr who gave Tammany its fighting spirit, fashioning a political instrument with which to rule New York and challenge Federalist control of the national government. Burr organized Tammany—or, as officially incorporated, "The Society of St. Tammany or Columbian Order in the City of New York"—around the inner circle of sachems who became the controlling body of the city's anti-Federalist party (known then as Republicans, later as Democrats), and he made sure it was prepared to do whatever was necessary to win.

In 1812, the Society built its first headquarters, or wigwam, at the corner of Nassau and Frankfort, and this hall and its successors became a symbol of the whole Tammany organization. The advent of Jacksonian democracy, along with the abolition in 1822 of property qualifications for New York voters (at least white male ones), required the Hall to reach out to the city's workingmen and, tentatively at first, to the growing number of immigrants.

By the time of Plunkitt's birth in 1842, the rising tide of immigration had made the Irish a constituency that couldn't be ignored. Native-born Americans of every political stripe had an almost instinctually negative reaction to the rapidly expanding number of papist foreigners. But some, like Fernando Wood, a prototypical urban boss—wily, pragmatic, unscrupulous—were able to swallow their distaste in the interests of political practicality. Wood quickly grasped that with their votes, the Irish held the key that turned the lock of electoral victory.

Over the years, a good deal has been written about Tammany Hall and the Irish. Much of it has proceeded on the notion that though (contrary to Plunkitt's boast) the Irish weren't born to rule, they were uniquely equipped to make full use of the American political system. According to this theory, thanks to the mass political movement begun in Ireland by Daniel O'Connell in the 1820s and continuing into the 1840s—a movement aimed at gaining civil rights for Ireland's Catholic majority and, subsequently, at repeal of the union with Great Britain—the Irish landed in America endowed with the organizational skills they needed to turn their numbers to immediate and full advantage.

There is no doubt that O'Connell mobilized the masses as no European political leader had before. But the exact relationship between that experience and the Irish involvement in Tammany is easier invoked than described. Take the case of Plunkitt. Residing in a shantytown in the vicinity of what is now Central Park, Plunkitt's family preceded, by a few years, the vast influx of Irish driven to America by the Great Famine of the 1840s.

The bulk of these emigrants were from the townlands of Ireland's south and west. They were steeped in the traditions and rhythms of a primitive agricultural economy. Deeply resentful, often violently so, of the Protestant ascendancy that had monopolized power and wealth in Ireland, a bitterness etched deep by the acid ordeal of the Famine, they poured into the port of New York, crowding into fetid cellars and hovels, swelling the dirt-floored shantytowns in which the Plunkitts had already taken up residence.

We have no records of what the Plunkitts and their neighbors thought about their prospects in America. There were no diarists or memorialists among them. But we know that as well as being a people of few material resources, their arrival in America brought about a powerful reaction. Of this they were quickly made aware. In 1844, soon after Plunkitt saw the first light of day, New York City elected John Harper as mayor. Harper, a co-founder of the publishing house that still bears his name, was elected on an anti-Catholic, anti-immigrant ticket. His victory was part of a nationwide surge of suspicion and resentment that coalesced into the largest and, for a while, most successful third-party movement in American history.

In New York City, as elsewhere, the battle lines were drawn: on one side, the mass of newcomers who had little to recommend them beyond the sheer force of their numbers; on the other, the descendants of the country's original white settlers, who were horrified and threatened by the invasion of hordes of foreigners who filled the almshouses and prisons.

It would seem that whatever effect Daniel O'Connell might have had, the Irish were drawn to American politics by purely practical and situational considerations. Like the Jewish immigrants who would create the American film industry, the Irish followed the path of least resistance. They went where they had the best chance of entry. Politics also allowed them to translate a real, if unquantifiable, cultural emphasis on sociability—on song and on talk—into a usable asset.

Plunkitt's own rise in the world is instructive in this regard. Bereft of education or connections, yet unwilling to resign himself to a lifetime as a Paddy laborer in the city's shambles, he set his sights on politics. He began, he tells us, "by workin' around the district headquarters and hustlin' about the polls on election day." Soon enough, after seeing for himself how the system ran, he went to a cousin and announced, "'Tommy, I'm goin' to be a politician and I want to get a followin'; can I count on you?' He said: 'Sure, George.' That's how I started in business. I got a marketable commodity—one vote."

The personal pragmatism encapsulated in Plunkitt's self-described entry into politics may well telescope and simplify a longer and more nuanced process. (Then again, maybe it doesn't.) Yet it is so utterly devoid of any patina of patriotism or idealism that it is hard to believe he made it up. In fact, in its unadorned directness it seems to summarize the oft-repeated assertion that, other than taking care of themselves, the Irish didn't know what to do with political power once they took it.

Plunkitt and many of the Irish of his time would have been bewildered by such a charge. They believed they knew perfectly well what to do with power: first, get it; and once you get it, keep it. They never claimed they had some master plan for socioeconomic reform, and they undoubtedly intuited that the American system looked far more benignly on corruption than radicalism, especially when practiced or preached by immigrant outsiders.

Living in a new country, in the aftermath of the Famine, the Irish employed political power as a buckler of community solidarity and survival, a means with which to shield themselves from the attacks of their enemies, and as a sword with which to strike back. They used the Democratic Party the way they used the Catholic Church: as a rallying point and redoubt, a place in which they gained the resources and discipline to recover from the shattering dislocation endured in their mass exodus from the ancient, familiar patterns of rural life to the freewheeling, winner-take-all environment of urban America.

There wasn't much room for great causes and grand ideas. Romantic Ireland never had much of a chance in the Hall. Tammany was about practical things: about jobs, bread, influence; about the neighborhood kid who needed a lawyer; about the fees paid a subcontractor; and about the hundred cases of champagne and two hundred kegs of beer waiting in the basement of the Hall for those who endured five hours of July Fourth speechifying. Neither Kelly nor Croker nor Murphy were ever in danger of being bathed in the heroic light of, say, a Charles Stewart Parnell. But unlike their cousins back in Ireland, the Irish of Tammany never became the impotent, disappointed romantics found in James Joyce's masterful story of post-Parnell Ireland, "Ivy Day in the Committee Room."

The men who ran Tammany commanded the loyalty of their followers because of their power to overcome the enemy at the polls and to disburse the fruits—or spoils—of their electoral victories. The greatest testament to their success was the ability of the Organization to survive their demise. The boss might die or flee or go to jail, but the Organization continued. As Croker put it, "A change is a good thing sometimes; but Tammany Hall will be here when we are all gone."

The bosses were very different men, and Tammany's fortunes varied under each. But they all promised to reward their followers with work. As far as they were able, they kept that promise. In the days before civil service, it is estimated that control of the city government meant 12,000 public jobs as well as the ancillary ability to squeeze additional jobs out of the private sector.

Nothing drew Plunkitt's hatred like the civil service. The man finds it hard to speak of it and maintain his sanity. But beneath the bluster and the blarney is a very modern concern. Plunkitt claims government jobs as a reward of political victory to be distributed among supporters in need of work. For them, it will provide a paycheck and, as important, a toehold on the ladder to respectability. Civil service defeats this process by restricting access to the already-blessed middle classes who are schooled in a knowledge of the mandarin arcana that, in Plunkitt's view, is the subject of civil service exams. ("State all you don't know, and why you don't know it," is Plunkitt's way of summing them up.)

It is not hard to imagine the perverse satisfaction Plunkitt would take in the appearance of affirmative action and the attempt of socially committed, good-hearted liberals to undo the strict civil service standards their intellectual ancestors worked so hard to put in place. While he would never approve a program insulated from the direct effect of politics, it is inconceivable that he wouldn't bless any effort to subvert the civil service and give the jobs to the people most in need of them.

At the root of much of Tammany's success was the identification with the city's immigrant poor and working classes. Plunkitt and others grew rich on it. As crass and self-serving as this often was, it was also real and powerful. The people weren't fools, at least, as Lincoln framed it, not all of the time. They heard and saw enough to know what Tammany was up to. On occasion their patience was exhausted and they voted to throw the rascals out. But they perceived in Tammany an institution that, if sometimes insincere, was never condescending in the way many middle- and upper-class reformers were.

There is a scene in Stephen Crane's novella, "Maggie, A Girl of the Streets," that sums up this awareness. A tough street kid wanders into a storefront mission "where a man composed his sermons of 'you's.' Once a philosopher asked this man why he did not say 'we' instead of 'you.' The man replied, 'What?'" Tammany never made this mistake.

Tammany was always *we, us,* always doing the people the service of treating them as if they were somebodies. Consider Plunkitt's small but revealing observation on the Wall Street janitors who determined the electoral outcome in the Battery district. Where a middle-class reformer might have seen a pack of ignorant, mop-wielding Italian immigrants, Plunkitt saw a proud collection of men who know the significance of their vote. "Even I," he confessed, "might have trouble holding them."

Or consider Johnny Ahearn, leader in the Fourth District on the Lower East Side. His constituents, Plunkitt tells us, were "about half Irishmen and half Jews," a division that bothered Ahearn not at all. According to Plunkitt, Ahearn was "as popular with one race as the other. He eats corned beef and kosher meat with equal nonchalance, and it's all the same to him whether he takes off his hat in the church or pulls it down over his ears in the synagogue." When Ahearn died, people in his district sat *shiva* and the street peddlers overturned their carts in a sign of mourning. Of how many reformers could this be said?

The people paid a price for their support of Tammany. Maybe in the end, in some ways, they might have been materially better off heeding the gospel of the reformers. But for all its excesses, for all its thievery and knavery, Tammany afforded the poor what the rich and well-off had denied them throughout history: respect.

Richard Croker said as much in his famous interview with W. T. Stead in 1897. Tammany, he said, was the only organization that met the poor man on his own turf and treated him as an equal: "Think of the hundreds of foreigners dumped into our city. They are too old to go to school. There is not a mugwump who would shake hands with them . . . Tammany looks after them for the sake of their vote, grafts them upon the Republic, makes citizens of them in short; and although you may not like our motives or our methods, what other agency is there by which so long a row could have been hoed so quickly or so well? If we go down into the gutter, it is because there are men in the gutter, and you have got to go where they are if you are to do anything with them."

Croker told a half-truth. Tammany worked the streets and gutters, but it didn't have to descend from any heights to do so. This is where Tammany came from, and though he retired to the life of an English country gentleman, this is where Croker began his existence in New York, in a shantytown not far from Plunkitt's. Neither Croker nor Plunkitt had any distance to travel to understand where the poor came from; it required no act of the imagination, no leap of sympathetic feeling. And because of this, they knew that as long as they didn't strut about with the refined hauteur of the upper classes, the poor were likely not only to forgive them their trespasses, but to cheer them on, the lead runners in a race the denizens of the slums hoped their own children would one day get to run.

The irony is that Tammany's end came not because it resisted the forces of economic progressivism and reform, but because it joined them. Under Charlie Murphy, Tammany swung its support behind a legislative agency that pushed government regulation and protection into areas it had never gone before. Murphy's protégés, Robert Wagner and Al Smith, became prototypes of a new kind of urban politician, streetwise as well as honest, promoting programs designed to improve the living conditions of the masses. Eventually, with the election of Franklin Roosevelt as president in 1932, New York's agenda became the nation's.

It is the received wisdom that Charlie Murphy's death in 1924 (fittingly enough, the same year as Plunkitt's) marked the beginning of the end for Tammany. The Organization fell into the hands of epigones who brought the Seabury investigation down upon their heads, eventually descending into associations with petty gamblers and big-time racketeers. Tammany was made irrelevant by the evolution of a new American political order and became a kind of vestigial organ, like the appendix, capable of doing harm but unable to make any positive contribution to the body politic. Finally, and mercifully, it was removed. Or so it is said.

There is, however, another version of Tammany's denouement that seems more in keeping with the true trajectory of its development. In 1922, with Murphy's blessing, the Bronx Democratic Organization chose as its leader Edward Flynn, an educated, well-mannered, suave Irish-American. Murphy obviously liked Flynn and saw in him, perhaps, the next stage of Tammany's existence. Leading an organization one step removed physically, psychically, and, in many cases, economically from the immigrant neighborhoods of Manhattan, Flynn had none of the flamboyance of a Jimmy Walker. Just as smart as Walker, Flynn was quieter, steadier, and divorced from the pervasive corruption Walker and company thrived on.

Flynn's highly efficient, disciplined Bronx machine won elections with even greater regularity than the New York Yankees, that other great Bronx machine, won pennants. Flynn's team played according to the old Tammany rules of district leaders and neighborhood captains, but Flynn had his sights set on a bigger game. He formed a close relationship with Franklin Roosevelt, helping him win the governorship of New York and then doing all he could to elect him president. Flynn stayed a trusted confidant of FDR. In 1944, it was Flynn who put Truman on the ticket for vice president.

Nobody ever accused Ed Flynn of not knowing what to do with power once he got it. He worked to put the New Deal in place and kept his full support behind the social legislation that brought an unprecedented degree of security and opportunity to ordinary Americans. With the passage of those reforms, he also helped open a path for his constituents to leave the Bronx and its urban precincts altogether, passing in to the greener pastures of the suburbs, the Promised Land the immigrants had come seeking.

Tammany didn't wither into extinction after Murphy died. Flynn took up the mantle, and wore it successfully, regally. He was the true last emperor. The machine survived long enough after his death to be an early and important supporter of John F. Kennedy, but the glory days were over. Everybody knew it.

What some seem to forget is that the machine conspired in its own demise. It supported the very legislation that removed its vital role as a quasi-agency of social welfare and legal aid. It bowed before the road builders and urban planners, with their cold-blooded schemes for demolishing the old neighborhoods and girding the city with highways whose sole intent was to ease the commute from the suburbs.

Plunkitt was lucky to pass away when he did. He went out attended by a full complement of friends, and even a few enemies. Sacred Heart Church, the *New York Times* reported, was crowded with politicians: "Among them were John R. Voorhis, Grand Sachem of the Society of Tammany; 'Big Tom' Foley, William Holly and John F. Curry, members of the Council of Sachems; Murray Hulbert, President of the Board of Aldermen; Charles H. Hussey, Tammany leader of the Third Assembly District; The McManus, who succeeded Plunkitt as leader of the Fifth Assembly District; Alderman Charles J. McManus; former United States Senator James A. O'Gorman . . ." All in all, a real-life last hurrah. A cortege of twenty-one automobiles followed the hearse from Plunkitt's home to the church.

Fate smiled on George Washington Plunkitt. It allowed him to travel from a shantytown crowded with Famine refugees to a life of comfort and, almost, respectability. He lived in a time when the city kept growing and booming, and the pie always seemed to get bigger and richer. The Depression, television, and the superhighway were hidden from him. Yet Plunkitt sensed trouble ahead. In words that ring with lament as well as prophecy, he saw a day when his world would disappear: "Ignorant people are always talkin' against party bosses, but just wait till the bosses are gone! Then, and not until then, will they get the right sort of epitaphs, as Patrick Henry or Robert Emmet said."

Part of that epitaph was already written at the time of Plunkitt's death. It was contained in his wise, intemperate, hilarious, outrageous little book.

Local Politics,
Irish-American Style

Be true to the neighborhood, and the neighborhood will be true to you.
—JOHN J. HANLEY, Sheriff of the Bronx, 1932

THOUGH I'VE ALWAYS BEEN AN ADMIRER of the late Speaker of the House, Thomas ("Tip") O'Neill, I've also thought that his oft-quoted dictum "All politics is local" is wrong. What he meant to say, as I see it, was that *his* politics—politics as practiced in the post-Famine tradition of Irish-American politicians—is local, and it's local because above all else it's personal, the entire organization depending on a network of face-to-face relationships. Admittedly, that's not as quotable as his original version, but it's far closer to the truth.

This was brought home to me a few years back when I was living in Brooklyn and went to join the local Democratic club. As a son of the Bronx Democratic Organization, I knew that the best way to express concerns about subway service or sanitation wasn't by writing indignant letters to the Grand Vizier in City Hall but by making friends with the neighborhood politicos.

The night I showed up at the club, a meeting of irate citizens was in progress. The object of impassioned conversation wasn't dirty streets or poor subway service. It was U.S. foreign policy in Central America. In the two hours I sat and listened, the discussion never came within 1500 miles of Brooklyn.

Looking around the audience of educated professionals—people like me—I knew no one was there for free legal advice or a lead on a city job. The politics being practiced reflected the lives of those who hadn't and, barring a general economic collapse, wouldn't come to the club in search of work or a lawyer. More than a few present in the room were required by their careers to change residences every several years. The upscale nature of their neighborhoods stayed the same, only the location—in New York, San Francisco, London, Paris, et al.—changed. Their politics, like their careers, was national and global.

The contrasting concentration of Irish-American politics on things local is nowhere better articulated than in George Washington Plunkitt's ruminations and fulminations. He mentions foreign policy only to dismiss it. On the burning national issue of the free coinage of silver, the center of William Jennings Bryan's 1896 presidential campaign, Plunkitt sums up Tammany's position by quoting Boss Croker: "What's the use of discussin' the best kind of money? I'm in favor of all kinds of money—the more the better."

The energetic flag-waving in which Irish-American politicians indulged wasn't insincere. Despite a core of dedicated radicals, most immigrant voters were to one degree or another glad to be in America and unready for revolution. But the machine's patriotism wasn't devoid of self-interest. There was no price to pay for patriotic gestures and speechifying. It didn't cost anything to root for the army, support the expansion of the fleet, or laud the country's aggressive spirit.

As Mark Twain pointed out during the war against the insurrection in the Philippines, if the United States was truly interested in overthrowing one party rule and clearing the way for honest government, it would send the marines to Manhattan, not Manila. That thought might well have crossed the minds of the Tammany sachems, which was why they could cheer with extra gusto for the interest Washington took in Asia rather than New York's Lower East Side.

The obsessive localism of Irish-American politics amazed Frederick Hackenberg, a German immigrant to New York who eventually rose to the rank of Democratic Party district leader. Hackenburg had been exposed to political theory in his native Germany and arrived eager to join the kind of national social democratic movement on the rise in his native country. Irish-American politics, he wrote in his memoir, *A Solitary Parade*, had a very different focus:

> Politics was not discussed in terms of principles, platforms, or ideas. It was entirely, thoroughly, and overwhelmingly personal. A leader was either a good man or a bad man. A good man took care of his constituents and supplied them with Christmas baskets and with jobs; he paid rents and prevented evictions. If he did not live up to these standards he was a bad man, working for his pocket, and was not destined to last very long in his position . . .

Perceiving the exact effects of the Great Famine on the urban enclaves of Irish America can be an uncertain business. But it would take an act of willful blindness not to perceive how the powerless victims of the British government's bureaucratic indifference (mixed with malevolence) and economic theorizing—all exercised at a safe remove from the devastated localities—came to America determined not to suffer the same fate. Statesmen and political economists could debate questions of tariffs and trade balances until they were red, white, and blue in the face, but the interest of the local clubhouses, as Hackenburg describes it, remained narrow and fixed:

> Living up to the requirements of personal charity and contract, the ward politician had no worries concerning the real business of government. No one cared how he discharged these responsibilities. The abstract ideas of political honesty and efficiency played no part in this scheme of things.

Eventually, the needs of the masses outgrew the resources of Tammany-style machines to serve or control them. There were just so many baskets of coal to distribute. But Tammany adjusted. Instead of sticking to defense, protecting its turf, warding off outside control, Tammany switched to offense, helping lead the campaign to alter the country's laws so that those at the bottom didn't have their faces ground into the mud.

The scope and substance of the agenda changed, but not its spirit. Tammany didn't put an Irish-American in the governor's seat in Albany until 1918, with the election of Al Smith, but his leadership in undertaking a pioneering agenda of social reform—worker safety, old-age pensions, child labor, decent housing—was rooted in neighborhood concerns. When Smith ran for president in 1928, it was a moment when international issues were almost completely absent from the campaign. Even when Tammany reached for the White House, its heart was in the neighborhood.

In an interview I did with William Kennedy (it's included in *Riding the Yellow Trolley Car*, a collection of his nonfiction), he described the stark determination of the Albany machine and its boss, Dan O'Connell, never again to experience powerlessness and the consequences of being at the mercy of others' charity (or lack of it), a resolve forged by the generations that passed through workhouses, immigrant ships, and shantytowns:

> When I grew up, there was no sense of morality in regard to politics. If you were Irish, you were obviously a Democrat. If you were a Democrat, you were probably a Catholic. If you were a Catholic, you obviously gave allegiance to the church on the corner, and to Dan O'Connell who was a pillar of the Church, inseparable from the bishop and the priests, and who was revered and prayed for. But Dan was also profiting from the whorehouses, the gambling joints, the all-night saloons and the blackout card games. He was in collusion with the grafters and the bankers, getting rich with the paving contractors.
>
> No matter what it was in town, wherever you could make an illegal dollar, that's where the Irish were, that's where the politics were, that's where the church was, that's where the morality was. And it was all fused. You couldn't separate it because the families were so interlocked, and the goodness walked hand-in-hand with the evil. It was viewed as a way to get on in the world. Objective morality didn't interest Albany. The Irish didn't care about it. They understood that they had been deprived and now they were not. Now they were able to get

jobs. In previous generations, when the Irish were not in power, they had not been able to get jobs. Their families starved, and starvation for them was immorality. So once they took power, O'Connell became a kind of saint. He became the man who would save your soul by putting you to work.

As far as I can tell, the morality behind machines in cities as disparate as Boston, Kansas City, Chicago, Jersey City, Albany, New York, and wherever Irish-Americans were in the political driver's seat, was the same. (And it's important to remember that their success as coalition builders often allowed the Irish to stay in that seat after other immigrant groups far exceeded them in numbers.) It wasn't lofty or theoretical. Jefferson would have been sickened at the dependence of the urban masses.

There were hacks galore. Corruption abounded. But the have-nots got their foot in the door, made one small step for themselves, one giant step for those to follow. Religious and ethnic barriers were challenged and breeched, while barriers of race were accepted, even strengthened. This was democratic politics in the raw, untouched by genteel considerations, untempered by education, steeped in circumstance, utterly imperfect, immediate, at its most human. No theorists need apply.

At a panel discussion on judicial corruption sponsored by the New York City Bar Association, I heard a participant, a law school professor, dismiss Irish-American political machines in toto as "venal collections of hacks, crooks, and hangers-on." ("The Organization" was the term that the members themselves usually preferred.) That summary indictment of the partisan apparatuses that, to one degree or another, controlled many of America's largest cities for extensive periods of their history is, I think, widely shared. While not entirely inaccurate— and let's not forget that even law school faculties have their own share of hacks and hangers-on—such a blanket appraisal is wildly, distortingly inadequate.

To measure just how inadequate, I would heartily recommend a close encounter with Teddy Fleming, leader of Jersey City's Sixth Ward, chairman of the Board of Chosen Freeholders, sheriff of Hudson County, self-labeled son of a bitch and subject of son Tom Fleming's memoir *Mysteries of My Father*. In reconstructing his father's rise from tough-talking, hard-fisted son of an illiterate Irish immigrant laborer to a top lieutenant and reeve of Frank Hague's all-controlling mayoral rule over Jersey City, Tom Fleming tells a real-life story that should be read, examined, and absorbed by every serious student of American political history and, especially, by the timid crew currently running the Democratic Party.

Neither hack nor hanger-on nor crook, Teddy Fleming was a full-time, full-service local politician, a "ward heeler" in the old parlance, who knew his people and precincts the way an Indian scout knew his way through the forest. Rather than merely attempt to measure or approximate the opinions or needs of the grass roots, Teddy lived as a blade himself, albeit an especially strong, iron-sided, crush-resistant one. Though the results of each election—overwhelming victory for the machine—might have looked predictable and easy, producing those results was anything but. "Jesus Christ himself couldn't keep these people happy," a wise and battle-scarred monsignor told Teddy.

Happiness never had much good press among Irish-Americans, at least in their prolonged assimilation into the national mainstream, a process that proceeded far more rapidly in the aftermath of World War II than in the century that had followed the Great Hunger. What counted was putting food on the table, keeping a roof overhead, finding some measure of security that wouldn't evaporate with the same horrifying suddenness it had when the blight obliterated the Irish potato crop. Irish-American politics was about security, not philosophy. Morality wasn't allowed to get in the way of electoral victory. (As one Albany pol famously put it, "Honesty is no substitute for experience.") Success depended on a single virtue: loyalty.

Teddy Fleming's loyalty was two-sided but equivalent. On one side was the boss, Frank Hague, who had to be listened to and obeyed or the game came apart. Occasionally, he could be defied, but Teddy had to choose his moments carefully and brave a barrage of threats and abuse. On the other side, Teddy's loyalty was to the people of the Sixth Ward. Unless they were served and satisfied, the machine ceased to function. It was a political system that Teddy summed up to the voters in simple, unadorned prose: "You are my people. Never forget that. If any of you need help, all you have to do is speak to me. I will do my utmost to serve you."

Never the smooth, seamless monolith it often appeared to out-siders, the political machine in Jersey City (or in any of the various urban locales that hosted similar organizations) was, Tom Fleming writes, "a churning mix of ambition and resentments and inertia over which leaders presided only by constant effort." That Teddy survived as long as he did, and even prospered, maintaining the loyalty of the eth-nic mélange of voters in the contentious Sixth Ward right up to the end, was a testament to the skills he'd acquired as a boxer, salesman, and veteran of some of the bloodiest fighting endured by American sol-diers in World War I. Teddy was a man of no illusions. He knew when to push and when to be patient, and he never violated his credo: He was there to help people through the litany of everyday woes—loss of a job, physical injury, the arrest of a child, a husband's abandonment—that wrecked individuals and families.

Tom Fleming's portraits of his father and the Jersey City machine are rendered in subtle hues. He refuses to find heroes where they aren't or to blot out the good in the interest of creating simple, easy-to-recognize villains. The same is true of his description of his parents' marriage, a tortured, contested union between two people from the polarities of Irish-American life—"shanty" and "lace-curtain." Kitty Dolan, Fleming's mother, was a product of "uptown" Jersey City, a world removed from the hardscrabble Sixth Ward. Though her life with Teddy began in romance, it endured as a long-running bitter argument over the whole tenor and trajectory of Teddy's political and personal life, ending at last in "residual tenderness." At the heart of the struggle were their progeny, two boys Kitty would have loved to see become priests and Teddy was determined to prevent from becoming "Mama's boys."

Fleming's *Mysteries of My Father* is a rich book. Rich in its tex-tured description of Jersey City politics. Rich in wonderful political anecdotes. (Frank Hague's last hurrah on a platform amid the surging, rebellious voters of the Second Ward is the stuff of epic poetry.) Rich in sympathetic understanding of Teddy and Kitty and of their tempestuous marriage. Rich in honest evocation of "the morally gray world of Hudson County politics." And rich in its power to bring alive the once vital, now vanished world of the big-city Irish-American political machine.

Teddy would be proud of his son's courage in confronting truths that are never easy to face. If more than a little chagrined at public exposure of family secrets (the bête noire of the lace-curtain Irish), Kitty couldn't help but be proud of her son's artistry. For my part, if by some terrible twist of fate I ever find myself in the middle of a political campaign, I pray it's being led by the likes of Teddy Fleming and not some law school professor.

In his novel *Roscoe*, William Kennedy renders in fiction what Tom Fleming records in his memoir. *Roscoe* is a brilliantly real and comic exposé, creating a portrait of the Albany machine in its heyday that is sympathetic and unsparing. Kennedy grew up surrounded by the local machine. As a young reporter he fought it. Better than any writer, Irish-American or otherwise, he understands it. At one point in *Roscoe*, he takes the reader inside the minds of the politicians pleading with Governor Franklin Roosevelt, then entering his 1932 campaign for president, to overlook the corruption in New York City brought to light by the Seabury investigation and choose a regular (as opposed to a reformer) to run for his seat as governor:

> John Curry and John McCooey [the bosses of Manhattan and Brooklyn, respectively] are likeable men; they take care of the money because there it is, as it always was. Somebody's got to take care of it. Just because you're born with money and don't need to accumulate any, don't mean you close out the less fortunate. Christ Almighty, Frank, it's only a few million, nobody'll miss it, don't drive your bowels into a stupor. The true question is jobs and families, the flower of our meaning, the source of our blessedness, we who have been chosen to raise up our

people. These people can't make it on their own, Frank, but they're our future, those tots of ours in carriages, little boys on the altar, darling girls playing hopscotch, God bless them all, the world is not Irish, Frank, and it was never Dutch, if you'll pardon the expression. We're trying to do right, elect progressive people who want to promote the general welfare of our great city and state, we need people who matter . . . who'll do what is good for them, and for us. That's all we ask.

Mixed in with obvious blarney (altar boys and darling girls) and subtle self-interest (officeholders who'll do good for the people "and for us") is a phrase as truthful as it is now unfashionable: "These people can't make it on their own . . ." Today, with the trauma of the Great Depression a faded memory, the national political faith is once again heavily invested in every person's ability, no matter how poor, deprived, or disabled, to go from rags to riches. Most of those whose lives are a saga of rags to rags are seen as suffering the consequences of their own inertia.

Contained in the local Irish-run political machines was an opposing idea: the laissez-faire ethic of free-market capitalism creates winners as well as losers (and during the Famine the losers among the Irish numbered in the millions). Even if by some miracle the playing field were made perfectly level, there would be large numbers, some temporarily, others permanently, hobbled and unable to compete. The local machines couldn't theorize these people out of existence or chalk their fate off to the gods of macroeconomics. The unemployed sat on the neighborhood stoops and stood on its street corners. Their wives and mothers came to the clubhouse to beg for work. Attention had to be paid

The evils, in Kennedy's phrase, walked hand-in-hand with the good. The poor weren't subject to the inquisition of their social betters to determine eligibility for assistance. They were helped. Immigrants weren't mocked for their ignorance. They were courted for their vote. Loyalty counted more than competency, connections more than merit. Appointments to public-sector jobs saved families from economic ruin. Working-class parents obtained the wherewithal to push their children into the middle class. A social safety net was eventually woven for the entire country out of materials manufactured in part by the machines.

Socialism was admirable, an ideal my own grandfather imagined might come in time, when workers put aside ethnic, religious, and regional differences, overcame the resistance of the propertied classes and its extensions—courts, banks, the army—and took firm and prolonged hold of the levers of power. What descendant of the working classes doesn't admire the wild hopes and valor of vagabond radicals like the Wobblies? *Better to die on your feet than live on your knees!* In the meantime, back in the Sixth Ward, there were the small and not-so-small everyday questions of putting bread on the table, caring for the infants and the old, getting sons and brothers out of trouble, finding a little fun, enjoying a clambake or a boat ride, keeping at bay the blue-nose reformers, and circumventing the societies dedicated to creating a respectable, respectful lower class that was well behaved and knew its place.

The machines were the enemy of Social Darwinism, the anti-eugenic party, an example of how outsiders can wield democratic politics to push their interests against insiders. They were also creatures of their times, not embodiments of urban politics in the "good old days" but a tactic of the marginalized in an era when government took no active role in protecting them from predatory capitalism and collective penury. For most of their history, they were conservative in nature, moderating the worst effects of the economic system instead of advocating its overthrow. But they weren't static. They evolved, replaced by the New Deal and the Great Society.

Tammany is gone. Frank Hague and Dan O'Connell molder in their graves. But corruption thrives. It was never the monopoly of local machines. Today's bribery and illicit deal-making are usually (though certainly not always) subtler, more sophisticated, and more lucrative. The executives and lobbyists who ride in golden circles upon the military-industrial-financial-congressional merry-go-round pluck more opportunities for personal gain than Plunkitt and his cohorts could have conceived.

In the opening decade of the new millennium, the question of who gets to run the government and to whose benefit is as fresh as ever. With global capitalism triumphant and its engine of "creative destructionism" praised by those fortunate enough to enjoy the creative part and escape the destructive, it seems to me that the underlying lesson of the old-style politics shouldn't be entirely lost. If ordinary people are to have any say in the exercise of power and the disposition of resources, local politics is where they must begin.

Life of the Party

He concedes that a morally pure society, with candidates unblemished with sin and vice, might exist somewhere, though he has never seen or heard of one, and can't really imagine what one would be like. "But I'll keep looking," he concludes.
—WILLIAM KENNEDY, *Roscoe*

PETER A. QUINN, MY FATHER, was a most imperfect man. Moody, often emotionally distant, capable of purple-faced tantrums that seemed certain—although they never did—to end in his death or the death of anyone in the near vicinity, he was also a good man. The older I get, the longer I've been around high-ranking politicians and corporate executives, the more I've realized his goodness. He was uninterested in wealth and power. He was devoid of pomposity and self-importance. A judge for twenty-five years in city and state courts, he approached his job with an equal sense of responsibility and humility. He was capable of laughing at himself and had a gut-seated sympathy for the poor, the powerless, and the disenfranchised.

Several times, learning that my father had spent his life in politics—Bronx politics, no less—strangers have responded jocularly, "You must be rich!" I've laughed along with them. My father died in 1974 with accumulated life savings of $16,000. At the same time, amid the hours

I've spent reading about Tammany Hall and New York's rampant political skullduggery, I wondered about my father's experiences in Bronx politics as an assemblyman, congressman, and judge, about the corruption he undoubtedly knew of and, perhaps, closed his eyes to.

When my father entered politics in the early 1930s, the leader (newspapers invariably referred to him as "boss") of the Bronx Democratic Organization was Ed Flynn. An intimate of Franklin Delano Roosevelt, Flynn ran a relatively "clean machine." It wasn't devoid, by any means, of the self-dealing and "honest graft" described long before by George Washington Plunkitt; but especially in comparison to Prendergast's machine in Kansas City or Hague's in Jersey City—or even the Tammany machine in Manhattan—it was free of an avaricious disregard for legality.

My father's political initiation came during the investigations of Judge Samuel Seabury into the multiple layers of graft, bribery, and venal shenanigans piled atop one another in the administration of Mayor Jimmy Walker. When bosses in other boroughs ordered their followers in the state assembly to vote against the continuation of the Joint Legislative Committee investigating the government of New York City, Flynn stood with Roosevelt and backed the bill. His overriding goal was to do what was necessary to protect FDR's chances of winning the presidency in 1932 from being harmed by the scandals in New York City. If that meant pursuing the investigations to their final conclusion and bringing public officials to justice, Flynn was willing to spin the wheel.

He did so at considerable risk. Serving as New York's Secretary of State, Flynn was convinced that he was being stalked because of Seabury's not-so-subtle desire to gain the Democratic presidential nomination for himself. "If he [Seabury] could embarrass Roosevelt's Secretary of State," Flynn maintained, "then he thought he could use that as a springboard to the presidency. He searched my records from the time I was born, but he found nothing and he never would admit that he found nothing."

I'm not the most impartial of observers in these matters. Belief in the Democratic Party was ingrained in me as a child, in much the same way that my religious beliefs were. By the time I got to college, and commuted to the same school over the same streets my father had forty years before, I made it a point to seek every possible opportunity to challenge the Church and Party as corrupt, obsolete institutions, guilty of every sort of transgression. "Every organization is made up of sinners," he told me.

He loved to argue and always encouraged it at the dinner table. As far as he was concerned, I was welcome to my opinions—which he kept telling me, annoyingly, I'd one day outgrow. But no matter what opinions I held, as long as I was living under his roof, I'd register as a Democrat and attend Sunday Mass—"period," as he liked to say. "End of argument. Next case."

The equation my father helped plant in my head between Catholic Church and Democratic Party meant that I perceived them as fulfilling parallel roles. In my mind, each seemed a source of certainty, a bulwark against evil and exploitation, a guide and protector leading us safely through the perils of today as well as eternity.

My experience of the party was secondhand. I watched my father go out to political dinners and events but rarely accompanied him. I heard the muffled rise and fall of his voice as he rehearsed speeches in his bedroom. I absorbed his faith in the New Deal from his conversations (and sometimes arguments) with friends and acquaintances. Once I heard him say, "It's enough to know that children are poor to know that they need help," and the words stuck with me, resonating with a line from a familiar prayer . . . *to Thee do we cry, poor banished children of Eve.*

My experience of the Church, in contrast, was up close, intense, personal, and pervasive. For families like mine, in those pre-Vatican II days, life revolved around the Church. The environment was sexually puritanical, ritually demanding, and often stultifying. It was also intensely comforting and secure, liturgically rich, a culture of moral absolutes, theological certainties, and religious devotions in which the answers to all life's questions were readily at hand.

As rigorous and rigid as that culture was, it had, in the form of the Virgin Mary and the saints, a soft center. God the Father was practically unapproachable, the gray-bearded patriarch from the Sistine Chapel, quick to anger and eager to dispatch evildoers to hell. The Virgin Mary was the opposite—patient, understanding, infinitely kind. The *Salve Regina* expressed her attributes best: "O clement, O loving, O sweet Virgin Mary." St. Anthony of Padua was typical of the kind-hearted intercessor who, along with the Virgin, was always there to help people both in their secular and spiritual needs. We prayed to St. Anthony when we lost something. If neither he nor the Virgin could assist, there was St. Jude, the patron of lost causes.

Many Catholics traditionally adopt a particular saint as their own special patron to be prayed to for guidance, protection, and assistance. My father's was Thomas More, the English lawyer and chancellor who was beheaded in 1535 for his refusal to consent to Henry VIII's divorce and remarriage. More was a rarity among saints. He was married and spent his career in public service. My mother's patron was Martin de Porres, a Dominican lay brother who lived in seventeenth-century Peru. Though he was only "blessed" (one step short of canonization), my mother treated him as the full-fledged saint he would eventually become. Martin was the object of my mother's constant pleas and petitions. She had obtained a relic of him, and when members of her family were sick or dying, the relic was touched to their flesh in hope of a cure. Martin was also odd among saints: He was a black man.

A child's formal introduction to Catholicism was through the Baltimore Catechism. The question-and-answer format was precise and direct. Existence presented basic questions to which God had provided the answers, all of them possessed and guarded by the One True Church. Other religious traditions—Protestant, Jewish, Zoroastrian, take your pick—were gravely deficient. But it was Protestantism and its degenerate and inevitable offspring of religious indifference that presented the real threat.

Unlike Jews or Buddhists, Protestants were interested in claiming our souls and separating us from our faith. They were nowhere near as threatening as Communists, whose object was the violent eradication of religion, but we stayed away from places like the YMCA because we'd been warned of the subtle but ever-present desire of Protestants to convert us. (And, yes, that glistening and seductive swimming pool we glimpsed through its portals seemed a perfect place to find oneself suddenly subjected to a Protestant baptism.)

In early childhood, I was confused by the mention of Protestants, and I wasn't alone. During a lesson about Thanksgiving, Sister Liguori, my second grade teacher, informed us the Pilgrims were Protestants.

A classmate raised his hand. "You mean they were Jews?"

It seemed a fair question. Like Caesar's Gaul, the Bronx we knew was divided into three groups: Italians, Irish, and Jews. If you weren't Catholic, you were Jewish. The Orthodox Jews we sometimes saw on the Grand Concourse or Pelham Parkway wore large black hats similar to the ones worn by the Pilgrims. The Bronx was filled with synagogues. Protestant churches were usually small and tucked away. Yet the near total absence of Protestants and our less-than-clear understanding of who they were (were Presbyterians the same as Protestants?) only served to heighten a sense of their subversive intent.

I can't recall a single instance of anyone in the neighborhood going over to the Protestant side. My father, on the other hand, in his career as a lawyer and politician, had known Catholics who'd attended "the better" universities, worked at prestigious law firms, married into the upper class, and changed churches. To my father, this was a kind of treason, a bending of belief to ambition, a betrayal that involved class as much as religion. It stirred something visceral inside him.

During his time in Congress, my father developed an acquaintance with a fellow representative, a Republican, who he eventually discovered had been born an Irish Catholic but had traded in his religion, party, and identity for more prestigious and socially advantageous affiliations. In the bar of the Mayflower Hotel, after hearing my father recite a passage from Shakespeare, he said that he found my father "unusually cultured for an Irishman."

"If I thought less of my saliva," my father said, "I'd expectorate in your face."

Those were uncommonly harsh words for my father. He always encouraged us to be respectful of other people, no matter who they were. When it came to those who abandoned their Catholicism to move up the social ladder, however, his feelings reflected a bitter disdain among the Irish that went back to the economic, political, and social benefits conferred on those who took communion in the established church. This act was given an added aura of ignominy during the Famine, when Catholics were converted at the hands of Protestant missionaries in return for a portion of soup.

The actual number of those who took soup (or offered it) was tiny, and far more Protestant clergymen were involved in providing relief than seeking converts. But "taking soup" was a phrase that summed up the continued sense of living in a Protestant country and culture that regarded Catholicism and its adherents as incurably superstitious, ignorant, and alien. The key to survival was loyalty. As well as the supreme vitrtue of machine politics, loyalty was the bedrock of the Church's power, the cement of neighborhood and family. As Micheal Tuberty has pointed out about Irish-American filmmaker John Ford, "His films lend themselves to a discussion of loyalty, such as the Pacific war and cavalry films and in terms of flaunting the norms of loyalty, such as *The Informer*." ("Informer"—i.e. the betrayer, the disloyal one—was traditionally the lowest epithet the Irish could hurl at one another.)

My father made friends easily with Jews and Protestants. He worshipped F.D.R., an Episcopalian. Baptist Harry Truman was a hero. In his last years, his best friend and golfing companion (and drinking buddy) was an old-line Brooklyn German Protestant named Harry Christman. My father wouldn't join any club that excluded Jews. He was an ecumenicist before the word had any popular currency. When a tiny congregation of Lutherans invited him to attend the dedication of its new church, he readily accepted. The monsignor in charge of our parish heard about it and called to tell my father that, as a prominent Catholic, his participation in such an event might be "a source of scandal to the faithful." My father thanked him for his opinion and went anyway, enjoying, as he described it, "a grand old time."

My father was clear with his children that, by being good Protestants or Jews, adherents of those faiths could enter heaven. But because we'd been born into the Catholic faith, ours was a tougher challenge. We'd been uniquely burdened and uniquely blessed. We had the real presence of Christ in the Eucharist, confession (at once a terrifying and reassuring sacrament that underlined our salvation was always in the balance, capable of being won or lost in a matter of minutes), the saints, and the Virgin Mary, priceless possessions others didn't have. We also had stricter requirements for salvation. The devil had it out for us. He coaxed us to take the easy way out. We were denied the luxury of a death-bed conversion, á la Dutch Schultz, whose baptism in the final moments of his life wiped away his gangster misdeeds and mortal sins.

In the early 1960s, a case came before my father involving a highly decorated Irish-Catholic detective accused of shaking down immigrant doctors who were practicing on their Hispanic clientele without being licensed in New York. If the doctors protested, they were roughed up. After the detective was convicted, my father was contacted by representatives of several Irish-American organizations—including a monsignor and fellow judge—all echoing the same call for leniency in sentencing. Nobody was killed, the doctors were violating the law, the detective had an outstanding record, and, *don't forget, he's one of our own.*

Unfortunately for the detective, my father didn't forget. A decade later, a veteran court officer vividly recalled to me how he was in the courtroom the day my father handed down a maximum sentence. In this thirty-year career as a court officer, he'd never heard a more fluent and ferocious tongue-lashing than the one my father administered. The detective's crime, my father said, wasn't merely an ordinary instance of racketeering, but an extraordinary betrayal of the public trust and a base and reprehensible repudiation of the immigrant struggle of his own ancestors. The detective learned the hard way that pressing my father's ethno-religious buttons raised rather then lowered the bar.

My father went to Mass each morning before work. He was punctilious in his devotions, saying the rosary, praying on his knees each night before he went to bed, observing the Lenten fast, and attending the Stations of the Cross. But when it came to the clergy, he was a skeptic, an attitude inherited from his father, who'd faced the efforts of Archbishop Michael Corrigan to stop Catholics from joining the Knights of Labor. When my father thought a priest was an idiot, or a reactionary, or a timeserver, he said so.

In the eighth grade, at St. Raymond's Grammar School, I expressed an interest in studying for the priesthood, a process that in those days began in high school. The priest in charge of vocations pounced on my interest with such enthusiasm that I was afraid to back out or express any doubts. How could I not be honored at the thought of God calling me to be a priest? Yet, at night as I lay awake in bed listening for God's call, all I heard was the soft flow of traffic and the distant rise and fall of police sirens.

Without any encouragement from me, my father bailed me out. He said no, he wouldn't allow me to attend the pre-seminary. When I told the priest what my father said, he was convinced I'd botched the communication. He took it upon himself to contact my father. The gist of what my father told the priest was that no boy of my age had a real clue what he wanted to be. If I had a true vocation, then I'd have it at eighteen, when I got out of high school. Sure enough, by that time, the nighttime voices I heard were sirens of the flesh, succubae whose suggestions were irresistibly seductive.

I never questioned my father about how he reconciled his belief with his anticlericism. We didn't have that type of relationship. He stood off from and above us, and he didn't invite any probing of his personal life. Yet, in retrospect, I think he balanced his faith and his often jaundiced view of those who ran it in much the same way he did his unwavering loyalty to the Democratic Party with his embarrassment or dislike of particular candidates or officeholders.

This was brought home to me on Election Day in 1956. My father was running for a judgeship in the City Court. Adlai Stevenson was the Democratic candidate for president, a fact I was constantly reminded of by the Stevenson pennant my father had tacked over my brother's and my beds. For the first time, he took us into the voting booth with him. Barely looking at the names on the ballot, he pulled all the levers on Row B, voting a straight Democratic ticket.

He told us to remember that the Democratic and Republican parties had, at any one time, roughly the same proportion of fools and knaves. Absolute perfection and moral purity were out of the reach of any individual or party, he said. But each stood for something different, and only together, as a party, as a coherent organization, could people see to it that justice was done for all. "It's the party that matters," he added as we left the polling place, "not the man. You've got to stick with your beliefs." Though he never said so, I'm certain he viewed the Catholic Church in the same light.

My father went into politics to find work. He graduated from law school in 1929, right in time for the Depression ("the luck of the Irish," he used to sniff), and the first time he got a steady income was when he was elected to the state assembly in 1936. But employment wasn't his only motivation. He inherited a healthy suspicion of great wealth from his father, and the Depression added to that distrust an abiding belief in government's responsibility to protect the non-rich from the failures and excesses of free-market speculation.

As a young lawyer trying to prove himself, he went to the 1932 Democratic Convention in Chicago, not as a delegate but to work behind the scenes for Ed Flynn. The Tammany regulars, upset with Roosevelt's support for the investigations into Mayor Jimmy Walker's administration, hoped to throw the nomination to Al Smith, who was more than willing to accept it. Flynn brought a cadre of Bronx Democrats with him to lobby the delegates and keep them in line for Roosevelt.

My father returned from Chicago more convinced than ever that Roosevelt was the country's best hope. During the campaign of 1932, my father gave speeches for Roosevelt while standing on the back of a flatbed truck that traveled around the Bronx. He wrote a piece of political doggerel that he recited and that he taught me as a child (to me it was poetry, and I still think of it as the first poem I ever learned):

A chicken in the pot
is something I ain't got
and I ain't got
two cars in no garage.
The wife ain't wearing silk.
Heck, the kids ain't got no milk,
and today the grocer told me,
"No more charge."
I'm stranded on a rock
and my benny's* in the hock
and the thought of winter covers
me with goosepelt.
But there's one thing that I got
Since things ain't been so hot:
I got my mind made up to vote for Roosevelt!

His friends and acquaintances often remembered my father as "cheerful" or "fun," words that don't immediately pop in to my mind when I think of him. At home, he felt freer to give in to the melancholy and depression that he normally held at bay. But I know where the public image comes from. I only saw him speak in public a few times, but he could move a crowd, make them laugh, and bring them to their feet.

Although the constraints of the Depression forced my parents to postpone their marriage for seven years, each continuing to live at home, my mother never remembered the days of their courtship as grim or despairing. Wherever they went, she said, whether it was a political function or a parish dance, "Your father was always the life of the party."

---

*"Benny" was New York slang for an overcoat. It probably derives from the Irish word *báinín* (*pron*. baaneen), or jacket or overcoat made of homespun woolen cloth.

Civil Service

There is no higher estate then the service of
one's fellow citizens.

—MARCUS AURELIUS

I HEARD ABOUT THE CIVIL SERVICE from my father. Over and over,
I heard about it. The two words were part of oft-repeated mantras:
*A civil service job brings security. You can't beat a civil service
pension. You can retire from a civil service job and still have a decent
number of years to live. There's nothing better than a civil service job if
you expect to raise a family. A civil service job isn't at the mercy of the
stock market or the economy.*

As usual with my father, a story went along with his observations:

*He's two years out of law school. June of '29, when he graduated,
has turned into December of '31. Unable to find a job, he hears that the
next morning, down at Foley Square, applications will be available for a
civil service exam to fill a half dozen or so positions as uniformed court
officers.*

*Aiming to be at the head of the line, he gets up early, takes the
subway to Foley Square, emerges into wind-slashed, snow-dusted, winter-
solstice gloom of Lower Manhattan, and is startled by what he thinks is
a milling crowd. Soon he discovers that what he thought was a crowd is a
line that coils around itself. Several hundred men are already lined up for*

applications, including several acquaintances from law school who look half frozen.

For my father, as for many New Yorkers whose lives were shaped by the Depression, the civil service always retained a special cachet. Working for the government didn't mean joining the ranks of a bloated, inert bureaucracy, a last resort for those without enough smarts or moxie to make it in the marketplace. The marketplace was a pile of rubble. Government helped families and communities keep body and soul together. It assisted the weak and the ruined, protected the poor, reigned in economic predators, put out fires, stopped crime, provided public transit, educated the young, and built and maintained a vast network of public works—parks, roads, tunnels, bridges, housing, aqueducts, etc.—that is the backbone of urban civilization.

Serving in the government was a highly honorable calling. Many of the men and woman who went into civil service jobs during the Depression as teachers, firemen, cops, court officers, inspectors, and clerks were smart, talented, and dedicated. They were grateful for the rest of their lives. They thought of themselves as civil servants, not bureaucrats.

For that generation, greed wasn't a virtue but one of the seven deadly sins, whose worst effects were visited not on individuals but on the community. The greedy you will have with you always. But when greed was elevated to a moral good, when outrageous monetary gain for some was put ahead of decency, mercy, and a modicum of security for all, the results were seen as corrosive of society's foundations, an erosion of values that eventually led to what we witness today: corporate executives whose first reaction to the news of the September 11, 2001 attacks was to perceive the temporary panic-driven slide on Wall Street as an opportunity to issue themselves more stock options. (Compare their ethic to the civil service ethic that firefighters and police officers followed into the Twin Towers, and then declare greed is the only way forward to a better future.)

Similarly, politics wasn't deemed a "high calling," but a necessary one. Those who made a living at it didn't have to justify themselves by claiming a selfless desire to offer some return for their good fortune in the private sector. Politics was about power, especially power over the public purse, and better that power was in the hands of people whose instincts you trusted, who were accessible, who believed in the capacity of government to help improve the circumstances of people's lives, than in those motivated by a doctrinaire denial of the ability of the government to do more than get out of the way of ruthless ambition and leave great wealth to do as it pleased.

I entered the civil service in part because of my father's exhortations. But there was more to it. After college, I was excused from the military draft because of the high number I received in the Selective Service lottery held in December 1969. I spent a brief stint as a media buyer at an advertising agency during the high tide of the two-martini lunch. (I was pulled down by the undertow on more than one occasion.) I served for a year as a VISTA volunteer in Kansas City, Kansas. I returned to New York and taught at a Catholic boys' high school but was a lousy disciplinarian, and discipline was what the boys' parents had sent them to receive.

Nixon was re-elected. There was a recession. Watergate was starting to unfold. The country seemed to be falling into a funk. I certainly was. I took a job as a messenger, first for a Manhattan real estate agency, then for a Wall Street law firm. I drifted through the days, riding the subways, ogling/observing the mutli-hued mélange of ethnic and racial loveliness resident in the five boroughs, watching the spectacle of the changing cloudscape above Manhattan, which altered in shape, form, and substance with each season.

I lived with my brother in a small apartment in the Bronx. Together, we made enough to avoid starvation or eviction. In all our growing up, my father had never asked us what we intended to do with our lives. Now, in clear reaction to what he was afraid was becoming incurable fecklessness, his generic endorsement of the civil service became specific and prescriptive. I heard the Foley Square story for the umpteenth time, but this retelling concluded with an instruction: *There's a court officers exam being given in a month. Sign up for it.*

For lack of a better idea, I took the test and passed. Within a few months, I was assigned to the Bronx Landlord and Tenant Court (L and

T, as it is universally referred to by its employees and combatants). The borough was spiraling into what seemed a bottomless decline. In my first year in L and T something like 100,000 notices of dispossess for nonpayment of rent were served, a number that continued to grow robustly in the time I was there. On the east side of the County Courthouse, the once Grand Concourse, the Bronx's version of the Champs-Élysées, was beginning to look like Berlin's Unter der Linden at the end of World War II.

Each morning I got off the bus at Joyce Kilmer Park, just north of the courthouse. In front of me was the Lorelei Fountain in honor of Heinrich Heine, the German-Jewish poet. The fountain had been sculpted in Germany at the end of the nineteenth century, but due to anti-Semitic sentiment ended up in the Bronx, as had many of the old German Jews who lived in the area. It is topped by the figure of *Die Lorelei,* the seductive and destructive Rhine maiden. Three marble mermaids rested on the statue's base. Gradually, the statue became covered with graffiti. One day I exited the bus and saw that the hands and heads of all the mermaids had been amputated.

I worked for three years in L and T. I hated it more with each passing day. Finally, I made a rare trip from the basement, where L and T was located, to my father's chambers on the top floor. I told him that I didn't like wearing a uniform and was tired of the work. In the face of what was happening across the Bronx, I said, I was depressed by the transparent inconsequentiality of what I was doing.

My father never lost faith in the Bronx. He was sure the new immigrants would eventually rise the way the old ones had. But he didn't talk about the Bronx. He didn't get angry. He didn't argue with a single thing I said. "Peter," he said in a calm, firm voice, "you never quit a civil service job. *Never.* I forbid it." I was twenty-seven, living on my own, but I obeyed. I didn't quit until after my father had died from lung cancer.

The civil service was good to me. The pay was more than adequate. The structure of a regular job was what I needed at that moment. After work, I began taking graduate history courses at Fordham University, an easy commute from the Bronx County Courthouse.

"You'll be glad you didn't quit, even if it takes you a while to realize it," were my father's final words of admonition on the subject of the civil service. Though I didn't end up with a career in the civil service, my father was not entirely wrong. I *am* glad for the experience. After several years in the Bronx courts, at a time when the borough was in the throes of an immense socioeconomic transition, I left with a dawning awareness: for the first time, I perceived the experiences of my ancestors—of displaced, unschooled, unskilled, newcomers—not as part of the dead past but as a chapter in a still unfolding epic. History took on flesh and blood in ways it never had before.

The Bronx is Burning

I saw the ramparts of my native land,
One time so strong, now dropping in decay,
Their strength destroyed by this new age's way,
That has worn out and rotted what was grand.

—DON FRANCISCO DE QUEVEDO,
"The Ramparts of My Native Land"

S EVERAL YEARS AFTER I LEFT THE COURTS, I returned. By then
Howard Cossell had already made his famous observation/declaration
to the entire country via a broadcast from Yankee Stadium that "the
Bronx is burning." The prosaic Bronx of my childhood, a synonym for the
boring stability of ethnic middle-class aspirants and arrivees, had been
apotheosized as an international synecdoche for urban decline. I was making
a living as a speechwriter for Governor Hugh Carey. It was a start on the
writing career that, at a deep level, I had always desired. I had moved to
Manhattan, geographically a short jump, but for anyone formed and
steeped in the outerboroughness of the Bronx, a journey akin to the
Mormons' Great Trek.

I rode the D train from the governor's office on Sixth Avenue to the
courthouse and spent the day with old friends in L and T. I took notes
and made them into an article entitled "The Bronx Is Burning" that, until
now, I never published. It was intended as a farewell to my dead father,

*my deceased self, my dying (so it seemed then) borough. In a few cases,
where I thought it appropriate and privacy should be respected, I altered
names.*

De mortuis nil nisi bonum.

The Bronx County Courthouse is divided into three parts. On the top
floors are the Supreme Court and the Surrogate's Court. Here, where
the courtrooms have a paneled elegance and a spacious grandeur, the
judges sit high above the proceedings, elevated and aloof, a full complement of clerks and court officers to protect them.

Down a few flights is the Civil Court, its quarters more cramped,
the halls noisier and dirtier, the atmosphere more hectic. A brood of
negligence lawyers wanders in and out of conference rooms attempt-
ing to postpone whiplash-fractured-finger-broken-nose cases and get
back to "Supreme," where the money is.

Last and least, jammed into the basement, is the Landlord and
Tenant Court. It consists of a clerk's office, a great battered barn of a
courtroom—Part 17, the calendar part—and five closet-like hearing
rooms, windowless, each with a shrunken version of a judge's bench, a
recording machine instead of a stenographer, and a lone court officer
to keep the records, call the cases, and maintain order.

The day begins in Bronx L and T with the posting of the calendar, a list of all the cases that will be called that day. "The calendar,"
says John English, chief clerk of L and T, "actually represents only a
small proportion of the complaints filed in our office. I mean, last year
130,000 dispossesses were filed in the Bronx, enough to cover the
entire population of Albany." (A dispossess is a legal complaint by a
landlord to recover rent he is owed and, if the money is not paid, to
take possession of the premises.)

"In many cases the tenant simply moves. In others, the landlord
and tenant settle out of court. In some, a fair proportion, unfortunately,
the building burns down, and that settles that. So just to get here represents something of an accomplishment."

English is a gruff man. Short, well-built, with a large forehead
and a crowded head of hair that comes disconcertingly close to his

eyebrows, he seems to be perpetually frowning. Each morning he pushes his way through the crowd outside his office to post the day's calendar. Today the calendar fills four sheets. Each sheet has two columns: Case and Disposition. The long columns under Case are filled with names: Proskow Realty vs. Ida Mendez, Friendship Realty vs. Oscar Alvarez, Goldmark Brothers vs. Arthur Johnson, etc. There are forty cases to a sheet.

"One hundred sixty cases," says English, "not bad, but no record. Our record was back in May 1974, during the Nixon recession. Howie Goldman, the calendar clerk, called 288 cases. Who knows, if things keep going like they are, we may break that record."

John English has been in the courts since 1945, first in Manhattan, then in the Bronx. "I asked to come up here," he says. "Back in the late 1960s, I was in charge of the record office in the Manhattan Civil Court. The quiet drove me nuts. Quiet, quiet, quiet, that's all you ever heard. I put in for a transfer to Bronx L and T. Everybody thought I was bonkers, and maybe I am."

Moving down the hallway toward Part 17, English answers some questions ("Take that into the clerk's office, and have it stamped"), dismisses others ("No, for Chrissake, this is not the criminal court"), and finally stops at the three small steps that lead down to the courtroom.

"This is as far as I go," says English. He stands momentarily in the doorway of the courtroom, lawyers, clerks, tenants, landlords flowing past him like a river around a rock. Then, with a smile that almost eclipses his frown, he says, "I keep having this nightmare that someday the last building in this borough is going to burn down and there'll be nobody left in L and T but me. The quiet will drive me crazy."

Howie Goldman, the resident clerk in Part 17, is sitting where he has sat every working day for the past fifteen years—next to the judge assigned to dispose of the calendar.

Judges are rotated through Part 17. They sit here for only a week at a time. Many of them have no particular expertise in the labyrinth of landlord and tenant law. That's why Howie Goldman is there. "All things passeth away," John English says, "but Goldman remains. He's seen every kind of L and T case, heard every kind of plea, every ploy and counter-ploy, every excuse, defense, and pretense. He's a living compendium of New York's housing codes, laws, and statutes. He'd put a computer to shame."

Goldman sits at the right hand of Judge Harry Kraf. On the other side of the mahogany bench, past the beaten but substantial guardrail, the two or three hundred people have yet to settle down to the rhythm of hearing the cases called. Babies scream; lawyers confer with tenants and landlords and other lawyers; a demented, disheveled old woman sits and talks to herself in a loud whisper punctuated with cries of "*Mañana! Mañana!*" Two cases have already been called, but nobody seems to have noticed.

Judge Kraf, a slight, bald, nervously impatient man, turns to Goldman: "Get some order in here, clerk, get some order—immediately."

Goldman speaks slowly into the microphone: "O.K., folks, no silence, no calendar. We'll sit here until there's silence." Then he puts his hand over the microphone, leans over the high, fortresslike bench, away from Judge Kraf, and says to the uniformed court officer sitting at the desk below him, "Hey Frank, why are spics so noisy?"

Frank Corado keeps writing. Sitting in his blue uniform, with its gold insignia, he finishes working on the paper in front of him. In his late thirties, twenty years Goldman's junior, Corado is stocky yet well proportioned. A heavy black mustache cuts across his handsome Latin face. He looks up at Goldman and shrugs. "I don't know why," he says. "But at least they don't eat Christian babies for Passover."

Goldman throws his head back with laughter. Corado and Goldman, in the twelfth year of battlefield cooperation, cantankerous friends, occasional drinking companions, constant rivals for the affections of every beautiful woman who passes through this court, now turn their attention to the milling, mulling crowd.

For the rest of the day, they will move in tandem, two parts of one machine, calling and processing cases with unflagging speed, rebuking the disorderly, disciplining the distraught, filling up the five calendar sheets with dispositions: Sent out for trial to 17C; Dismissed—No appearance by landlord; Default judgment—No appearance by tenant; Adjourned; etc.

Throughout it all, throughout the screaming, crying, yelling, Corado will keep a careful watch on Goldman, making sure he's not too angry, too excited, too near his third coronary. And Goldman will never take his eyes completely off Corado, never allow someone to become physically or verbally abusive.

"*Silencio!*" Corado booms out in a thundering voice that brings people up short and causes Judge Kraf to jump up slightly in his seat.

"*Silencio!*"

In 1972, the Landlord and Tenant Courts in the five boroughs of New York City were reorganized into the Housing Court. The new name never caught on, yet the changes in procedure and organization were substantial.

"The old system was based in common law," explains John English. "The court was here so landlords could recover rents and their property. By the early 1960s, when the housing situation started to get out of hand, the court had about as much relation to conditions in the Bronx as the House of Lords."

With the rapid deterioration of the Bronx's housing stock, the massive influx of new, desperately poor immigrants, and the gathering exodus of the middle classes, the Landlord and Tenant Court began to sink under the sheer volume of cases that came before it. Tenants organized massive rent strikes. Landlords walked away from buildings. Entire neighborhoods began to vanish. Vandalism, arson, and abandonment grew to catastrophic proportions.

"By the early 1970s," says Howie Goldman, "the Bronx was like Vietnam, and this place was Saigon. In one year alone you had film crews here from the BBC—they shot something called 'The Bronx is Burning,' I think—and from West Germany, France, and Japan. If it kept up I figured eventually I'd have a shot at an Oscar."

Before 1972, one Civil Court judge sat in Part 17 and called the daily calendar of cases. He attempted to settle some cases, adjourned a few others, and, if there was time, tried one or two himself. But most cases that could not be settled or adjourned were sent out for trial. There was one trial judge. Like his counterpart in Part 17, the trial judge sat in L and T by rotation.

The court was hopelessly choked. There were delays of up to seven and eight months before a case came to trial. In addition, judges often felt frustrated that the law restricted them to considering questions of rent and possession, leaving the wider issues of rehabilitation and repair to city agencies with few enforcement powers.

Everybody seemed to recognize the situation was out of control. "My first day here in 1970," says Frank Corado, "I walk into Part 17 and I can't believe my eyes. Let me amend that: *I tried to walk into Part 17.* It looked like a crowd scene from the French Revolution. You had the Young Lords, the Black Panthers, and a cast of thousands.

"I push my way through the courtroom. And then, when I turn around at the front of the room, I realize that Frank Corado—a 175-pound Puerto Rican in a blue uniform—is supposed to keep this whole thing under control. My knees began to knock."

Finally, the State legislature passed a bill to reorganize the court. A chief administrative judge was appointed to preside over a citywide Housing Court. The court's jurisdiction was extended to include questions of a building's condition and tenants' right to repairs and decent services. Tenants could now deposit their rents with the court until the landlord made needed repairs.

In each borough, the chief judge was empowered to appoint Housing Court hearing officers. (They are called judges although they lack the full authority of judges; they cannot, for instance, order an arrest, sign a warrant, or hold someone in contempt.) In the Bronx, five hearing officers were appointed. The calendar judge had five back-up parts: 17A, 17B, 17C, 17D, 17E. The hearing officers were permanently assigned to their parts, and once a case was assigned to a specific part it stayed there.

Jerry De Angelo, a rotund, dour court officer, red-faced and sandy-haired, stands in the doorway of Part 17E, his left hand on the doorknob, his left foot holding the door open. The corridor in which the hearing parts are located is choked with traffic, here and there a battered bench or half-broken chair, the detritus of some higher court, is propped against a wall. De Angelo's deep roar of "17E, Friendship ver-

sus Ramirez," repeated three times, briefly silences the conversation/
argument of the crowd.

Inside 17E, the Hearing Officer, Judge Trussel, sits in a space-
starved courtroom. Counsel's table is pushed flush with his unelevated
bench. Between this arrangement and the door is the court officer's
desk and two benches for witnesses or spectators. Although windowless and small, the room is noisy, a ventilation system in clanking competition with the hubbub from outside.

Friendship Realty vs. Matilda Ramirez originated in November,
1980, with a complaint filed against Miss Ramirez for non-payment of
two months' rent. Miss Ramirez answered the complaint, and the case
was put on the calendar for December 1st. It was subsequently
adjourned for a week so Miss Ramirez, a welfare recipient with two
children, could obtain a lawyer. South Bronx Legal Services, a publicly-
funded organization, agreed to represent her. On December 8th, the
case was assigned to Part 17E. It was the last of twenty-one cases to be
heard there that day. Miss Ramirez said she had not paid her rent
because her three-room apartment, for which she paid $280 per month,
was roach-infested, had a broken toilet, and a stove but no oven. There
were no lights in the building's stairways, she maintained, and no lock
on its front door.

Judge Trussel directed that a housing inspector be sent to the
building, and the case was adjourned to December 28th. On that day,
with Miss Ramirez in court, the inspector confirmed her allegations.
He also noted that the building, 2229 Valentine Avenue, had four
unoccupied apartments in which the windows were broken and water
leakage was severe. The judge ordered that Miss Ramirez deposit with
the court the rent she owed—now $1,120—and that a list of repairs be
drawn up. The landlord would have to petition the court to vacate this
order. Miss Ramirez would be notified of his action and could appear
in court to stop him.

Now, three months later, the landlord's lawyer, Charles Marks, is
making a motion to vacate the original order and allow the landlord to
get his money. The repairs, he claims, are completed.

"Your Honor," says Marks, "this is not the tenant. This man has
no legal status here." Marks stares straight ahead at the judge. From

the left side of the table, an intense young man, his voice tight and qua-vering, says, "Tell him to shut up, Judge, tell this thief to shut his mouth or I'll show him who got status and who don't."

Judge Trussel looks over the top of his black glasses, his eyebrows arched in mock surprise: "Now, just one minute. First of all, this is a courtroom. We don't make threats here. Second, Mr. Marks raises a legitimate question. Who are you and . . ."

"I'm Carl Ruiz," he says, cutting the judge off.

"He's not mentioned in the lease," says Marks. "He has no stand-ing here."

"Shut up," says Ruiz to Marks, who still stares straight ahead.

"Now stop that," says Judge Trussel. "This is a courtroom, not a . . ."

"He's the common-law husband of Miss Ramirez," Marks interjects.

By now, Jerry De Angelo has left his desk and placed his blue bulk behind Mr. Ruiz's chair. He stands there with his arms folded.

"Where is Miss Ramirez?" asks Judge Trussel.

"She's sick," answers Ruiz.

"And her lawyer?"

"He said he wouldn't come unless she showed up, or had a doc-tor's note but she don't have time to get one. But she asked me to come here because this thief—he done nothing to do repairs."

"That's a lie," says Marks. "I have the super right here—Mr. Kemjian—the repairs are done—done in good faith and my client is entitled to his money."

"Judge," says Ruiz, "the building is a shit hole."

"Mr. Ruiz, this is a courtroom, not a street corner. First of all, Miss Ramirez should be here. I should vacate the order on that fact alone. Yet Miss Ramirez has shown good faith to date and this involves a substantial . . ."

"This is a travesty!" protests Marks, interrupting the judge. "A travesty and an outrage!"

"Please, Mr. Marks, please. I am adjourning the case to April 5th, that's only five days. The money is still here. Nobody will lose anything by this short delay. Case adjourned to April 5th. Call the next case."

"She'll be here, I promise," says Ruiz.

"This is an outrage," interjects Marks. "How can I expect my client to keep coming back here to suit the convenience of people who . . ."

In the hallway outside, Jerry De Angelo can be heard bellowing: "17E, Pincus Brothers versus Jasmine." He shouts it three times.

Every work day at 5:00 P.M. Jerry De Angelo goes into John English's office and signs out. "In the old days," De Angelo says, "we left when our part finished its cases. It was a real incentive to get things done. But downtown decided to make us sign out at five, so now there's no reason to push hard."

De Angelo waits for his bus on the southeast corner of 161st and the Concourse. He takes the bus to 200th Street, where he keeps his car, then drives home to Nyack.

Now in his early forties, De Angelo has been a court officer since 1968, in L and T since 1975. He began his career as a high school teacher but quit because he felt the work was too hard, the pay too little, the students too unruly. He thought about becoming a cop, but his wife talked him out of it. He became a court officer instead: "It's nine to five, no homework, good benefits, and the pay is O.K.

"The real problem is the tedium and all the bullshit. You sit in the goddamn room all day listening to the same story, the same whine, the same con job. You heard that lawyer today, right? You know that, if he wanted to, he could have put up a real stink and forced the judge to have a hearing right there. But he didn't want to. First of all, an adjournment gets him another fee for a court appearance. Second, the repairs were probably never done. Eventually, the lady will give up and move. She'll disappear into some other sinking wreck of a building, farther north, and the landlord will get his rent. I've seen it happen a hundred times. In L and T, only the forms change; the bullshit remains the same."

De Angelo pauses as a police car, its siren screaming, passes up the Concourse. No bus in sight, he walks a few yards toward the corner of 161st Street, and points eastward, in the direction of the Criminal Court Building. "I came from over there, originally," he says. "St. Angela Merici's Parish. In my lifetime I've seen the whole thing change. It's remarkable when you think of it. Look at this place. It's like the Bronx was in a war—and lost.

"The whole thing, I guess, is crazy. Here's a place where everything has failed. There's no jobs. The schools stink. Drugs are everywhere. The place is burning down. And what do the geniuses in government do? They rewrite the landlord and tenant law and throw in five hearing officers. Big freaking deal."

Once—it now seems a lifetime ago—I stood here in the late afternoons with Jerry De Angelo and some others who are now dead or in other jobs. I remember the first day, in the early 1970s. A skinny kid in a blue uniform, I had been overwhelmed by the parade of anger, bewilderment, and despair that filed in and out, endlessly, of the part to which I had been assigned.

In a small courtroom, I sat behind a desk, with badge and billy club, another Irish cop, first line of defense for a society that could not employ these people, that was unwilling, or unable, to give them hope, that was content to see this area consume itself in fire and violence so long as the proper forms were filled out and the city of shining glass towers was saved from the encircling rot. Bunched up there in a fetid, miserable room, I felt all my fine notions of humanity crumble and die. In an atmosphere thick with rumbling, threatening resentment, I'd looked into the ignoble, uncomprehending, angry face of poverty. The law, I explained, says this. The judge, I explained, orders that. Sit down, I explained, or I'll knock you down.

The landscape of history that I'd learned in school—great, sweeping social forces, progress, suburbanization, integration—disappeared. It was replaced by something more intimate and more frightening: a young mother who wept and wept in my courtroom; a punk who shouted that my mother was a whore; a timid man who spoke no English and threw up across my desk and trousers; a foul-breathed drunk who said he would kill me. People hated my guts and, in rooms where violence and despair were thick and real and awful, they'd told me so. Eventually, I hated them back. And after hatred drained me of my resentment, I felt nothing. This job was the same as any other job. At night, I would stand on the corner of 161st and board my bus and dream of never coming back, until finally the dream came true. Away from here, away from these courtrooms, dispossesses, legal forms, abandoned buildings, fights, and hatred, I re-entered a world where balanced and respectable opinions didn't cost so much.

From where Jerry De Angelo and I now stand, in the shadows of a cold, gray dusk, the Bronx County Court House looks like a solid piece of granite. Its great bulk still dominates this area, a rectangular complement to the circular mass of Yankee Stadium behind it. Built in the early 1930s to mirror the Art Deco splendor of the Grand Concourse, a monument to order and optimism, it frowns fifty years later in mute rebuke on the perversity of history.

Around the courthouse are eight enormous marble blocks. On each is carved some great moment in the history of the law. On the one across from us, Moses, his robe ribboned with graffiti, holds the Ten Commandments aloft. He is leading a huddled, frightened crowd northwards, out of the Bronx.

In the distance, up near 170th Street, an apartment building is burning, sparks shooting up, disappearing into early night.

A pillar of fire.

Cast a Cold Eye:
William Kennedy's Albany

⬯⬯

> . . . for Cities
> Are Men, fathers of multitudes, and Rivers & Mountains
> Are also Men; every thing is Human, mighty! sublime!
> —WILLIAM BLAKE, *Jerusalem: The Emanation of Giant Albion*

I GREW UP 150 MILES SOUTH OF ALBANY, on the other side of the Hudson. Despite that distance, I recall the parish world of my childhood as proximate in time and spirit to the town that William Kennedy has raised to literary fame. Both were dominated by ethnic and religious loyalties, in which the Irish (though a far smaller percentage of the population in the Bronx than in Albany) held political sway. As a matter of fact, my connection to Albany was closer than even these similarities allow. My father served nine years in the state legislature, from the mid-1930s to the mid-1940s. His recollections of New York's capital made it seem a magical place in my mind.

A few decades later, in 1979, when by grace or tribal destiny I found myself working as a speechwriter for Hugh Carey, an Irish-American governor from Brooklyn, I was disappointed by my first view of the state's capital city and reminded again of how good a raconteur my father was. But Albany is a funny place. It grows on you. And if you read Kennedy's books—and anyone interested in Irish-Americans, or urban history, or politics, or human nature should—then it will do more than grow on you. His saga of Albany's characters and their shenanigans will seed themselves in your mind, real, unreal, and surreal entwining inextricably around each other, and haunt your imagination.

Kennedy's literary odyssey began in good Irish fashion when, as a young man, he turned his back on the parochial world of pols and prelates and left Albany for Puerto Rico. But, also in good Irish fashion, he has said that he remained a prisoner to the place:

> I understood that Melville went to school here. I understood that Henry James touched down here, in one of his less cosmic moments. Bret Harte was born here, and left immediately. Those kinds of moments, that's about as much as you used to expect out of Albany. But then I began to figure that it couldn't be all that bad . . . I was writing in Puerto Rico about myself and my wife and my ancestors trying to understand it all, and then I realized I didn't understand, and that was it. That ignorance was the main drive: to come back at some point in my life, settle in and do some research in the library, and try to understand. I never expected that I would stay forever.

His "Albany Cycle" (eight novels and counting) has put the city on the literary map where, if the progenitor of the James brothers (William and Henry, not Jesse and Frank) had not abandoned Albany for New York City and points east, it might have arrived sooner. But it wasn't a case of overnight fame. The first two, *Legs* and *Billy Phelan's Greatest Game*, won critical praise but didn't score large sales. After being initially rejected by a dozen publishers, the third, *Ironweed*, brought the cycle—and the cycler—riches, prizes, and the attention of Hollywood. (The film version, for which Kennedy wrote the screenplay, starred Meryl Streep and Jack Nicholson.)

I knew Bill Kennedy only through his fiction until I met him in the flesh on January 6, 1984, a date fixed in my mind by its liturgical and literary associations, the Feast of the Epiphany in Orwell's nightmare year. It was a day or two after Governor Mario Cuomo had delivered the annual State of the State address to the legislature, a time of supreme agony for his anonymous scribes, of which I was one. (Governor Carey could care less who knew he had speechwriters; Governor Cuomo played it like King Tut with his tomb. Mum's the word.) The process of assembling the address (no one person writes it, which is one of the reasons it always stinks) was made more arduous and torturous by the fact that 1984 was a presidential election year and Cuomo's star was being carefully watched by the magi of the national media.

During periods of welding and riveting various pieces of boiler-plate, I read and re-read Kennedy's sublime trio of novels. When I wasn't laughing or slowly intoning chapters and scenes to savor the richly intricate, inventive language, I was madly copying down sentences and paragraphs, plumbing their rhythms, trying to enter and master the momentum of his prose. After a day spent in the Governor's office with the monstrous regiment of lawyers and apparatchiks dedicated to murdering and mummifying clear, lively prose, fifteen minutes of reading Kennedy was usually enough to restore my faith in the power and glory of language.

My admiration for Kennedy's work was shared by a group of mostly wannabe Irish-American writers (Isaiah Sheffer and Gene Secunda made up the Judeo-Italian contingent) who met for lunch on the first Friday of each month. The First Friday Club, as it came to be called, was based on a religious devotion popular in our pre-Vatican II Catholic childhoods that promised to those who attended Mass nine First Fridays in a row the presence of a priest in their last moments, thereby ensuring the sacraments of Penance and Extreme Unction, definitive protection against eternal damnation. ("Fire-proofing," as it was called in the Bronx.)

I have made the First Friday devotion (the religious version) several times in my life. I have done so even after a priest friend dismissed it as the ritual equivalent to getting your ticket punched. He's probably right. But I enjoy going to Mass, and why take chances? More important, who says God never punched a ticket or two?

On a secular level, the putative benefaction of the First Friday Club was that those members who attended nine consecutive lunches would be attended in their end-of-days by a bartender who'd pour a parting glass of their favorite concoction and offer perhaps a farewell toast. *Good night and joy be with you all.* The reasoning seemed sound to me. Sure, this was more ticket punching, but why go to heaven with a thirst? And that goes double for below.

The serious intent of the First Friday Club was to bring together its mix of Catholics (lapsed, collapsed, and practicing), non-Catholics, and raving pagans to talk about writing. Which is what we did: *talk*. The group's only successful writer was Dennis Smith, an ex-fireman whose moving account of his years in the South Bronx, *Report from Engine Co. 82*, had been a national bestseller, which he followed with several best-selling novels. Dennis didn't drink. After he finished lunch, he left and went back to his writing. The rest of us lingered over whiskey and stout as long as we could—or until the office or the spouse called looking—and talked and talked about writing. (There was a separate and distinct women's branch of the First Friday Club known as the Legion of Mary. It was led by Mary Tierney and Marcia Rock.)

We discussed with increasing frequency and fervor the work of Bill Kennedy, and since I was a part-time resident of Albany, I agreed to write and invite him to lunch with the First Friday Club at a time and place of his choosing. He wrote back that, yes, he would meet with us on January 6, at Lombardo's on Madison Avenue, in Albany, which as any Kennedy fan knows is where Billy Phelan takes Francis, his father, after bailing him out of the cooler. (Vide *Ironweed*: "Francis registered to vote twenty-one times before the state troopers caught up with him and made him an Albany political celebrity. The pols had paid him fifty by then and still owed him fifty-five more he'd probably never see.")

Those who rode the train to Albany that day included (but were not restricted to): the late Kevin Sullivan, a tall, elegant Joyce scholar and ex-Jesuit; Terry Moran, professor at NYU, ex-Marine, native son of once-unfashionable Brooklyn's only marginally unfashionable (at least of this writing) Red Hook district; Tom Dunne, an ursine-sized educator, lawyer, and bon vivant, and brother of the city's top uniformed cop; Mike Patterson, ex-*Daily News* reporter, ex-gubernatorial press secretary, and the world's leading expert on films of the 30s and 40s; Sgt. Ed Burns, spokesman for the NYPD (the voice on the radio that reported "the successful apprehension of the perpetrators") and the sire of Ed Burns, actor and director; Tom Quinn, my twin, the best storyteller I've ever met (he practiced on me for nine months in the womb), and the person who would replace me among the governor's speechwriters; and the brothers McCourt, Malachy and Frank, the latter still teaching and brooding upon the literary egg that would one day hatch *Angela's Ashes* and global celebrity.

Bill Kennedy later told me that he thought the First Friday Club was some sort of genteel literary group that would query him for an hour or two about religious symbolism in *Ironweed* and the like. He barely talked at all. He laughed mostly, as we all did, and enjoyed the drink and dueling soliloquies that prevented us from noticing the afternoon of the Epiphany slip away into the pink, pinched glint of Albany's frozen twilight. We went on strike for the day against our serious workday selves and enlisted in the endless frolicsome one-upmanship of storytelling—salacious, slanderous, scatological, theological—a melee of poems, jokes, songs. The McCourt brothers put their not-inconsiderable stage skills on display, *Ironweed* style: "an antisyllable lyric they sang, like the sibilance of the wren's softest whistle, or the tree frog's tonsillar wheeze." We never ate lunch. I can't remember if we even ordered it.

What I do remember from that day in Lombardo's is a mix of certifiable fact and subconscious projection, a melding of the corporeal and fictional: living people mingling with the characters from Kennedy's world, imbibing together, dilating and digressing, whistling and wheezing, and discovering how much they had in common. The past brought the present a round of drinks (and the present returned the favor). *The word became flesh. And dwelt amongst us.* Marcus Gorman, Albany's noted communion breakfast intellectual and mouthpiece for Legs Diamond, took a seat next to Kennedy, offering observations with the same surgical detachment as he had in the book. Martin Daugherty, son of Edward and Katrina (she of the flaming corsage) regaled all present with stories of his old man, the playwright. Roscoe Owen Conway descended from the eleventh floor of the State Bank building and handed out absentee ballots (five per customer).

"Does the fact I never really existed disqualify me?" Francis Phelan asked.

"If our democracy is to continue," Roscoe said, "then it must include everyone, fictional as much as real. On such great principles does our polity endure."

There's magic aplenty in Kennedy's books. The dead have a hard time staying dead, especially in Albany and not just at election time. The consequences of what they took for truth continue to shape our world. Their saintliness or silliness will be felt forever. They rise and walk among us. Sometimes they take flight. Consider the exhumed remains of Amos Staats in *Quinn's Book* when exposed to air:

> His face had begun to swell: cheeks, forehead, neck, eyelids all rising as might a loaf of leavening bread, a shocking sight from which we could not take our eyes. And then he exploded . . . upward and outward, his hands and face disappearing beneath a great grayish puff of dust tinged with pale blue that ascended fully six feet above the coffin and spread over all in a melancholy haze.

As Francis Phelan becomes aware in the cemetery-situated opening of *Ironweed*, "the dead, even more than the living [are] settled down in neighborhoods," all the distinctions of this world continued into the next, "the privileged dead" resting for eternity apart from "the flowing masses, row upon row of them under simple headstones and simpler crosses." Roscoe remembers the ghosts at Tristano—Elisha Fitzgibbon's estate—as "two old men [who] came out in the middle of the night and sat by the fireplace in the Trophy House and drank brandy and talked and looked out at the moon until the sun came up on the lake, and then they got up and went away." And Roscoe does, too, in the end— goes away, that is—on the night boat across the River Styx, circling "back to the entrance of the main salon, the orchestra was still doing

Wagner, but was now into the love theme; or was it the death theme? One of those."

The cast of characters that Kennedy fables into flesh is so vividly imagined that I, for one, find it impossible to believe they live and die only on the page. His power to inseminate all the inhabitants of his stories with an inner momentum makes it seem that their existence isn't restricted to print—that they have traveled a good deal to get there and will go on traveling once their earthly part is played—and gives his cycle the energy of a perpetual motion machine.

This illusion was given additional substance when an apparition appeared at the window of Lombardo's: a Depression-era vagabond, hands clasping the threadbare collar of his coat tight around his throat, pressed his face against the window. Kennedy waved him in, offered him a chair, and ordered him a straight whiskey. "Please welcome," he said, "Rowdy Dick Doolan."

I immediately recalled Rowdy Dick's brief but vivid appearance in *Ironweed*, when he attempts to steal Francis Phelan's shoes, attacking him with a meat cleaver. Failing in his felonious assault (but not before severing two-thirds of Francis's right index finger and "an estimated one-eighth of an inch of flesh from the approximate center of his nose"), Rowdy Dick receives a fatal crack on the head from Francis.

Rowdy Dick didn't say much that day. He stared at the torn and ruined shoes he'd tried so violently and unsuccessfully to replace. Imprinted across his face, amid nicks, scars, and webs of red, protruding veins, was the permanent perplexity of a life gone awry; hemophilia of the spirit, the wound that never heals. It was easy to see that Bill Kennedy understood Rowdy Dick's predicament; easy, too, to perceive Rowdy Dick's momentary contentment at this reprieve. His lips spread with that silly, sappy, tentative smile that the dead wear when they come to spend time with the living, even if only for a few hours in the crepuscular gloom of an upstate afternoon.

"Any place beats the grave," was about all that Rowdy Dick said, "even Albany in the dead of winter."

*   *   *

Winter or spring, during my six-plus years as gubernatorial scribe, I saw a lot of Albany. I jogged its streets late at night (late is part of a speech-writer's fate). My peritropal jaunts were propelled by the sad and dreary loneliness of my hotel room in a downtown that was a shrunken shadow of what it was when Billy Phelan "made a right turn into the warmth of the stairs to Louie's pool room, a place where even serious men sometimes go to seek the meaning of magical webs, mystical coins, golden birds, and other artifacts of the only cosmos in town." Dear Louie and the place where Louie dwelled were gone, long gone, alas.

Stronger than the push of escaping the cinderblock celibacy of a room in the Best Western motel was the pull of exploring the city that, though large parts have been done in by the malpractice of road builders and urban planners with their mania for the double and triple bypass, still beats with cosmic intensity in the expanding universe of Kennedy's cycle. His novels are a Baedecker to what came before the life was sucked out of America's mid-sized cities, before the old ticker, the commercial heart of downtown, and the arterial networks of trolleys and trams that circulated its pedestrian lifeblood were ripped out.

Thanks to the pharaonic ambitions of Governor Nelson Rockefeller, who was embarrassed by the down-at-the-heels condition of this faded Hudson River town and frustrated by his quadrennial inability to remove himself to the imperial capital on the Potomac, almost a hundred acres at the center of the city were cleared to make way for a massive new marble heart called the South Mall. (It was eventually re-named in Rockefeller's honor.) Nine thousand people—"who in their entirety," wrote Kennedy, "cast a cold eye on tomorrow because there was never enough heat in the joint tonight"—were displaced.

Those who got the collective boot were the inhabitants of The Gut, Albany's night town, the reduction stuck to the bottom of the city's melting pot lovingly evoked in *Roscoe*:

> . . . bartenders and waitresses, burglars on relief, family outcasts and runaways, semiaffluent winos who could still pay rent, motherless queens, hula dancers, B-girls and strippers, horseplayers doing their best to die broke, dishwashers aspiring to be short-order cooks, good-time girls learning what it takes to go pro, and all the flakes, flacks and

flukes who get around to putting their heads on the greasy pillows just as the sun was also rising on the rooftops of The Gut . . .

The gutting and malling of Albany's gizzards resuscitated what it didn't destroy. Block after block of nineteenth-century brownstones were brought back to Victorian dignity, including the ex-rooming house on Dove Street in which Legs was shot to death ("'Honest to God, Marcus,' he said going away, 'I really don't think I'm dead.'") and which is now owned by the chronicler of gangster deeds and demise, William Kennedy.

Its role as the state capital gives Albany an advantage over other upstate New York cities whose depleted or vanished manufacturing base has sucked away their souls. Albany still has its soul, which resembles the hobo jungle in *Ironweed*, a spiritual core of "essential transience and would-be permanency." Its transience is underlined by the comings and goings of politics and legislators and governors— today's big shots, tomorrow's hobos. Its permanency is partly anchored to the government buildings done in styles from Athenian to Star Trekkian (the State Theater is called The Egg but to my eyes its tilted ovoid shape has more in common with a UFO). More permanent is the Hudson River that the city stands beside, a majestic flow that will still stream seaward when the crystalline and Carrara precincts of the Capitol, stone heart and all, have joined their flesh-and-blood inhabi- tants in the dust.

Maybe Kennedy's novels won't endure as long as the river. But as long as women and men read books, the Albany Cycle will also be part of the city's soul. Visitors will come from afar to search out his streets and characters, and if they're lucky and alert enough to what's going on around them, they might be joined at lunch the way the sojourning First Friday Club was all those years ago when Legs Diamond, sandwiched between pious Alice and sexy Kiki, showed up in Lombardo's, his arrival heralded by the bagman for the Albany machine, "a dandy and curmud- geony and a wily and wise old Irishman," as Kennedy describes him, "who had read his Yeats and Wilde as well as Croker and Tweed."

The entire crew who filled up the backroom of Lombardo's was known to Kennedy: showgirls, sports, yeggs, and the "men I'd been raised with, men who knew my father and my uncles; tradesmen and sportswriters and other lawyers and politicians and factory hands who like pinochle and euchre, and salesmen who like to bowl and drink beer, and, of course, of course, Jack Diamond."

Kennedy knows/appreciates/understands these people better than anyone. He forgives them their trespasses and posts bail for their felonies. He refuses caricature. He sympathizes with their quest for mercy. He loves their empowering/crippling incapacity to take themselves or their world too seriously. He laughed with the rest of us when Hattie Wilson, mistress of The Gut, wobbled upward and stood precariously atop her chair, her callipygian assets on full display, and announced, "One way or another, everybody's an idiot, and that goes double for the geniuses."

Games have an important part to play in this Albany world of Kennedy's. They fill the pages of his books. Cards, dice, horses, bowling pins, bats, balls, and chickens. (Chickens, yes, chickens supremely so; as recounted in *Roscoe*, the Swiggler versus Ruby is the most brilliant knockdown cockfight in American literature.) The object of these games is more than amusement and fun. In a different fashion but with the same purpose as religion and politics, games are about taking control of chance, facing down the odds, and being delivered from evil. The goal, Frances Phelan will tell you (having learned the hard way), is "to beat the bastards, survive the mob and that frightful chaos, and show them all what a man can do to set things right, once he sets his mind to it." (And that goes for the chickens, too.)

Billy Phelan never showed up at our lunch. Though I loitered a few times in front of where Louie's pool room used to be, I never saw even a vaporous wisp of sewer gas that might be construed as a ghost. But in the several times I've read Kennedy's account of Billy's greatest game, I've come to see that Billy's greatness lies not just in the skill with which he plays, nor merely in his intensity, but in his style, the purity and intensity of *how* he plays. Style is the signature of the soul. It distinguishes great players from mere winners. Winners can only win. The great can win or lose, but always, always with style.

The importance of style is correctly (if with a tinge of Teutonic arrogance) summarized by "a young, half-drunk playwright named Weissberg," who is introduced to Legs Diamond during his brief visit to Weimar Germany to score drugs. Weissberg speaks of his desire to travel to America and study Legs's life, dissect it, and use it as the raw material of his art:

> I want only the opportunity to write what I believe, which is that there are similarities among the great artist, the great whore, and the great criminal . . . In all these professions is the willingness to withhold nothing from one's work. All these, when they achieve greatness, have also an undeniable high style which separates them from the pedestrian mob. For how could we all tell a great criminal from a thug in the alley, or a great whore from a street slut, if were it not for style?

Legs's riposte is to draw his chair close to Weissberg's, until their knees touch, and fire his pistol in the small space between the playwright's feet. Weissberg wets his pants. Coming face to face with a great stylist can intimidate as well as inspire.

Upon reading in the book section of a great metropolitan newspaper an academic's categorization of Kennedy as a "regional writer" (ah, yes, the academic mind, forever reverberating with Teutonic hubris!), I thought of Weissberg's attempt to deconstruct Legs's style. Kennedy is a regional writer for sure—that is, if Melville is a travel writer and Hemingway a sports writer. True, Kennedy's novels are not free of categorizations of their own. Marcus Gorman, for instance, categorizes Legs as an "indignant liar." But Marcus has a deep sense of irony, and academics, as claimants to all that is analyzable, categorizable, deconstructable, lack a true sense of irony and are, along with horseshoe crabs, the most humor-challenged creatures on the planet. (Anglo-Irish essayist Hubert Butler saw this coming a generation ago when he commented that scholars were ceasing to be humanists and becoming clinicians.)

If we must pigeonhole Kennedy, then let's at least name the pigeons correctly and make sure they're plugged in the right holes. Kennedy is—and I'm sure Herr Weissberg concurs—a great stylist. He withholds nothing from his work. He is also a great comic writer. I have rarely seen that mentioned in reviews of Kennedy's novels: how hilarious they are, how filled with jokes and terrific one-liners. But his comedy is never frivolous. It serves the larger purpose of keeping everyone awake and alert on the redemptive journey at the heart of all serious comedy, the journey we are keyed into with the quote from the *Divine Comedy* at the beginning of *Ironweed*: "To course o'er better waters now hoists sail the little bark of my wit, leaving behind her a sea so cruel."

Along with playwright Eugene O'Neill, Kennedy is the supreme chronicler of the Irish-American experience. This was made clear to me by Bill Hanlon, a character who could be in one of Kennedy's books but isn't because God got to him before Kennedy and caused him to be born into life instead of literature, a condition in which he continues to this day. Hanlon, a sardonic, scholarly Irish-American scion of the working class-endowed with a stainless-steel intelligence, labored beside me in the satanic mills of speechwriting. He is a writer of consummate skill and possesses of editorial skills that never dull, not even amid the choking exhaust of the four-score-and-seventh cigarette chain-smoked in the wee, wee hours of the state capitol's haunted chambers (ghosts are ubiquitous in Albany).

A near miss of a Jesuit, Hanlon's command of literature is prodigious. (Should he ever escape into one of Kennedy's novels, he'll have his own table in the Rainbow Room at the Kenmore where he'll lecture on Henry James.) He pounced on Kennedy's work before I did, devoured the original trio of the cycle, and, in blunt, authoritative style announced to me, "Kennedy nailed the Irish-American tribe like nobody before." He said he was done talking to me until I read the novels. I did what he told me. Thank you, Bill Hanlon.

It wasn't until Lombardo's, however, when Kennedy brought Legs over to the table, that I understood the writer's special genius in joining the yin and yang of the Irish-American soul, shanty and lace-curtain, criminal and respectable, the lurking ambivalence that's been there from the time of Famine and before, an inherited sympathy with the outlaw, uncle to the nun, cousin to the cop, brother to the bishop. Legs didn't fire a pistol between anybody's feet. His presence was punctuation enough. He sipped his drink, and collectively, in silence, we thought, *Yeah, the lines between legal and illegal are drawn in sand, not concrete, and hell, it depends on who's making the laws where the line goes, and who's out and who's in.*

Once, in Chicago, I sat with a Mayo man, a handsome, learned carpenter with emphatic eyebrows; the seventh son of a seventh son, he told me. My carpenter friend, he of the Savior's trade, recalled as a boy saying the rosary every night with his family. His father led it and always ended with the same prayer: "Lord, protect us from the long arm of the law." Legs would have understood that prayer, I think. And the Fenians. And Michael Collins. And Jack Duggan, the Wild Colonial Boy. I know Kennedy does.

There is no need to be Irish-American to appreciate Kennedy, as there's no need to be Jewish-American to appreciate Philip Roth or African-American to savor Toni Morrison or American-American to revel in John Updike. But for myself, I know that in reading Kennedy, I felt that I was encountering Irish America in all its full-blown aspects for the first time in fiction. Not ethnic navel-gazing or phony baloney, sentimentalizing self-praise. Not an apologia pro whoever the Irish-Americans are. Not a search for excuses. Not a slice but the pie: the hilarity, profanity, decency, brutality, piety, stupidity, fidelity, pugnacity, gallantry, bigotry, prolixity, fluency, carnality, generosity, immorality— the totality—of this peculiar people on their particular journey.

Kennedy presents the whole megillah, singularity and universality, *untermenschen* of the British Isles striving in the New World, if not to *über-alles*-ness, then for sufficient control to ward off hungers great and small, the kids starving, or their parents reduced to begging. No way, pal, not in the land of milk and money, not in this life or the one to come. We'll always have the votes and plenary indulgences to see to it. The ward boss and the bishop will be ours. Ourselves alone, if that's what it takes. (And no one should forget that as hard as the Irish could be on those outside the tribe, they were always hardest on one another.) Ourselves, more likely, with enough other votes to swing the election our way, keep the enemy at bay, now and at the hour of our death. Amen.

Kennedy is the poet of this complex people, their Homer. Nobody has caught their voices the way he has, their Americanness, their gut-seated hatred of pretense, snobbery, and aristocracy; and their Irishness, their subtle, stubborn, successful resistance to subordination and annihilation. He has nailed their cadences and nuances, their supreme resentment annealed in the furnace of defeat, poverty, famine, emigration, and articulated so succinctly by Felix Conway, father of Roscoe, in his deathbed resistance to surrendering his grievances and dying like a Christian. Felix tells the attending priest: "None of us is worth an old man's piddle and we never could be, because the whole world is fixed against us, Father. The whole damn world is fixed." (And it will stay fixed, Felix might have added; only we'll do our best to ensure that it's fixed in our favor.)

"Epiphanies come true when you least expect them," says Roscoe. Mirable dictum, they even come true on the Feast of the Epiphany in a royal flush of ghostly visitations and earthly realizations; Legs with the frankincense, Kiki Roberts with the myrrh, and Patsy McCall, Albany boss, with (what else?) the gold. On January 6, 1984, at our epiphanic lunch—a day, to quote from a certain Albany-based Irish-American writer, that "would seem to have been invented by a mind with a faulty gyroscope. It had the quality of a daydream after eight whiskeys"—I understood something that I'd never before been certain of: whatever it took, no matter how long, I was willing to pay the price of becoming a writer.

III. FAITH AND IMAGINATION

Father Daniel F. Ryan. S.J.,
in his army chaplain's uniform (1944).

Confessions of a
Bronx Irish-Catholic

> No Catholic breaks with Rome casually.
> —JOHN O'HARA, *BUtterfield 8*

I WAS BORN IN 1947, IN GREENPORT, on the northeast end of Long
Island, exactly a century after my first Paddy ancestor set foot in
America. My birth was a reproductive and geographic accident.
My father had been defeated for re-election to Congress the previous
November and, as my mother told the story—to my father's perpetual
embarrassment—her final trip to help close his Washington office
ended up with her pregnant—with twins. The twin part wasn't discov-
ered until August, while my parents were vacationing on Shelter
Island. In view of the fact that my mother was forty and my brother and
I reached a collective in-womb weight of sixteen pounds, the local doc-
tor told her to stay put, which she did.

I was supposed to be born in the Bronx, a destination to which
I was delivered shortly after the incidental nativity on Long Island.
Yet, if the geographical circumstances of my birth were dictated by
chance, the Irish-Catholic identity into which I was born seemed as
certain as the beads on my grandmother's silver rosary and rolled off
the tongue with the predictability of the theological mysteries—

glorious, sorrowful, joyful—that she honored with those beads.

I lived my childhood in the Bronx aware that I was an Irish-Catholic. But I never gave it much thought. Ethnicity was basic to the place, like asphalt and elevated trains. Everybody in the borough, at least everybody I knew, had an identity other than "American." If you didn't know what you were, somebody else did, and if you found yourself in a neighborhood where you were something everybody else wasn't, you ran a good chance of getting your you-know-what kicked.

It wasn't until I spent a summer semester at University College, Galway, in the mid-1970s, that I discovered I wasn't really Irish at all. Arriving there on my first prolonged stay in Ireland, I expected not so much a warm welcome as a joyous reunion with the long-lost relatives my family had been separated from a century before. I quickly discovered that the separation was permanent.

My fellow students saw me as indelibly American. Some were good-natured about it. Others—including some professors—were vehemently contemptuous of Americans in general and Irish-Americans in particular. A literature teacher I had, who went out of his way to avoid Irish-American students, told me he was "embarrassed by the racism, jingoism, and intellectual poverty of Irish-Americans." It was my first face-to-face encounter with the negative stereotyping of Irish-Americans. (Over the years I would encounter plenty more, in Ireland, America, and Great Britain.)

Intellectually, my experience at UCG was a turning point. When I returned home, instead of focusing excessively on the history and culture of Ireland—topics that will always remain of consuming interest to me—I began to look more intently at the Irish entry into America and the epic implications for the country they left and the one in which they arrived. I became absorbed in the story of the Famine Irish and their mass descent on New York, a saga of which my own family had been part. Out of this came my decision to write *Banished Children of Eve*.

Along with the professional desire to write about the Irish passage into America—about how the Irish were profoundly altered by America, yet at the same time successfully resisted dissolution and oblivion—I was increasingly drawn into a personal reconsideration of my relationship with the Catholic Church, an institution central to the post-Famine experience of Irish America and to my own family's sense of Irishness.

The Catholic Church of my childhood prided itself on its imperviousness to change. Maternal in the lush embrace of its liturgies and devotions, wreathed in incense and swathed in the Latinate cadence of a ritual language divorced from the taint of ordinary life, the Church was firmly masculine in its leadership of adamantine opposition to evil and error in whatever forms they assumed—false faiths, worldly corruption, moral laxness, communism, and the dangerous, if seductive, appeal of modernism.

Though my college-educated parents were skeptical to a remarkable degree about the hierarchy (a much rarer attitude among Catholics in the fifties than today) and were amused rather than influenced by the fulminations of our own local prelate against certain movies or books, they were extremely loyal to their faith and attentive to its practice. They also saw to it that all their children attended Catholic schools, which I did in the Bronx from Saint Raymond's Grammar School to Manhattan Prep, Manhattan College, and the last stages of study for a Ph.D. at Fordham.

Old St. Raymond's, the grade school I attended, is still there, at the corner of Castle Hill and Metropolitan Avenues, a square, red-brick edifice typical of the frill-free structures that have been a part of almost every New York Catholic parish for the last century and a half. (A new school was added in 1951 but, after the second grade, boys were divided from the girls and sent to the old school.) My father graduated from St. Raymond's in 1918, and I graduated in 1961, but we had the same art teacher, Miss O'Neill, the daughter of former Bronx sheriff John O'Neill.

In the eighth grade I sat in the same desk my father had, its oak top set in a cast-iron filigreed frame that was bolted to the floor. It was unalterable, permanent, like the religion we learned while we sat in it, or the lessons about color and perspective that Miss O'Neill hadn't changed in nearly half a century. My teachers ran the gamut from those unsuited by temperament and training to be teachers to extraordinary educators who did a heroic job of not only instructing us in the basics but instilling a love of learning. There was usually neither time nor space for cosseting individual students.

At St. Raymond's, the typical class included forty-five to fifty-five students of wildly varying abilities, often from widely different economic and ethnic backgrounds. With scant resources and no assistants or special support services, teachers concentrated on seeing to it that, at a minimum, every student mastered the skills needed to pass a civil service exam or qualify for an entry position at Con Edison or the telephone company.

The use of corporal punishment in schools like St. Raymond's has been covered to the point of parody. What's left out is that this was often a piece of the immigrant cultures that looked to these schools to train their children. The use of physical punishment frequently reflected the wishes of parents and families intent on having their children gain the discipline and knowledge they needed to rise in the world, even if it required force and intimidation. Most of us didn't report the punishments we received at school on the certainty our parents would repeat them.

Intellectually, while rote learning took precedence over the development of a capacity for creativity, the results weren't entirely regrettable. Few graduated without knowing the difference between adverbs and adjectives or the requirement of subject and verb agreement. My wife, for example, educated by Ursuline nuns in the South Bronx, had drilled into her a mastery of English grammar that, in my estimation, ranks her among the best copy editors I have ever encountered.

George Carlin recently told an interviewer that he is indebted to the Dominican nuns who taught him in grammar school. They were, he said, educated women who taught him to think for himself and "equipped me to question the very faith they were doing their best to teach." I feel a similar gratitude to the De La Salle Christian Brothers, my teachers from grade school through college.

Though not without their faults, the Christian Brothers who taught me were mainly well-educated, fair-minded men who encouraged me to think for myself and gave me my skill as a writer. There was never anything obscurantist or blindly sectarian in how they taught or what they taught. In college, the curriculum they used was based on the Great Books program developed at the University of Chicago. We were required to read ancient and modern thinkers and writers in the original texts and grapple honestly with their theories and assertions. Never once in my professional career did I find that my Christian Brothers education put me at a disadvantage.

Beginning in 1962, the Second Vatican Council changed forms and practices that Catholics had long assumed were unchangeable. The ultimate effects of the council will probably not be definitively clear for another century (you can't be a Catholic and not take the long view). But as the flying buttresses of the old counter-reformation order swayed and crumbled, John O'Hara's remark that no Catholic leaves the Church casually seemed out of date. Priests and nuns returned to lay life in large numbers. Seminaries emptied. Catholics increasingly ceased the practice of their faith without nailing ninety-five theses to the door or undergoing great inner turmoil.

At the same moment the Council opened the windows of the Vatican and shook its foundations, the Irish-Catholic immigrant community created in the wake of the Famine was collapsing from within. The election of John Kennedy as president in 1961 signaled the end of any significant barriers to Irish-Catholic entry into the American power structure. The need for internal cohesion and discipline in the face of a common enemy had disappeared. Mainline Protestantism was fading even faster than Catholicism and, in the end, it is fear of a common enemy rather than mutual admiration or affection that keeps most tribes together.

In 1967, during my junior year at Manhattan College, I stopped going to Mass and ceased being a practicing Catholic. Although I never announced it to my parents, I had decided that Catholicism was a rapidly disintegrating relic of a pre-modern mindset and, eventually, would be a curiosity in a category with Zoroastrianism. Done with Catholicism, I was no more attracted to any other faith than Stephen Daedalus in *Portrait of the Artist*, who upbraids a friend for supposing his apostasy implied an embrace of Protestantism: "'I said that I had lost my faith,' Stephen replies, 'but not that I had lost my self-respect.'"

I began my return to religious practice several years later when, as a VISTA volunteer in Kansas City, Kansas, I attended services at an African Methodist Episcopal church. The depth of belief I encountered there, the difference it made in people's lives, the hope, faith, and dignity it instilled, the strength of social consciousness, the emotional intensity of the worship and music, put a large hole in my smug dismissal of religion as bereft of continuing relevance to modern life.

Several years later, my graduate studies gave me a fuller appreciation of the complexity and richness of Catholic culture and thought. Similarly, I reached what I considered a balanced understanding of the Church's role in Irish history that neither set it on a pedestal as the repository of the national soul nor divided it as the bane of everything truly Irish. I was content to think of myself as a "cultural Catholic," interested in the integral role of Catholicism in Western culture but uninvolved in its practice as a living faith. Then, in a New York minute—I'm not kidding; I was waiting impatiently for a long-overdue bus—something happened.

I was looking up at the windows of the apartment building across the way. I was thinking about all the different lives being lived behind them, each convinced of its own significance, each caught up in tragedies and joys of no consequence to the universe, laughable in their smallness, and doomed to instant obliteration by death and the immense, amoral indifference of the cosmos.

In the time it took to turn and step onto the bus, I was convinced otherwise. No lights, parting clouds, or angelic voices. No sudden grasp of logical arguments I hadn't understood. No *De profundis* in the style of Gerard Manley Hopkins: "I did say yes/ O at lightening and lashed rod." Just this, felt for the first time: the certainty that Jesus isn't a prophet, a moral teacher, a saint, history's greatest holy man, but the living Christ, present in every moment of time, equally, always, and as real as the cold sensation in my hand of the metal handrail, the coins and tokens clanging at that moment into the fare box, the wide, brown, handsome face of the bus driver.

The Church in which I now practice my faith is different in profound and superficial ways from the Church of my childhood. The sense of suffocating insularity—a mix of defensiveness against Protestant disdain and assurance of our own moral superiority—is gone. Despite the best efforts of Popes John Paul II and Benedict XVI to restore a top-down order and banish debate, debate goes on. American Catholics have been profoundly influenced by the political society in which they live and function, and while they listen to their bishops and priests, they weigh other opinions and make up their own minds. No encyclical, fiat, or anathema will change that.

The hunger of traditionalists for a return to the status quo ante Vatican II has no appeal to me. I remember that Church. The changes the Council brought were desperately needed. The desire to restore the rituals and trappings that existed before the council strikes me as akin to the practices of the "Bundle Christians" discovered by nineteenth-century missionaries to Japan. Descended from converts made by Jesuit missionaries three centuries before, these Japanese Catholics had wrapped their sacred icons and statues and hidden them away during a period of persecution. Over time, they forgot what was inside and worshipped the bundling.

The equation of Irish and Catholic, so basic to my childhood, isn't as attenuated as between Irish and Democrat, but neither is it as iron-clad as it once was. Yet it is far from dead. Catholic higher education seems more vibrant than ever, and I've been surprised over and over, on visits to various campuses, by the numbers of students at Mass and by the interest in Irish as well as Irish-American writing and history.

Still to be reckoned with are the long-range effects of the sexual abuse crisis. There's no doubt about the profound damage it has inflicted on the entire Catholic community—foremost on the thousands of children raped and molested whose lives have been warped and ruined. The sum total of pain inflicted by the betrayal by Church leaders is incalculable. The laity's disillusionment with the hierarchy's incompetence and secrecy, which allowed the problem to fester and spread, and with its halting, circle-the-wagons response, is extensive and, probably, permanent.

Coupled with the precipitous decline in priests, the end result of the sexual abuse crisis might be greater empowerment of the laity and a more democratic understanding of ministry and authority. In the words of the King James Bible: "The wind bloweth where it will, and thou hearest the voice thereof, but knowest not whence it cometh, and whither it goeth: so is every one that is born of the Spirit." The Spirit has been known to throw some pretty tricky and unexpected pitches, as it did with the arrival of John the XXIII in the papal throne.

Equally, the ultimate outcome of the weakening tie between Irish and Catholic (which appears far more advanced in Ireland than America) remains to be seen. Though the dominant Irish presence in the priesthood and religious orders has demonstrably waned—and seems unlikely ever to return to what it was—the vast majority of Irish-Americans, it seems to me, will continue to practice the Catholic faith, although in more syncretic and free-spirited ways than their grandparents.

I've made peace with my Bronx Catholic childhood. Contra the assertion of my good friend Frank McCourt, the Irish-Catholic childhood isn't the most miserable of all. I was blessed as well as burdened, graced more than cursed. Yet I find little to lament in the loosening identification of Irish with Catholic. As well as idolatrous, the equation of religion and nation is, in the end, poisonous to both. Breaking the reflexive association of religion and ethnicity, however, isn't the same as saying that religious values are formed in a vacuum, divorced from history and devoid of cultural content. My faith is rooted in my Irish-Catholic heritage. It couldn't be otherwise. That's who I am.

For me, the significance of this identity—and the core of what will always keep me Catholic—is contained in the example of a Maryknoll nun I met almost a half century ago when I was a child vacationing with my parents on Shelter Island. The daughter of a wealthy, politically powerful Irish-Catholic family, she was preparing to leave for the overseas missions.

Although I sometimes recalled the attention and affection she focused on my brother and me, I didn't see her again until several years ago when I was looking through a Maryknoll publication and came upon an article in which she was featured. She had aged a good deal—as I have—and though she had shed the traditional habit I remember her in, she was still doing the work she set out to do. Refusing to be silenced by the threats from the military or the murder of other nuns, she was still working to achieve the Gospel message of justice, equality, and mercy.

To the loaded and sublimely subjective question of what it means to be Irish and Catholic, I find the intimation of my answer in that nun, in the willingness not to wallow in a romanticized notion of a collective past, not to deny the assorted and sordid sins of Catholic clerics, institutions, and laypeople, but to get on with living out the essential work of the Gospel and embracing those whose everyday struggle for dignity and survival is being waged at this very moment.

Sic Transit

> He, then, is perfect who does the work of the
> day perfectly, and we need not go beyond this
> to seek for perfection.
> —JOHN HENRY CARDINAL NEWMAN

WHATEVER THE FUTURE HOLDS for American-Catholics, it is clear that the Irish-led urban, immigrant institution formed during the mid-nineteenth century is rapidly vanishing. The physical evidence is embedded in the mounting number Catholic churches now derelict or facing closure scattered across the urban landscape. These include St. Brigid's, on the Lower East Side of Manhattan, which was built by Famine immigrants in 1848 and was where my grandparents were married and my father baptized.

Although I had no inkling of it at the time, I was there for the opening of the last chapter in this urban saga. In the early 1950s, when, like my father and his father in their day, I was enrolled in parochial school, our parish of St. Raymond's in the Bronx as well as the Archdiocese of New York were both flush with parishioners, piety, and political power. It felt like the best of times. At the opening of St. Raymond's new school building in 1951, my father shared the stage with Cardinal Spellman, the Archdiocese's ruling hierarch, and delivered the main remarks.

A former Democratic congressman and newly minted judge, privately critical of Spellman's Republican leanings, my father steered clear of controversy. Instead, he focused on the Church's role in providing generations of immigrants with spiritual sustenance and material support in their struggle to make a place for themselves in a city that once regarded them as incurably poor, ignorant, and foreign.

Though sometimes softened by the romance of memory, the struggle my father cited, which began with the influx of Famine immigrants, changed New York. Driven by the numbers of Irish who entered the port, a city of 312,000 in 1840 ballooned to 726,400 in 1865. That same year, one out of every four New Yorkers was listed as Irish-born and, according to the estimate of Church historian Jay P. Dolan, Catholics, once a tiny minority, were "somewhere between three hundred thousand and four hundred thousand, almost one half of the city's population."

The Irish weren't the only immigrants pouring into mid-nineteenth century New York—Germans, many poor and Catholic, also arrived in large numbers—but it was their ragtag condition that alarmed city residents. The Irish in New York, wrote Bishop John Hughes in 1849, were "the poorest and most wretched population that can be found—the scattered debris of the Irish nation."

It's no exaggeration to divide the history of the New York Archdiocese into before and after John Hughes. Born in County Tyrone in 1797, Hughes immigrated to America and worked as a laborer. He entered the seminary in Maryland at a relatively late age and rose quickly through the ecclesiastical ranks, becoming an auxiliary bishop of New York in 1838 and bishop four years later.

Hughes took it as his mission to prevent the disintegration of his flock by equipping it with the discipline and organization needed to survive in a hostile and brutally competitive environment. The most immediate challenge was erecting churches for Catholic worship. During his twenty-two-year tenure (he was made an archbishop in 1850), churches were erected at the rate of about one a year. Yet even at this pace, with churches growing larger and grander as they followed the city's expansion northward, many parishes still counted twenty thousand or more Catholics within their boundaries.

Every bit as important in Hughes's eyes as an adequate supply of churches was the creation of a system of Catholic education. The religion of Famine immigrants was a lightly practiced pastiche of Celtic folk belief and Catholic ritual. In the city's common schools, Catholic children not only lacked the opportunity to learn about their faith, but heard it mocked as "Papist superstition" and were proselytized by Protestant teachers and texts.

Wary of America's tradition of anti-Catholicism, the Church had been eager to avoid attention. Hughes had no such compunctions. He embraced controversy. He knocked down the attempts of lay Catholics to hire and fire their pastors and to run parishes along the congregational lines common among Protestants. Dismissive of the small community of Italian-Catholics and oblivious at best to the even smaller African-American one, his fierce nature turned incandescent when confronting the Protestant establishment.

He attacked the countrywide evangelical crusade being waged by some Protestants and confronted the sectarian bias of those in charge of the city's public schools. In the end, unable to achieve his goal of public funding of Catholic education, he declared that "the benefits of public education are not for us" and established an entirely separate system of church-funded schools.

Tribal chieftain as much as churchman, with a strong claim to being the original in-your-face New Yorker, Hughes welcomed the chance to work with politicians he found friendly. His cordial relationship with Republican Governor William Seward, which grew out of Seward's support during the school controversy, led Hughes to heed Seward's request as Secretary of State in the Lincoln administration and plead the Union cause in the Vatican. It was Hughes's last mission. Tired and ill, he was embarrassed by the awful spectacle of the 1863 Draft Riots that seemed to undo so much of what he had achieved and confirm the worst stereotypes of the Irish.

When Hughes died in January 1864, his work, like the new cathedral he had begun on the outskirts of the city (dubbed "Hughes's folly"), was unfinished. But he had cleared the ground and set the foundations for his successors to build upon. They were helped in no small measure by the mutually beneficial relationship between the city's large bloc of Catholic voters and the Democratic Organization headquartered in Tammany Hall.

Personal relationships were at the heart of the arrangement. Precinct captains, district leaders—right up to the boss himself—were often loyal parishioners, and a word from the local pastor was part of an old-style affirmative action that could trump bureaucratic procedure and result in a job or promotion, or keep a son or brother out of jail. Tammany, in turn, could be relied on to support the use of public funds for Catholic charitable institutions, oppose actions harmful to Church interests, and keep the working class in the political mainstream, away from the sway of radicals and anti-clerics.

The relationship between parish house and political clubhouse had a formal enthronement of sorts on November 21, 1876, when "Honest John" Kelly, the leader who picked up the pieces after the fall of the Tweed Ring and put Tammany back in business, married Teresa Mullen, niece of Cardinal McCloskey, the first American prelate raised to that rank. There were dissenters, for sure, foremost among them Father Edward McGlynn, a radical and highly popular priest whose endorsement of reformer Henry George in the mayoral contest of 1886 brought him into open conflict with Archbishop Michael Corrigan. But mostly the relationship endured.

The structure Hughes put in place proved highly viable. A distinct community, observant and loyal, drew strength and identity from local parishes. The tidal wave of Italian immigrants at the end of the nineteenth century that followed the German and Irish enriched the city's Catholic culture, as did smaller communities of Poles, Croats, Spaniards, French Canadians, et al., but did little to alter the operation of the institutional Church, which remained firmly in the hands of an Irish-dominated clergy.

Catholic schools never educated anything close to a majority of Catholics, yet along with a sense of structure and moral context, they offered a sizable number of children from immigrant families the skills they needed to rise into the middle class. They also turned out impressive numbers of graduates who went on to become priests, brothers, and nuns, expanding the personnel available to staff a far-flung and self-contained network of schools, hospitals, nursing homes, and orphanages.

The high point came around the same moment that my father and Cardinal Spellman shared a stage at St. Raymond's. Following Hughes by almost exactly a century, Spellman enjoyed the status of establishment insider—a perfect bookend to his predecessor's reputation as firebrand outsider. A manager and CEO by temperament, who preferred pulling strings over indulging in public donnybrooks, he wielded his considerable clout in private meetings with political and financial power brokers. (Still, shades of Archbishop Hughes, he found himself in a nasty public squabble with Eleanor Roosevelt over the perennial issue of public funding for parochial schools.)

When he took over in 1939, Spellman inherited an archdiocese with a staggering debt—for the time—of $28,000,000. Partly through his own managerial skills and partly aided by the New Deal and the remarkable post-war success of urban Catholics, Spellman returned the archdiocese to fiscal health and then some. He built new schools and hospitals, staffed by a ready supply of religious vocations, and became a major source of financial support for the Vatican.

Under Spellman, the Cardinal's residence behind St. Patrick's Cathedral reached its zenith as "the Powerhouse," an appellation that highlighted the role New York's Cardinal Archbishop played in matters of church and state, from influencing Rome's selection of other American bishops to helping city hall choose commissioners and high-ranking officials, especially in the heavily Catholic police and fire departments. The skills he displayed in maintaining a cooperative relationship with Spellman—described by some as the American Pope—undoubtedly contributed to Mayor Robert Wagner's eventual selection as the U.S. representative to the Vatican.

Never the unswerving reactionary critics caricatured him as, Spellman was progressive on racial matters, a bridge builder between Catholics and Jews, and a defender of Jesuit John Courtney Murray's advocacy of religious freedom, a position Spellman successfully championed at the Second Vatican Council. But his instincts were decidedly conservative. He was suspicious of those who questioned the social or economic status quo. (He tolerated Dorothy Day and her radical Catholic Worker movement because he suspected she might be a saint.) A supporter of Senator Joseph McCarthy, he was unbending in his anticommunism.

Spellman's political inclinations threatened to become an issue in the 1960 presidential contest between Vice President Nixon and Senator John F. Kennedy. In contrast to many ordinary Catholics, who saw Kennedy's election as a chance to avenge the humiliating rout of Alfred E. Smith in 1928, and to Richard Cardinal Cushing of Boston, an unabashed Kennedy partisan, Spellman preferred Nixon. Officially neutral, Spellman made no secret that he regarded Nixon as a devout anticommunist who would be a bulwark against a rising generation's desire for dangerous and needless—in Spellman's eyes—experimentation, the very desire Kennedy seemed to embody.

Angered by what he regarded as Spellman's duplicity, Kennedy gave no public hint of his resentment. He accepted Spellman's invitation to the Alfred E. Smith dinner, an annual affair Spellman hosted both to display his status as a major political player and to raise funds for the archdiocese's charitable endeavors. Spellman's body language might have been intended to confer his imprimatur on Nixon, but Kennedy's wit deflated its significance. He congratulated the Cardinal on using the occasion to bring together two politicians whose differences were so sharp and deep—Vice President Nixon and Governor Nelson Rockefeller. Kennedy carried the evening and the election.

Kennedy's presidency represented a real and symbolic triumph for Catholics in general and the Irish in particular. In terms of education and income, a majority of Catholics were rapidly shedding their lower- and working class status, and meeting or exceeding middle-class standards. As more and more upwardly mobile, college-educated Catholics followed the new highways to the suburbs, the century-old, tight-knit world of urban Catholicism, with the parish church and school at its center, unraveled.

The Second Vatican Council, which opened in 1962, changed the language of the Mass from Latin to the vernacular and ended meatless Fridays, alterations in the everyday touchstones of Catholic identity that were the tip of a deeper and more significant transformation in the Church's attitude toward other Christians, Jews, and non-believers. Simultaneous with the decline of the old-fashioned nativist fear and loathing of Catholicism signaled by Kennedy's election, the Church itself started to dismantle the defensive walls erected in the counter-reformation.

It would be wrong to interpret the problems that now beset the Archdiocese of New York as the collapse of the work that John Hughes started. The Church's challenges are rooted in success, not failure. Arriving as strangers in a strange land, millions of Catholic immigrants were comforted, educated and cared for in Church-run institutions. The Church assisted in creating an environment in which the newly arrived and their children—often poor and still steeped in the village ways of their peasant ancestors—could catch their breath and come to grips with the disorienting realities of a sprawling, winner-take-all society. The idea of a social safety net that was pioneered in New York reflected in no small part the influence of Catholic social teaching.

Although it doesn't often interact or intersect with the elite levels of New York's cosmopolitan culture (and never has), Catholic life in New York continues to be vibrant, at least at the parish level. Local churches are frequently a touchstone for different cultures and classes, the place in which immigrants, working-class ethnics and college-educated professionals share more than just the same sidewalks. The liturgies are celebrated more vibrantly than in my childhood, when the priest had his back to the congregation and the Mass was in Latin. Ironically, at the same time that the sexual abuse crisis and its mishandling by the hierarchy have grievously wounded the morale of Catholics, it has made many of those who remain in the Church both more critical of its leadership and more committed to bringing about the goal of lay empowerment envisioned by the Second Vatican Council.

The old order has had its last hurrah. Politicians stop by the Cardinal's residence to pay their courtesies, not to consult on appointments. The Church's ethnic composition has been made richer but more complicated by a wealth of new immigrants, including Puerto Ricans, Dominicans, Haitians, Mexicans, Chinese, Africans, and Vietnamese. The critical shortage of priests promises to grow worse. The dislocation caused by shifting demographics has driven the Archdiocese's recent decision to close parishes and schools—some, like St. Brigid's, dedicated by John Hughes himself. It is aggravated by a decision-making process that still relegates the laity's role to "pray, pay and obey."

I think my father was right all those years ago when he pointed to the Church's role in caring for the least. Bishops come and go. The city continually molts its old self and renews its pursuit of the extravagant. But amid the whirlwind of ambition and celebrity, the need will always be great for institutions and congregations whose mission stays the same: to heal souls as well as bodies, comfort the sick and dying, welcome the stranger, shelter the homeless, defend the poor and disenfranchised, and insist on the God-given dignity of every person. To the degree that the Church and its members seek their perfection in this work, the future will never be in doubt.

The Catholic Imagination

Crumble, crumble
Voiceless things;
No faith can last
That never sings.
　　　　　—LASCELLES ABERCROMBIE,
　　　　　"The Stream's Song"

T HE LATE ED SHAUGHNESSY, as profound and insightful a student of Eugene O'Neill's work as will ever pass through this vale of tears, stood perpetual watch against faith-based literary enthusiasts eager to claim that, though O'Neill wasn't exactly a church-goer, he was in his heart a loyal Catholic. Shaughnessy was fond of pointing out that O'Neill himself anticipated this brand of parochial expropriation in his masterpiece, *Long Day's Journey into Night*.

In the play's last act, James Tyrone and his son, Edmund, go another round in their endless verbal sparring. Edmund mocks the old man's Irish-Catholic chauvinism; "Yes, facts don't mean a thing, do they? What you want to believe, that's the only truth! [Derisively] Shakespeare was an Irish Catholic, for example."

Old man Tyrone stands his ground. "So he was," he tells his son. "The proof is in the plays."

Shaughnessy found no proof of a secretly-practiced Catholic faith in O'Neill's life. Yet, in his book *Down the Days and Down the Nights: Eugene O'Neill's Catholic Sensibility*, Shaughnessy carefully dissected the profound influence of post-Famine Irish-Catholicism on O'Neill's mind and imagination. Acolyte of Freud and Nietzsche though he was, O'Neill didn't regard sin as a historical curiosity. Even in a world without God, the old religious definitions still held true. Sin separated us from one another. We suffered because of it, and we inflict that suffering on others.

Describing another famous artist-apostate possessed of the same Catholic sensibility, literary scholar Beryl Schlossman writes of James Joyce that "his Catholicism, often dismissed as an artifact, is at the source of his symbolic vision and its imaginative constructs; it led him to read the writings of the great mystics and perhaps to conceive of his own experience of language in their terms."

In the end, it seems easier to identify elements of a Catholic "sensibility" or "imaginative constructs" in specific artists than to agree on a universal definition. Is there really a fundamental and unitary imagination that underlies the philosophical, political, and creative differences among Catholics as diverse as Antonin Scalia, Mary Gordon, Hans Küng, Ted Kennedy, Mother Angelica, the College of Cardinals, et al.? Or is the very notion of a shared imaginative base an outdated concept that can no longer—if it ever did—describe or contain the disparate viewpoints and emphases of all who call themselves Catholics?

Prior to Vatican II, I think, it was easier to conceive of a single Catholic imagination, especially perhaps in the U.S. where the Irish-dominated Church forged a unified religious identity from a welter of disparate ethnic groups. We Catholics distinguished ourselves from the plethora of Protestant denominations through the uniformity of our rituals, dogmas, and, most visibly, our shared sacramentals—rosaries, scapulars, religious statues—and the habits of old, the distinctive dress of priests, nuns, and brothers that retains its popularity in two places: Hollywood, which often seems at a loss for identifying anything as Catholic unless clothed in costumes that have been part of wardrobe departments since *Going My Way*; and EWTN, often referred to as the Catholic Channel, where the old habits are, well, still habitual.

Even at the height of the Tridentine regimen, beneath the carapace of outward conformity, there existed different emphases and viewpoints which, at a minimum, reflected what John O'Malley has described in his book of the same title as "four cultures of the West." O'Malley encapsulates those cultures as the prophetic, academic, literary, and liturgical. Each has shaped and been shaped by the Church, he writes, and each enjoyed a dominant moment. Although these cultures have sometimes overlapped and intermingled, they've also given rise to imaginative expressions as different as a monk's cell is from a chapel in the style of the high baroque.

Though founded in Jerusalem, the Church undertook, in O'Malley's words, a "massive appropriation . . . of the cultural reality of the Greco-Roman world." Here is St. Gregory the Great on the Catholic education he received at the hands of Origen: "For us there was nothing forbidden, nothing hidden, nothing inaccessible. We were allowed to learn every doctrine, Greek and non-Greek, both spiritual and secular, both divine and human. With the utmost freedom we went into everything and examined it thoroughly, taking our fill of enjoying the pleasures of the soul." What was true for the upper classes was true for the lower as well, especially the *pagani*—the *paisanos* or country people—whose imaginations and practices incorporated much of their pre-Christian heritage.

The expression of the Catholic imagination in Western culture has been carried out in staggering variety, in high art and folk art, in the classicism of St. Peter's in Rome and the modernism of the *Sagrada Familia* in Barcelona, in the mysticism of St. Teresa of Avila and the existentialism of Gabriel Marcel. Here in America, if Catholicism has produced little memorable in the way of architecture, or music, or painting, it has nurtured the imaginations of some notable literary figures.

Paul Elie's book, *The Life You Save May Be Your Own*, is a strikingly incisive examination of four of those writers: Thomas Merton, Dorothy Day, Flannery O'Connor, and Walker Percy. Elie weaves their stories together masterfully, never confusing the reader or leaving loose ends. He distills what they sought and found in the Catholic Church as "a place of pilgrimage, a home and a destination, where city and world meet, where the self encounters the other, where personal experience and the testimony of the ages can be reconciled."

In Elie's incisive telling of these writers' lives, it becomes apparent that imagination was a vital component of their Catholic faith.

Dorothy Day, for instance, read and reread Dickens and Dostoyevsky with the same intensity and scrutiny that she did scripture, finding parables to guide her life. Elie also makes clear that for these writers in particular—and by extension, I believe, for Catholics in general—imagination is a means toward more than enjoyment or entertainment. These are side effects. The end is enlightenment, to find in our world of death and disappointment—of catastrophes visited on us by nature and our own moral blindness—some confirmation or clue of the divine presence.

Imagination isn't the same as religious faith, obviously—or there wouldn't be so many imaginative atheists and agnostics. And it isn't the same as mental relaxation, a trip through the fun house of the subconscious, the rigors of intellectual inquiry thrown aside in favor of treating the mind to a day at the beach. The subconscious is lazy and disordered. Turning the mud of the imagination into the clay of popular entertainment or the more lasting substance of art, into something capable of conveying meaning and resonating with our shared human experiences and expectations, is hard work. That's true across the board, for believer and non-believer alike.

What's different for the Catholic artist is the context of that labor. It's not a matter of dressing up a creative work in the traditional trappings of Catholic practice. Often, I think, especially in the movies, films get categorized as "Catholic" because there's a crucifix on the wall or somebody's wearing a miraculous medal. I once attended a seminar on "religion in the movies" in which Alfred Hitchcock's *The Wrong Man* was described as his most "Catholic film." As far as I could tell, the only thing Catholic about it was Henry Fonda fingering his beads during his trial and staring at a picture of the Sacred Heart when his innocence was about to be proved. Martin Scorcese is frequently identified as a Catholic filmmaker, but, as I see it, more often than not what people mean by this is the rich texture of his movies, the color, movement, and ritual, which I'd ascribe as much to Scorcese's love of opera as his Catholicism.

What do I mean, then, by the context in which Catholic artists labor to express faith through imagination? Not strict adherence to dogma, although I can't imagine a Catholic artist who rejects Christ's divinity and the basic tenets of the creed. The context is the set of shared presumptions about the world and human behavior with which Catholics in general and Catholic artists in particular approach the disjointed, sometimes absurd, often disturbing experience of reality.

Here, in the first decade of the twenty-first century, in a post-Holocaust, post-Cold War world, post-Vatican II Church and post-modern society—we seem to be in a post-everything era—let me suggest sin, holiness and mercy as three elements common to "the Catholic imagination." (Nota bene: I said "common to," *not* "that define." I leave that job to far more learned minds.) The first two elements—sin and holiness—probably seem obvious. The third—mercy—might seem less so, but, for me, divine mercy, which runs so counter to the prevailing spirit of religious and secular fundamentalism, resonates at the very center of the Catholic imagination.

Sin is where we all start. There is neither Catholic faith nor imagination without it. Sin, says the dictionary, shares a root with the old English verb "to be." We are sinful from the moment of our conception, the Church teaches, imperfectable. Sin separates us from God and one another. But it is also the cause of our redemption, and it is an invitation to free ourselves from the tyranny of the perfect, to accept ourselves as we are: broken, fragile, constantly in need of forgiveness and the capacity to forgive others.

The prayer of the Easter Vigil describes Adam's primal sin, the root of our imperfection, as "O happy fault, that merited so great a redeemer." Adam's sin, the "*felix culpa*," isn't condemned but celebrated as *certe necessarium*—"truly necessary." The human experience, as Catholicism sees it, isn't split into two distinct, exclusive halves, the sinful and the unsinful. Graham Greene prefaces his novel *The Heart of the Matter* with a quote from Charles Péguy that asserts the sinner is more of a Christian than anybody except the saint.

I was reminded of this while reading the reviews of Norman Sherry's third volume of Greene's biography. They paid a great deal of attention to his sex life. In several instances, the implication was: Here was a so-called Catholic writer who spent most of his life in flagrant violation of the Church's teachings. How hypocritical. And how typical. Too bad, I thought to myself, that Greene wasn't around to read these reviews and chuckle at their fundamental misreading of Catholic teaching, that sin, indeed, was, is, and will always be the heart of the matter, the ever-present root of our ever-present longing, the origin of our search for redemption.

In his astute analysis of seventeenth-century English Puritanism, *The Company of Saints*, Michael Walzer traced the rise of our modern political parties to the Puritans' sense of organization which removed traditional bounds of class and geography to unite its followers around a shared and transcendent idea of election, of being drawn together by their uniqueness. The Catholic imagination is, to some degree, the mirror image of the company of saints. Although referred to as a communion of saints, the Church is more truly a communion of sinners, pope, peasant, and Ph.D. in the same boat, members of that greatest democracy of them all—the classless, numberless democracy of sin.

For Catholics, sin is ubiquitous. But so is forgiveness. Hell exists. But it might be empty. Evil is real but mingles with good, and no human being is either *all* good or *all* evil. We are mixtures of both, and who is saved or damned is beyond our knowing. Thomas Merton put it this way: "In the end it comes down to the old story that we are sinners, but that this is our hope because sinners are the ones who attract to themselves the infinite compassion of God."

Side by side with sin is holiness. That, I think, is the conundrum of the Incarnation. The fallen world has been raised up. The redemption isn't an event far off in the future. It's already taken place. The profane has been made sacred. Think of the gospel passage from John in which Jesus spits in the dust and makes mud with which to cure the blind man. Spit and mud turned into the stuff of miracles. The Incarnation doesn't get much more basic than that.

Alone among the great monotheistic faiths, Catholicism is a lover rather than a breaker of images and icons. This is reflected in the success with which the Church grafted onto Christianity the classical as well as popular culture of the pagan world, turning the great edifice of the Pantheon in Rome into the Church of All Saints, and the faerie-haunted streams of pre-Christian Ireland into holy wells. The grafting was made possible by the Catholic understanding of the Incarnation, which not only licenses but impels us to seek God in the material—yes, even in mud and spit.

Certainly, there have always been two forces at odds in Catholicism: immersion in the world and renunciation of it, appreciation of the flesh and aversion to it, the embrace of the immediate and the flight from it. That tension is built into the lives of creatures suspended between the temporal and the eternal, between time and timelessness, and the Incarnation is where these parallel lines finally meet and run together, the point at which the Creator undertakes full and unqualified immersion into the form of the created . . . *et incarnatus est* . . . "and He became flesh."

The Catholic Church's wealth of visual art put a special focus on the physical representation of the incarnate Christ—of the naked child and the nearly nude figure on the cross—a prominence largely lacking in other Christian churches. The art historian Leo Steinberg, in his book *The Sexuality of Christ in Renaissance Art and in Modern Oblivion*, sees in the Catholic art of that era the expression of "full Christian orthodoxy" as applied to the Incarnation. Renaissance art, he writes,

> harnessed the theological impulse and developed the requisite stylistic means to attest to the utter carnality of God's humanation in Christ. It became the first Christian art in a thousand years to confront the Incarnation entire, the upper and the lower body together, not excluding even the body's sexual component.

The deepest meaning of this "utter carnality" is captured for me in a scene from William Kennedy's novel *The Flaming Corsage,* in which Edward Daugherty encounters Cappy White coming down Broadway in Albany with a growler of beer beneath his arm. Cappy, Edward recalls, had a son, Bitsy, "a softspun boy born without ears, who'd earned candy money eating live frogs for a nickel [and] went up in flames in church while lighting a candle for his mother, Mamie." Already obese—she weighed "maybe five hundred pounds"—Mamie grew even heavier with grief.

"When she died," Edwards remembers, "Cappy knocked out

siding and two doors, then backed up a derrick to lift her out of bed and carry her to her own funeral. After that he took himself to bed and stayed there, leaving it only to buy food and beer. Hermit of Main Street, punished by the gods for marrying fat and cherishing a freakish child. What peculiar shapes love takes."

There is no better summation of the mystery, majesty, and contradictions of the Incarnation, of "God's humanation" in our emotional miseries and physical infirmities—in the full brokenness of the world—than Kennedy's phrase: *What peculiar shapes love takes.*

The Catholic celebration of the Incarnation—full and unqualified—grounds the Church. It is the basis of Catholic insistence on the Real Presence. It is also the reason, I think, that there is so little Catholic writing on the Second Coming and the last days. Many Christians don't share that reticence. The publishing sensation of the last decade has been the *Left Behind* series of eschatological novels, which have sold nearly fifty million copies detailing a right-wing Christian fantasy about the end of the world, the Rapture, and the battle of Armageddon. In contrast to this trend, when I scanned a list sent me by a friend of some eighty titles he uses in a course on the Catholic novel, I was unable to recognize any apocalyptic sagas.

The materialism of Catholicism is materialism with a difference, however. It isn't a mirror that reflects back on us, but a looking glass—of the type Lewis Carroll wrote about: a window on another world, another reality. We feel the water and oil used in the sacraments, taste the bread and wine, not just to enjoy them for what they are, but to plumb our belief that they aren't just what they seem to be but, in ways that defy the limits of language, signs of God's real presence among us.

I knew an Irish-American playwright, a lapsed Catholic, who raised his children Catholic because he believed the Church was the last institution left to awaken the imagination of the young to a sense of holy mystery—or, as he called it, "sacred enchantment"—affirming a realm of realities reason couldn't contain. I'm not holding up this playwright as a role model. He got the true order of things precisely backwards, at least from a faith perspective, making belief an instrument of imagination, rather than vice versa. Yet, in his hope that the Church could offer his children an intimation of the world as a place of sacred enchantment, that it could teach them to know they stand on holy ground, he evinced a more Catholic imagination than some practicing Catholics I've encountered.

Look around: Where once the Catholic imagination found profound expression in the material—in painting, building, sculpting—it has largely receded into irrelevance. Catholic material culture is more a heritage than a living tradition, a concern of curators more than creative artists. Is this because we've ceased to see the world as a holy place? Maybe not entirely. Yet, to some degree, I think, the ascendancy of scientific rationalism, which in so many ways has helped us lead better lives, has also left Catholics as much as non-Catholics with a sense of the vast, indifferent universe we inhabit.

The prima facie evidence would certainly seem to support that view: brothels filled with children, tsunamis, war, ethnic cleansing, an entire continent ravaged by AIDS, a billion members of our species who live every day on the borderline of starvation. Yet, faced with this evil, it is in the uncompromising emphasis on God's mercy, and on the ways that His mercy is expressed through the presence of the Virgin Mary and the saints and, before all else, through the person and presence of Jesus Christ, that the Catholic imagination stands apart.

Almost twenty years ago, in his book *The Thanatos Syndrome*, Walker Percy wrote, "It crossed my mind that people at war have the same need of each other. What would a passionate liberal or conservative do without the other?" The war Walker Percy referred to rages on more bitterly than ever, to the point that polar views of religious right and secular left not only frame much of the argument over belief, morality, and public policy but, in my view, put into sharpest relief the centrality of divine mercy to the Catholic faith as well as imagination.

Fundamentalism is easy to caricature as a uniform sect of idiots, bigots, and reactionaries. While these types are undoubtedly present, they can also be found, to one degree or another, in most mass movements and belief systems. Not all fundamentalists come in for ridicule, however. Fundamentalists of the quietest Mennonite type are often respected by those who otherwise scoff at literal readings of religious texts. As long as they stick to their knitting—or quilting—and appear socially quaint instead of politically querulous, they're acceptable, even admirable.

While all fundamentalists share a belief in the literal truth of scripture, the Anabaptist branch is even more literal than the conservative political branch, rejecting all forms of violence in obedience to Jesus's injunction to love our enemies and turn the other cheek. The literalness of political fundamentalism, on the other hand, seems especially focused on the most symbol-rich book in the Christian scriptures, *The Book of Revelation*, which is interpreted as an exact road map of God's plan. What God has in store, as they say in Texas, ain't pretty, at least for the bulk of humanity left behind after the Rapture, when the Anti-Christ will bring to bloody conclusion the unholy ways of the human race.

While it's important to acknowledge the nuances of fundamentalism—itself in some measure a reaction to a highly aggressive form of secularism—and to avoid lumping together in a single, indistinguishable mass of fanatics a movement that includes pacifists, social progressives, and people of real charity, it's impossible to ignore how many of its proponents substitute certainty for mystery, and revenge for mercy. In its extreme version—the version, unfortunately, that prevails among fundamentalist televangelists and radio preachers—God seems a supersized version of us humans, more powerful, vindictive, and nastier, a cosmic Jerry Falwell equipped with apocalyptic weapons.

On the other side of the divide, although agnostic in spirit, the secular left is certain in its practice. At best, it treats the mystery of divine love as a harmless myth; at worst, as a dangerous delusion that can impede human progress, particularly in the medical sphere. Secularism claims toleration as its central tenet. But it's a qualified toleration. It says, Go ahead and believe what you will, just as long as it has no effect on any significant part of your public life, is never asserted outside of church, and remains a private eccentricity. Not all secularists behave this way. There are non-believers who've reached their agnosticism after hard struggle and, at the same time, respect the rights of believers to make their case in the public square.

More often than not, however, secularists are contemptuous of any public expression of belief and eager not just to separate church and state, but to make the church isolated and irrelevant. I encountered this attitude a few years ago while at lunch with a fellow novelist and editor. In the middle of a good-natured discussion of our backgrounds, I mentioned that I was raised an Irish-Catholic.

He laughed. "You're not *still* a Catholic?" he asked.

"Still," I said, "Sometimes very still."

This time he didn't laugh. "A practicing Catholic?"

"Yes," I said. I knew our discussion had hit a roadblock.

"A believing Catholic?"

When I answered positively for the third time, the conversation steered back to literary matters, but I could read his reaction in his face. There was surprise as well as disappointment, as if entire areas of potential conversation had been closed off and our lunch was going to be less relaxed and open than he'd first supposed.

At present, a prime flash point for the conflict between fundamentalists and secularists is the teaching of Darwinism in public schools. The argument is obviously more than a dispute over a single scientific theory. It's a contest over how to view existence. Ironies abound. Many of the same people who attack evolution simultaneously back an agenda that, in its worship of the disruptive, merciless operations of free markets, free trade, and globalization, supports an economic form of "survival of the fittest," a phrase Herbert Spencer coined and Darwin endorsed. Within the liberal camp, many people, while still espousing social justice and solidarity, seem to exhibit a growing faith in a neo-eugenicist ethic that rests on a belief in the power of science to engineer the next stages of human evolution, weeding out the causes of mental and physical diseases and perhaps those who carry them.

In the eyes of some bioethicists, all human behavior reflects evolutionary adaptations that have been translated into our genetic structure. Thus there's a selfish gene, a cooperative gene, on and on, a gene for every attitude from altruism to xenophobia, each in some way related to our struggle for survival. The concept of an emotion unrelated to this process, of an impulse to mercy that overrides notions of utility or fitness, is hard to place in this scientific equation. Darwin himself, while he believed charity and mercy had a social value in human relationships, could find no basis for them in nature. The utter lack of mercy, he wrote, would be "about the blackest fact in natural history" were it not for the truth that natural selection and species survival necessitate the ruthless and relentless destruction of individuals.

Fundamentalists are correct, I think, in their perception of Darwinism's corrosive effects on the moral sanctions that respect and protect the individual human person. But their response is to retreat into an untenable defense of the Bible as a work of science and to offer a view of the human future every bit as merciless as Darwin's, with sinners and non-believers wiped out in a catastrophe of the kind that rendered dinosaurs extinct. Catholics mostly tiptoe around the problem, I think. While accepting the scientific validity of Darwinism, with all it says about the brute realities of existence, Catholics quietly maintain, simultaneously, a benign view of nature, its tooth-and-claw cruelty and violence more aberration than rule, with a loving God somehow hovering over it.

Ironically, it was Gerard Manley Hopkins—like Darwin, a former Anglican divinity student—who marked his conversion to Catholicism with the imaginative triumph of "The Wreck of the Deutschland," a poem-cum-credo that confronts head-on the raw facts of nature in order to assert the primacy of divine mercy in the life and thinking of the Church. But he didn't do so by averting his eyes from the faith-draining, hope-breaking implications of a jungle-like universe. In the high summer of Victorian England, the Anglican clergy was rife with amateur naturalists who looked at creation as reflecting the order, stability, and good sense that a hierarchical God imposed on it. Darwin rejected that model of nature, and so did Hopkins.

The context of Hopkins's poem is a tribute to five German nuns driven into exile by Bismarck's anti-Catholic legislation, who drowned when their ship—the *Deutschland*—was wrecked off the coast of Wales in 1875. Today, after a century that included two world wars, which killed upward of sixty million people, the mass murder of European Jews, the gulags of Soviet Russia, the genocides in Cambodia and Rwanda, and other assorted persecutions and state-sponsored programs of collective homicide, Hopkins's concern for five nuns might seem quaint, even trivial. In language as strong, original, and rich as any in the English tongue, however, Hopkins forces us to confront the nasty and inevitable end we all face:

> . . . flame,
> Fang, or flood goes Death on drum, . . .
> Flesh falls within sight of us, we, though flower the same,
> Wave with the meadow, forget that there must
> The sour scythe cringe, and the blear share come.

Hopkins doesn't sugar-coat the shipwreck, instead putting front and center the murderous capacity of the world to destroy fragile human beings:

> . . . the sea flint-flake, black-backed in the regular blow,
> Sitting Eastnortheast in cursed quarter, the wind;
> Wiry and white-fiery and whirlwind-swivellèd snow
> Spins to the widow-making unchilding unfathering deep.

Men and women die senselessly. Children perish before their parents' eyes. Prayers for a miraculous delivery go unanswered. The innocent are destroyed along with the sinful:

> They fought with God's cold—
> And they could not and fell to the deck
> (Crushed them) or water (and drowned them) or rolled
> With the sea-romp over the wreck.
> Night roared, with the heart-break hearing a heart-broke rabble,
> The woman's wailing, the crying of child without check—. . .

These lines express, I think, the post-modern consciousness as it sees our human predicament today: alone amid an accidental universe, ether without end, stars dying and being born in a random, ultimately purposeless process of following out the cosmic consequences of the Big Bang. Hopkins doesn't end there, however. The very power of his language—language, as Flannery O'Connor described it, "heightened and unlike itself"—the momentum it builds, the way it causes the mind to move past the single meaning of words, and beyond what is on the page, is every bit as magical as the work of that other contemporary of Darwin, Lewis Carroll.

The truth, Hopkins posits, isn't found by looking away from nature but by looking deeper, by following belief with imagination, by seeking God not apart from pain, doubt, despair, death, but in the midst of it, riding "time like riding a river." Sin and holiness meet here, in Hopkins's imagination, not in a single end-of-time eschaton, but in the existence of each person, in introspection that doesn't end in egotism but allows us to sense the limitless reach of the Incarnation:

> The girth of it and the wharf of it and the wall;
> Stanching, quenching ocean of a motionable mind;
> Ground of being, and granite of it: past all
> Grasp God, throned behind
> Death with a sovereignty that heeds but hides, bodes but abides; . . .

For Hopkins, this sovereignty, though often terrifying as death always is, teaches the human heart not so much to seek God's mercy as submit to it:

> Wring thy rebel, dogged in den,
> Man's malice, with wrecking and storm. . . .
>
> With an anvil-ding
> And with fire in him forge thy will
> Or rather, rather then, stealing as Spring
> Through him, melt him but master him still: . . .
>
> Make mercy in all of us, out of us all
> Mastery, but be adored, but be adored King.

In the poem, Hopkins uses the word mercy five times, a clear allusion to the five wounds of Jesus's passion: "Five! The find and sake/And cipher of suffering Christ." This is neither a cipher to be decoded nor a mystery to be solved, but a truth that can only be denied or accepted. For me, the whole Catholic faith and imagination springs from this acceptance, this reconciliation of worldliness and holiness embodied in the Incarnation and consummated on the cross that makes us givers and receivers of mercy, both. And once accepted, how is it possible for the Catholic imagination not to embrace and explore the human condition honestly, to seek God in one another, in our nobility and squalor, in our infinite ability to break each other's hearts?

Gabriel Marcel imagined a "metaphysic of hope" by which Christians' belief in the eternal significance of every human life is a bulwark against a Malthusian ethic of reproductive profligacy that robs the individual of any meaning other than in furthering the survival of the species. Anticipating Marcel, and the mass destruction of human life carried out in the name of eugenic perfection, ethnic purity, and the economic millennium, Hopkins imagines in "The Wreck of the Deutschland" what I would call a "metaphysic of mercy."

In Hopkins's telling, the shipwreck is neither an act of divine retribution against a godless crew nor a small but revealing glimpse of nature's pitiless contempt for single lives. Hopkins poses this question:

> Yet did the dark side of the bay of thy blessing
> Not vault them, the million of rounds of thy mercy not reeve
>   even them in?

Several stanzas later, he answers with this vision of a God who acts:

> With a mercy that outrides
> The all of water, an ark
> For the listener, for the lingerer with a love glides
> Lower than death and the dark;
> A vein for the visiting of the past-prayer, pent in prison,
> The-last-breath penitent spirits—the uttermost mark
> Our passion-plungèd giant risen,
> The Christ of the Father compassionate, fetched in the storm
>   of his strides.

If I had to choose a single part of the Catholic imagination to give to the non-Catholic world as representative of the rest, it would be the Christ that Hopkins describes. The instinct toward mercy, the instinct Darwin couldn't find in nature, is for Hopkins the purpose of Christ's presence among us, the essence of His "humanation"; and the lashings of storms and man-made savagery should cause us not to turn away or find God absent or see His intent as revenge or retribution, but to seek Him in all the peculiar shapes love takes, amid the chaos and pain of the human condition, this God of ours who goes "lower than death and the dark," to "the uttermost mark," to the farthest depths, "with a mercy that outrides the all of water" to gather us in.

And here in this time of division in the Church, of corruption and suspicion and scandal, if I had to choose one part of the Catholic imagination for Catholics to cherish and explore and, above all, to make part of our dealings with the world and one another, it would be the merciful Christ of whom Hopkins sings to us: *Our passion-plungèd giant risen . . . Let him easter in us.*

Holy Orders

A man becomes a saint not by conviction that he is better than sinners but by the realization that he is one of them, and that all together they need the mercy of God.

—Thomas Merton, *New Seeds of Contemplation*

Few professions have tumbled in public estimation as far or with the same conclusive thud as the Catholic priesthood. The descent began with the mass exodus following the Second Vatican Council and was given new and hurtling velocity by the prolonged season of ugly revelations of sexual misconduct, which, as well as bankrupting entire dioceses, has splattered a mass of innocent priests with its septic effects.

The distance that the reputation of the priesthood has fallen is testament to the heights it once rested upon, an elevation attained in part thanks to the movies. Hollywood created the urban, Irish-American archetype of the movie priest: holy but not impossibly pious, a great friend to young boys (the girls, the presumed source of temptation, were left to the nuns). Across several decades, it did its best to place him firmly among its pantheon of other male archetypes, laconic cowboy, hardboiled private eye, etc.

The movie priest could be sporty and quick-talking, the way Frank McHugh played him in *Going My Way*, or a rock of incorruptibility like Father Flanagan as played by Spencer Tracy in *Boys Town*, or a working-class hero like Father Barry in *On the Waterfront*, portrayed with great conviction by Karl Malden. But always he stood out, couldn't be bought or cowed, and wouldn't let down his flock. Even the whiskey priest of Graham Greene's *Power and the Glory*, as brought to the screen by John Ford, became in the person of Henry Fonda more hero than hopeless case.

The movie priest was originally designed and built under the direction of the same Catholic pressure groups that imposed the production code on Hollywood and did their best to ban sexual suggestiveness from America's movie theaters, saving non-Catholics and Catholics alike from impure thoughts and their inevitable corollary, impure acts. (Whether they wanted to be saved is another matter.) The imposition of the movie priest on the collective imagination was an exercise of Catholic power, driven largely by Irish-Americans, and represented a highly effective backlash against the pornographic libels spread by hugely popular anti-Catholic propaganda such as the nineteenth-century tract *The Awful Disclosures of Maria Monk*.

The flesh-and-blood priests I've interacted with all my life never conformed to the archetype. Many performed their duties with the unenthusiastic efficiency of mid-level bureaucrats or corporate cogs. A few were hopeless reactionaries. Most were intelligent, caring, good men frequently worn down by the ceaseless expectations of parishioners who presumed the instruments of God's supernatural presence must be supernatural themselves. If they were sometimes perfunctory in their preaching and seemed more resigned than inspired in their ministry, they were nevertheless usually benevolent and sympathetic, attuned to human imperfection, and my relations with them were never tainted in any way by sexual advances or attempted seductions.

Unlike doctors, of course, priests are supposed to aspire to a higher standard than "do no harm." But that's not a bad place to begin measuring any profession, and if I can say truthfully that no Catholic priest has done me harm, I can also state unequivocally that there have been priests who have done me immeasurable good, far more good on many more occasions than I can record here, and that goodness has

been a part of my life from the time I was a small child to the present
moment.

None of the priests who have influenced and changed my life has been
an exact replica of the Irish-American movie priest. Two have been
Italian-American. Two have been gay. The only one vaguely reminis-
cent of the archetype was Father Daniel Ryan, a Jesuit, who was a
Boston-born son of Irish immigrants. Father Dan, which is how my sisters and brother and I always addressed him, taught my aunt psychol-
ogy at Fordham University. The two were best friends for the rest of
their lives, and he became a part of our family.

In the 1930s, Father Dan was sent to instruct seminarians in psy-
chology at the Jesuit College in Rome. He conducted the classes in
Latin. He was a gifted linguist who taught himself Russian at the end
of his life so he could read Dostoyevsky in the original language. A
chaplain in World War II, he was among the most relaxed, unauthori-
tarian, unmilitary men I've ever encountered.

Father Dan served as confessor at America House, the home of
the national Jesuit magazine, while the French Jesuit and paleontolo-
gist Tielhard de Chardin was staying there and working at the Museum
of Natural History. (Chardin died in New York on one of his visits.)
They had long conversations in French and developed a friendship. Yet
Father Dan wore his learning lightly. He was the one adult from my
early life who took children seriously, always listening with genuine
attentiveness, never in the saccharinely dismissive or abruptly condescending fashion of most grownups.

Toward the end of his life, Father Dan was stationed at Fairfield
University, in Connecticut. He had grown frail. I accompanied my aunt
when she drove him back from our apartment after Christmas. For the
first time, he allowed me to carry his bag to his quarters. His furniture
consisted of a bed, a desk, and a bookcase. The only decorations were
a crucifix above his bed and a mantelpiece filled with scores of post-
cards that my sisters, brother, and I had sent him over the years.

Father Dan was a worldly man, not in the sense of being owned
by his possessions—he had next to none—but in the ease with which

he moved among people. He loved a good cigar. He savored a single shot of rye whiskey. He and my aunt took us to plays and movies and showed us New York. He engaged taxi drivers, waiters, and doormen in deep conversation. He seemed to find everyone interesting. He had a wonderful, resonant laugh. When at the end of a visit, he made the sign of the cross over you, there was never anything perfunctory about it. You felt it as a blessing of forgiveness and approbation, an invitation to resist evil and do good, and not be discouraged when you didn't. Father Dan was the most nonjudgmental person I have ever met.

At the end of World War II, Father Dan was briefly posted to Jamaica by the Jesuits, where he developed an interest in the culture and struggle of blacks. He became a devoted reader of *Ebony* magazine, the black version of *Life*, a publication I wasn't aware of until he passed on a copy. He was a member of the Catholic Interracial Council, which was founded by a fellow Jesuit, but quibbled with its name. "Catholic Interracial," he told me, "is a tautology." After I looked up tautology, I agreed. More than sympathetic to the plight of African-Americans, he was vocal in his admiration for what he described as the spiritual dignity they had maintained through centuries of relentless oppression.

Other priests I encountered shared Father Dan's concern. The first time I remember hearing about the Civil Rights movement was from the pulpit of St. Raymond's. In 1960, Father John Flynn challenged a packed house at the twelve o'clock Mass to embrace the example of the "Negro Protestant minister" (gasp!) Martin Luther King and see his struggle for equality in the light of the Gospels. Four decades later, Father Flynn is still in the Bronx, part of a remarkable cadre of nuns and priests—many Irish-Americans among them—who have never wavered in their commitment to the poor and marginalized.

The sacrament of Holy Orders, which belongs exclusively to those ordained as deacons, priests, and bishops, is closed to women. It remains to be seen if the growing shortage of priests will bring about a reordering. I suspect the Church will feel compelled at some point to reach an accommodation by which married men will be admitted to the priesthood. Eventually, I believe—and not as distant as it might seem now—the urgent promptings of the Holy Spirit will lead to the ordination of women. Likewise, the current huffing and puffing over gays in the priesthood can't negate the fact that there were, are, and will always be homosexual priests whose piety, probity, and loyalty deserve respect and gratitude rather than slanderous distrust and squalid witch hunts.

I'm not a theologian. But I will always be a Catholic, and being a Catholic means being patient. Ours is an un-apocalyptic church. We persist in the everyday, in what is called in the liturgical calendar "ordinary time." Though we might feel a twinge of nostalgia for the days when Holy Orders were synonymous with the Irish-American movie priest (heroic and handsome to boot), we recognize that life is complex and imperfect, that good and bad are threaded in the same tapestry, that saints are canonized for their exceptional holiness because holiness as a hallmark of any life will always be exceptional, that most of us stumble through the unholy, disordered mess of existence, inevitably falling back to sin, which is why we—pope, priests, and the rest of us—go to confession not just once in our lives, but over and over.

City of God,
City of Man

Does it matter? Grace is everywhere . . .
—GEORGE BRESSON, *The Diary of a Country Priest*

O NE OF THE RARE TIMES THAT *I have had the opportunity to recognize publicly the impact a Catholic priest had had on my life was when I was invited to give a lecture at Fordham's Lincoln Center campus to mark the retirement of the University's president, Father Joseph O'Hare, S.J., who although by no means a movie priest has the good looks to be cast as one.*

A fellow child of the Bronx who never lost his New York accent or his Irish sense of humor, Father O'Hare was the editor of America when I first met him. He did the mitzvah both of accepting the articles I submitted for publication, which were among the first I ever got into print, and encouraging me to keep writing. "Fordham and the Rise of Gotham: City of God, City of Man" was delivered in his honor and in gratitude for his reminder of the difference one good priest can make.

A quarter of a century ago, in 1979, I was working as a graduate assistant in the history department of Fordham University when Father Joseph O'Hare, S.J., as editor of *America* magazine, began publishing my articles. The first, entitled "An American-Irish St. Patrick's Day," was read by Dr. Kevin Cahill, a Fordham alumnus, who brought it to the attention of Governor Hugh Carey and, to make a short story even shorter, I was hired to be his speechwriter.

I spent the next six and a half years working for Governors Carey and Cuomo, living alone in a hotel room in Albany and getting to know the midnight cleaning crew in the capitol. My hair fell out, and I developed chronic back pain. I was subsequently hired by Time Inc., which begot Time Warner, which begot AOL Time Warner, which made me party to one of the greatest corporate merger disasters in business history, with a 401K approaching single digits.

None of this would have happened to me without Father O'Hare. In other words, instead of being entitled "Fordham and the Rise of Gotham: City of God and City of Man," this might as easily—and *more* accurately—be called, "Father O'Hare and the *Fall* of Peter Quinn."

The first in this series of lectures in honor of Father O'Hare's retirement as President of Fordham University was delivered by eminent urban historian Kenneth Jackson. Truth in labeling requires I stress that I'm *not* a historian. Neither am I an urbanist or a professor. I'm not even a journalist. By day, I'm a corporate editor and writer. Though it's true that neither I nor any of the CEOs I've written for has been indicted, it's also true that the role of corporate apologist isn't one that recommends itself to widespread credibility.

By nights—early mornings, actually—I'm a historical novelist. The term is impossibly compromised. Does it imply a historian writing as a novelist? Or a novelist as a historian? And which is worse: novelists making up history or historians choosing fiction over fact?

In view of my credentials—or lack of them—I won't try for a highly detailed account of the institutional role Fordham has played in the life of New York or to correlate its role with the city's rise to global prominence. Instead, I'd like to consider three individuals—John Hughes, Edgar Allan Poe, and Michael Manning—who were all connected to the village of Fordham between, roughly, 1846 and 1850, during the college's formative first decade. Neither Hughes, Manning, nor Poe attended the college. But Hughes, the archbishop of New York, not only figures prominently in its history, he founded it.

Edgar Allan Poe was born in Boston, raised in Richmond, educated at the University of Virginia and West Point—neither of which he graduated from—and spent most of his career as a writer in Philadelphia, New York City, and Fordham. He lived a few years in obscurity in Baltimore with his aunt and her daughter, Virginia, whom he eventually married and who died in Fordham. In 1849, while traveling from Richmond to New York, Poe died in Baltimore. For this, the city eventually named a football team in his honor—The Ravens. (Though Poe was interested in foreseeing the future, there's no indication he ever anticipated the invention of football. His poem "The Raven" was conceived in Richmond and completed in New York.)

Like Hughes, who was born in County Tyrone, Ireland, and Poe, whose paternal great-grandfather came from County Cavan, Michael Manning was Irish. His exact place of birth is unknown. It's said he was from County Kilkenny, but there's no record of what town or village, or what occupation—if any—he had. His level of education was, at best, probably rudimentary. It's possible he was illiterate. He arrived, it's thought, in Fordham in 1847—six years after Hughes opened St. John's College and one year after the Jesuits and Poe, who'd arrived at almost the same time, in the spring of 1846.

If Thomas Carlyle was right, and history is nothing more than the biography of great men, then Michael Manning is a figure of no historical significance. Yet, though little is known about him or his wife, Eileen Purcell, also of Irish birth—their paper trail consists of a single death certificate—they had several children while they were in Fordham. Their oldest, Margaret Manning, born in Fordham on a site now occupied by Theodore Roosevelt High School and baptized in the college chapel, was my paternal grandmother.

Both born to the Irish peasantry, Manning and Hughes traveled very different paths. Hughes became a de facto chieftain of the American hierarchy and archbishop of the fastest growing Catholic diocese in the world. The Tyrone of Hughes's childhood, in the first decade of the nineteenth century, was still reeling from the aftermath of the bloody and unsuccessful rebellion of 1798. Sectarian feelings weren't merely hardening but taking on new militancy. Protestant evangelicalism was on the march.

Hughes migrated to America at age twenty, in 1817, part of the swarm of Catholic laborers who left Ireland in the agricultural depression that followed the boom years of the Napoleonic Wars. He joined what historian Peter Gray has described as the advanced guard of a mud-splattered proletarian army whose spadework dug the country's canals and put in place the foundations of America's industrial transformation. Hughes, however, was a spalpeen with a difference. He wanted to be a priest, and eventually, against great odds and thanks to the intervention of a Protestant convert and American-born saint, Elizabeth Seton, he was successful.

The Church in which he took holy orders was a small archipelago of dioceses amid a Protestant sea, largely left alone because it was so inconspicuous. The hierarchy was drawn mostly from families of English-Catholic stock, descended from seventeenth-century colonists and French refugees from the revolution. The year Hughes was ordained, in 1826, was the same year, coincidentally, that Edgar Poe matriculated at the University of Virginia.

The university Poe was entering was the creation of its founder, Thomas Jefferson. Then in the last months of his life, Jefferson took great satisfaction in the establishment of this school, and like its founder, the university was given to radically innovative ideas. Students were allowed—and even encouraged—to choose among electives. They were offered training in the mechanical arts and in agricultural science. Attendance at chapel was optional. Modern languages were preferred to ancient ones.

The object was to produce a new generation of men in the mold of Jefferson himself, gentlemen farmers of independent mind imbued with an appetite for practical improvements and material progress. The very architecture of the school buildings, which Jefferson designed, reflected a certain vision of what America should be, a blend of the classical and the bucolic, a setting that embodied proportion and balance, in which citizen squires would be prepared to participate in a process of republican progress.

There was an elephant in the parlor, of course, which wasn't much discussed. Like most of his classmates—and like Jefferson himself—Edgar Allan Poe's status and leisure rested on the foundation of human slavery. Poe's foster father, John Allan, a parsimonious

Scotsman, built a business that traded in all kinds of merchandise. This included, as one account puts it, "horses, Kentucky swine from the settlements, and old slaves who were hired out at the coal pits till they died."

There was another problem with Jefferson's rustic Enlightenment vision of America. His loathing of cities as concentrations of the worst decadence and ignorance of European civilization—a loathing which didn't prevent him from enjoying his years in Paris—had little effect on the gathering momentum within American society. America's cities were beginning to grow at an increasingly rapid pace, and with the completion of "Clinton's Ditch"—the Erie Canal—in 1825, one city in particular swelled in size and significance. From a Jeffersonian perspective, the rise of this urban agglomeration was bad enough. Size alone wasn't the problem. Worse was the volatile human mix that New York was coming to contain.

For the first time, many of the immigrants weren't moving on from the cities to help tame the frontier. They worked temporarily on projects like canal digging or, as John Hughes did, on turnpike building, but more and more they stayed in the cities, gathering in neighborhoods in such large numbers that issues of public sanitation and safety soon took on frightening urgency. America confronted an incursion of foreigners noticeably different from the bulk of those who'd arrived up to that point. Everything about Irish-Catholics seemed strange and alien —their accents (and in some cases, their Gaelic language), clothes, work habits, social conduct, and tendency to stay together.

Particularly disturbing was their religion. Anti-Catholicism was a pan-Atlantic part of English-Protestant culture, quiescent at times but always there beneath the surface. Ingrained through centuries of struggle against Catholic Spain and France—fueled by a brew of myth and history, by the ominous specter of superstition, cruelty, priestcraft, political oppression, and moral debauchery—anti-Catholicism spanned the wide and sometimes bitter divisions among Protestant sects.

Ireland's pre-Famine migrants were not in the rigorist, church-going mold of their post-Famine descendants. Priests were few. Religious practice was lax and heavily laced with Celtic folk religion. But the Catholic identity of pre-Famine immigrants to America was sufficient to sound alarms among—as the United States's first wave of European immigrants liked to refer to themselves—"native Americans."

The nativists not only sounded the alarms, they set the fires. First, in the spring of 1834, to the Ursuline Convent in Charleston, outside Boston, where, prompted by the Reverend Lyman Beecher—the father of Harriet Beecher Stowe—a mob succeeded in burning out the nuns and their students. It was a situation rife with the potential for ethnic conflict and social turmoil, and into it came John Hughes.

From the start of his career as a priest, Hughes broke with the accomodationist tradition that Catholics in America had followed. He fought with Protestants, responding in kind to the growing chorus of invective directed against "papists and popery." He fought with the hierarchy, both with Bishop Kenrick in Philadelphia and Bishop Dubois in New York. He fought with the laity, crushing the trustee movement that aspired to run the Catholic Church along the lines of congregationalism. He fought with German-American Catholics, judging them querulous loudmouths given to intellectual arrogance. (The Irish, needless to say, were well behaved, soft-spoken, and, as always, humble.)

Naturally Hughes fought with the Jesuits whom he'd induced to move from Kentucky to Fordham in 1846. In his book *Fordham: A History and Memoir*—an intriguing, insightful discussion of Fordham's evolution—Father Raymond Schroth describes how bad it got:

> At one stage . . . Hughes became so fed up with [the Jesuits] that the president of the [college's] board of trustees . . . told the Jesuit president that the best thing for the Jesuits to do was to give the archbishop a year's notice and then get out of town.

Hughes first arrived in New York in 1837, as co-adjutor to Bishop Dubois, whom he quickly pushed aside. It's no exaggeration to say that this was a perfect marriage of the man and the moment, and like a truly perfect marriage, it was fiery, passionate, and contentious. More Irish chieftain than Christian churchman, Hughes wouldn't turn the other cheek. He wouldn't forgive his enemies or bless those who cursed him. He wouldn't settle for anything less than what, in his view, was his people's fair share of the city's power and riches. He wouldn't allow anything to stand in the way of his people's possession of the full rights and opportunities due to every American citizen.

Hughes was not in any sense—modern or otherwise—what we'd call a "multiculturist." His people were the Irish. He never tried to disguise that. But, in his own forceful, impolite way, by challenging the power, presumptions, and privileges of the elite, by demanding instead of standing hat-in-hand to ask, he was opening a new chapter in American history and, particularly, in the progress of its greatest city.

Hughes was adamant in his aims. His complaints in the public schools controversy were specific and material, and when he didn't get everything he wanted, he took the radical step of creating a parallel system of parochial schools, a move that flew in the very face of nativist concern over Catholic separatism.

Hughes's arrival in New York in 1837 drew a good deal of notice. The arrival of Edgar Allan Poe that same year drew none. Like thousands—perhaps millions—of New York writers and artists since, Poe was battling poverty and obscurity. Two years before, he'd secretly married his thirteen-year-old niece, with the girl's mother, Poe's aunt, as the only witness. He drank to excess and took opium.

Most significantly, he worked, constantly, writing and rewriting his manuscripts. He wrote literary criticism, poetry, and short stories for various journals. His muse was often the rent. While his aunt-cum-mother-in-law helped support him by taking in borders, Poe began to turn out stories that were different in tone and substance from the prevailing literary style. He described grizzly murders, psychological terrors, primal fears, erotic urges, plumbing the deepest recesses of the human soul and mind.

At a period when American technical prowess was—literally —beginning to gather steam, and talk of telegraphs, railroads, and factories was reviving people's hopes after the Panic of 1837, and nurturing one of those perennial and inevitable rebirths of national optimism, Poe traveled in another direction, inward and downward, into the dark, subterranean catacombs and tunnels beneath the temple of progress.

Poe and Hughes may have passed on the street. New York was a small enough town, its commerce concentrated enough, for that to have happened, and though they were very different individuals, with different tastes and values, from different religious backgrounds, the fact that they were both in New York, both struggling to realize their dreams, said something important about what was taking place.

The city of man was up for grabs. This wasn't a place where caste or privilege would go uncontested. Whether an uprooted Irish spalpeen or a disinherited son of the Virginia slavocracy, you could become something different in New York. Hughes set out to remake the city, Poe to re-invent himself. In the process, they were clearing the way for generations to follow, for men and women very different from them, the inhabitants of shtetls and Italian hill towns, Central-American villages and the slave cabins of the South, for people who wanted the space to be different from what the reigning expectations said they must be.

Hughes was trying to create a space for the Irish, and while it would be a distortion to ascribe to him loftier and more universal motives, he wasn't unaware of the wider ramifications of his actions. During the school debate, he told the Common Council that if Catholics quietly accepted what they saw as injustice, their example would set a dangerous precedent. "While it is the Catholics today," he said, "it may be the Universalists, or the Jews, or the Baptists, or the Unitarians tomorrow who may suffer."

By 1841, Poe had given up on New York. To paraphrase a famous lyric, "If you can't make it here . . . there's always Philadelphia." There, at last, he found a degree of long-sought literary success as the editor of *Graham's Magazine*, the first truly mass-circulation publication in the United States, with a subscriber base that rose from 5,000 to 40,000 under his direction.

Hughes was also looking outside the city, not to start a magazine, but for a place to relocate the archdiocesan seminary and to establish a Catholic college. He wanted it to be a safe distance from the flesh-pots of Gotham, but not *too* far. Two years previously, with that purpose in mind, he'd purchased Rose Hill, an estate of approximately 100 acres in "the Manor of Fordham," in lower Westchester County, for

$30,000. He spent another $10,000 to house St. Joseph's Seminary and St. John's College.

The college formally opened on June 21, 1841, the Feast of John the Baptist, with six students. Hughes had built the college with two expectations. The first came to pass a few months later when the tracks of the New York and Harlem railroad reached Fordham. The second—his appeal to the Jesuit superior general in Rome to staff his college with Jesuits—didn't. The superior general turned him down.

The Jesuits were already committed to St. Mary's College in Kentucky and an educational venture near the American capital, in a swamp called Georgetown. It had been Hughes's hope to create an institution of such quality that it would attract the sons of the Catholic elite as well as Protestants interested in first-class education.

Disappointed as he was, Hughes was more and more preoccupied with events in the city itself. Irish Catholics continued to arrive in the United States in growing numbers, and the backlash against them grew with it. In May 1844, tensions boiled over. Nativist attacks on a Catholic neighborhood in Philadelphia erupted into what one historian has described as "a brutal ethno-religious war." Gun battles raged for three days. Two Catholic churches were attacked and one burned. The militia was called out. Thirteen people were killed and scores wounded.

New York's nativist community was incensed. They planned a rally in City Hall Park, where a delegation from Philadelphia would present an American flag supposedly "trampled by Irish Papists." Hughes called on Mayor Robert Morris and issued him a blunt warning. "If a single Catholic church is burned in New York," he said, "the city will become a second Moscow." When the astounded Mayor asked him, "Your grace, are you afraid that some of your churches will be burned?" Hughes replied, "No, I'm afraid that some of *yours* will be." This is one of the first identifiable examples of the New York negotiating style known as "in your face," and the only instance I know of where a clergyman of any denomination threatened to burn the city down—the Reverend Al Sharpton *not* excluded.

The college Hughes created in Fordham Manor was a gesture to the future, to the creation of an educated Catholic elite. But his immediate concern was the burgeoning number of impoverished Irish-

Catholic immigrants arriving in the city. The progress he'd made in establishing the infrastructure of his diocese was about to be overwhelmed by an event that would change every aspect of life in New York—politics, housing, entertainment, policing, sanitation, religion, race relations, education, the city's very destiny itself.

In the fall of 1845, the potato blight struck Ireland. This is neither the time nor the place to chronicle what occurred or discuss the controversies that rage around it to this day. For our purposes, it's enough to know that, among the horde of emigrants who left Ireland between 1845 and 1855 was Michael Manning. Given the unpredictability of sailing schedules and the volume of immigrant traffic into the port, it's highly unlikely anyone was there to meet him. According to family legend, he came to Fordham because he had relatives already living there, or perhaps they were relatives of his wife, Eileen Purcell.

Because the date is unclear, I'd like to use my novelist's license to suppose that Michael arrived not in 1847 but in 1846, on a day in June, let's say, sometime between May, when Edgar Allan Poe rented a cottage in Fordham with the hope of improving his young wife's health, and July and August when, as so richly described in Father Schroth's book, the Jesuits arrived from Kentucky.

For Michael and the Jesuits, coming from famine Ireland and rural Kentucky, Fordham was a step up. For Poe, coming from Manhattan, it was a step down. It wasn't that Poe had anything against the Bronx, as so many Manhattanites do. The Bronx was a half-century in the future. But Poe hadn't come to New York to escape a national catastrophe like the Great Famine or to create a college that could rear up leaders for a disorganized—in many ways, traumatized—immigrant community.

Poe was in pursuit of that most seductive of all American prizes, which remains at the heart of New York's allure and is captured in a four-letter word beginning with F—*FAME*. "I love fame—I dote on it—I idolize it," Poe wrote. "I would drink to the glorious intoxication. I would have incense ascend in my honour from every hill and hamlet . . . *Fame! Glory!*—they are life-giving breath and living blood." No incense greeted Poe from the hills or hamlet of Fordham. He'd arrived back in New York in the spring of 1844, ready to give the city a second try, but found himself once more living on the edge. When fame finally came with the publication of "The Raven," it came too late.

He was drinking heavily. He found it harder to write, and when he couldn't write, he couldn't make a living. Virginia's tuberculosis was entering its critical last stage. In his masterful, if dated biography, of Poe, *Israfel*, Hervey Allen describes Poe's move to Fordham:

> Far from being a restful, and a quiet retirement, Fordham, in 1846, was to Poe a place of confusion. There was, of course, Virginia. He was torn between his pride and the trammelings of poverty. His health and unstrung nervous condition precluded any work, except, intermittently, perhaps, upon a few poems.

The one place Poe seems to have found some comfort was among the Jesuits of St. John's College. Poe informed a friend that he liked the Jesuits because they were "highly cultivated gentlemen and scholars, they smoked and they drank, played cards and never said a word about religion." It's comforting to know, isn't it, that after 150 years, at least some things at Fordham haven't changed?

Most of the Jesuit fathers were French, a language in which Poe was fluent. But among the many interesting facts I learned from Father Schroth's book is that in their company was a recent entry to the Society named Michael Nash, who'd been born in Kilkenny, Ireland, in 1825. That makes Nash about the same age as Michael Manning and explains a piece of oral tradition in my family.

According to my father, his mother told him that Michael Manning used to earn money cobbling the boots of the Jesuits. Since there was never any other mention of Michael Manning as a cobbler, that struck me as strange. But in view of the fact that Nash was from the same county, Kilkenny, and about the same age as Michael Manning, an explanation suggests itself: the Irish were taking care of each other. Whether he was a cobbler or not, Michael Manning needed a job, and Michael Nash saw that he got one. Thus was born the Bronx County Democratic machine.

I'm surmising here, making an educated guess, which is all you can ever do with the faceless poor. Their lives are hidden in statistics and summarized in charts. Sometimes they stare out of old photographs of streets or crowd scenes, or they dart between the words of histories and newspaper accounts. In the aftermath of the Panic of 1857, for example, an editor of the *Collegian*, the campus publication, recorded looking out his window and seeing people coming onto the grounds of Rose Hill to beg for food.

Were Michael Manning or any of his family among them? Was he ever so poor he had to beg? When my father was a little boy, and Michael was old and blind and living with them in a tenement on East 7th Street, he told his grandfather he wanted to visit Ireland. "No member of this family will step foot there again," Michael Manning said with an adamant and unusual edge of bitterness, "until they've hanged the last landlord." It was the only time my father ever remembered hearing him speak of Ireland.

Wandering around the village of Fordham, it's possible that Michael Manning exchanged pleasantries with Poe. Although Michael Manning drank, he did so in moderation. He could have been in a barroom with Poe, for whom moderation was a challenge. It's possible Manning, Poe, and Hughes were all on the Rose Hill campus on one of those festive occasions, such as the first graduation on July 15, 1847, when 2,000 people gathered to see the first four graduates get their degrees.

Hughes was there for sure. He spoke. If Poe and Manning were around, it's hard to imagine they would have ignored the spectacle. Poe's wife, Virginia Maria, had died in their Fordham cottage the previous January, and he often wandered the neighborhood in search of some diversion.

At this point, Hughes's biggest challenges were still ahead. The graduation on the lawn of Rose Hill, in the summer of '47, occurred at the moment when the Famine immigration was taking on the trappings of a mass rout. In 1847, more than 120,000 Irish came to the United States. In 1851, the number was more than 200,000. The Archdiocese of New York was every day acquiring new congregants to whom it remained woefully unprepared to minister.

In the spring of '48, the immigrants imported Asiatic cholera in their intestines. It had already killed tens of thousands in Ireland and now did the same in America. The disease had come to Ireland from

India in the bowels of British soldiers who'd been sent as reinforcements in the wake of food riots and rumors of revolt. Eventually, the cholera would travel as far west as Cincinnati, where it would kill the beloved boy child of Harriet Beecher Stowe. She would seek an outlet for her grief in novel writing. Such were the unintended consequences of nineteenth-century globalization.

In 1849, Poe was among those afflicted by cholera. It weakened but didn't kill him. Instead, another consequence of Irish migration did. Not long after a deadly riot at Astor Place—another portent of the direction in which the city was traveling—Poe left Fordham for Richmond to woo an old love. He was apparently successful in that endeavor, and he set out for Fordham in late September to put his affairs in order. He sailed to Baltimore, where he intended to entrain for New York. He never made it. Abandoning his recent sobriety, he had one drink, then another.

Baltimore was in the midst of an election in which the local nativists were determined to stop the growing number of Irish from taking political power. It was a struggle taking place up and down the East Coast, and the tide seemed to be running with the nativists. Poe was a pawn in that contest. Rounded up by nativist thugs who had scoured the city's dives in search of inebriates who could be taken from poll to poll to vote again and again, he was detained in a basement for several days. There, eventually, some concerned friends found him, ill and unwashed, surrounded by drunks and derelicts. They removed him to a hospital where he died on October 7, 1849. In one of his last poems, he wrote, "And the fever called 'Living' / Is conquered at last."

Hughes lived another fifteen years, long enough to witness the searing and destructive violence of the Draft Riots of July 1863. Throughout his years as archbishop, Hughes made it seem as if the masses of Irish Catholics did whatever he told them. It was a fiction, but a useful one. Protestants were more than willing to believe it.

When the revolt got underway, the elites joined together in demanding that Hughes order it to cease, and he was confronted with the choice of either doing what they said, which would both lay bare the real truth of how limited his power was and acknowledge that the bulk of rioters were Catholic, or stay silent. He didn't say anything in public until Friday, when the riot had almost burned itself out. Richard Shaw writes that, "The effect of the riots upon his spirit intensified what was his last illness." Depressed and enfeebled, fretting over all the work that remained to be done—symbolized perhaps by his half-finished cathedral on Fifth Avenue—he died the following January.

Michael Manning had the longest life. At some point, he moved out of Fordham to the Lower East Side of Manhattan. He survived into the first decade of the twentieth century, totally dependent on his daughter and son-in-law, my grandparents. He died with no reason to expect that a grandson of his, my father, would one day graduate from Fordham Law School and represent the Fordham district in the United States Congress; or that a great-grandson would attend graduate school at Fordham and—the age of miracles has not passed—be invited to speak in honor of Fordham's president, a fellow child of the Bronx.

John Hughes, Edgar Allan Poe, and Michael Manning each came to Fordham for different reasons. But I believe that there is shared meaning in their stories and that it touches very directly on what brings us here. There's a scene in Hervey Allen's biography of Poe that suggests where to find those parallels. Allen writes:

> As Poe paced the arches of the High Bridge through the spring and summer nights of the year A.D. 1847, the mysterious sleeping world seemed to cut away from beneath his feet, while over his head marched flashing rank on rank "the armies of unalterable law." He pondered upon it all, upon himself, and upon the place of man in the scheme of things, and he essayed to solve that mystery, which his own exalted ego whispered that he could solve. He could not bear to think that even God should elude him.

In Poe's day, the High Bridge and the water system it was part of were engineering marvels. The bridge was the final link in a vast project that brought clean water from Croton to the Collecting Reservoir on 42nd Street. Dug by Irish laborers over a four-year period, it not only secured the vital water supplies the city needed to grow but embodied the power and the promise of a rising metropolis.

Today, the High Bridge is a battered remnant of what it was in the 1840s. A portion of its arches was amputated by the Army Corps of Engineers in the interests of navigation on the Harlem River. Few of the thousands of motorists who travel beneath it each day on the Major Deegan Expressway or the Harlem River Drive have any idea of the importance it once had.

The physical city keeps changing. The metropolis, outside of which Hughes wanted to place his college, eventually engulfed it. Fordham returned the favor, implanting itself at Lincoln Center. Neighborhoods rise and fall. Great structures are built, destroyed, fall into decay. The city of men and women changes with it. Immigrants arrive each day. The wealthiest and most skilled are welcomed. The poorest and most desperate sneak in illegally and are exploited. Certainly, those of us descended from the Famine Irish must count ourselves lucky that our ancestors arrived before immigration controls were in place.

Writers and artists starve and dream. People despair and give up. Immense fortunes are accumulated. Fame is won and lost. An omnipresent and elusive God is sought, denied, found, and ignored. Today, we are where Hughes, Poe, and Manning once were, suspended between the human city and the holy one, pondering our place, asking the questions they asked:

> Whose city is it?
>
> Who belongs and who doesn't?
>
> What does God have to do with it?

Fordham University is now an intrinsic part of this city, physically, psychically, and spiritually. It is interwoven into the fabric of New York. It counts among its alumni and students the descendants of the early immigrant waves and the newer ones. It provides a unique perspective from which to ponder our place in the scheme of things—a tradition of Jesuit humanism that insists human beings are more than the sum of their DNA; that a just society must have as its purpose something more than personal indulgence, wealth accumulation, and the "shock and awe" of unrivalled military power.

New York wouldn't be as great as it is without this Jesuit institution, as rich in human voices or choices. By gathering people of different traditions, from different places, and with different ambitions in the shared pursuit of truth and meaning, Fordham reminds us that we are each capable and called to create a city and a world in which the possibilities for beauty, knowledge, hope, faith, and love belong to the poor and the outsider as much as the comfortable and privileged, to all those still searching for their place.

Ad majorem Dei gloriam.

IV. SILENCE AND HISTORY

Viola Murphy, with bobbed hair, in her senior year
at Our Lady of Angels Academy (1925)

The Triumph of
Bridget Such-a-One

I dreamed that one had died in a strange place
Near no accustomed hand;
And they had nailed the boards above her face . . .
And left her to the indifferent stars above . . .

—W.B. YEATS, "A Dream of Death"

WALKING THROUGH THE WOODS outside Concord, Massachusetts, in the spring of 1846, amid his solitary experiment in living close to nature, Henry David Thoreau was driven by a sudden storm to find shelter in what he thought was an uninhabited hut. "But therein," Thoreau recounts in *Walden*, he found living "John Field, an Irishman, and his wife, and several children," and he sat with them "under that part of the roof which leaked the least, while it showered and thundered without."

Thoreau pitied this "honest, hard-working, but shiftless man," a laborer probably drawn to the area to lay track for the railroad and now reduced to clearing bogs for a local farmer. He also "purposely talked to him as if he were a philosopher, or desired to be one. But alas," Thoreau lamented, "the culture of an Irishman is an enterprise to be undertaken with a sort of moral bog hoe."

Field "heaved a sigh" at Thoreau's suggestion that "if he and his family would live simply, they might go a-huckle-berrying in the summer for their amusement." Field's wife neither sighed nor spoke. A woman of "round greasy face," her breast exposed to suckle an infant, she "stared with arms a-kimbo" at the Yankee in their midst. The Fields left no account of this visit. Yet along with weighing the bewildering improbability of Thoreau's suggestion, it is probable that there were other matters on their minds.

By the spring of 1846 the condition of Ireland was well known. The country was on the edge. Hunger was widespread, and though the Fields may well have been illiterate, they must have shared with fellow immigrants a growing fear of what might happen if the potato failed again, as it had in 1845. Perhaps they had already received pleas from relatives still in Ireland who had sold their livestock or fishing nets to buy the American corn the government had imported. "For the honour of our lord Jasus christ and his Blessed mother," one contemporary letter writer to America cried, "hurry and take us out of this."

The Fields themselves were part of a steady stream of Irish who had been heading to North America for more than a century. The so-called Scotch-Irish—mostly Presbyterians from Ulster—were the first to come. They settled in large numbers in Canada and the American South, especially on the westward-moving edge of settlement, away from the low country with its established churches and plantation economy. By 1790 there were at least 250,000 Scotch-Irish in the United States.

After 1815 and the conclusion of the Napoleonic Wars, a steep fall in prices caused an agricultural depression in Ireland. At the same time, the start of widespread canal building in the United States and the laying of the groundwork for the country's industrial emergence drew more Irish Catholics, men whose sole marketable skill was their ability to wield a spade and whose religion, poverty, and numbers made them immediately suspect. The rough, brute work of canal building presaged the role that unskilled Irish labor would play in railroad construction, road building, and mining. Subject to cyclical employment and low wages, often living in shanties, the Irish were prized for their hard work and resented for what was seen as their proclivity to rowdiness and labor militancy.

The numbers of unskilled Irish in the cities along the Eastern seaboard grew. They lived where they worked, near the docks, foundries, and warehouses, in decaying housing that the former residents had fled or in flimsy, crowded structures erected to bring a maximum profit to their owners. By the early 1840s the increasing presence of the Catholic Irish helped prompt such prominent Americans as Samuel F. B. Morse, the inventor of the telegraph, and Lyman Beecher, progenitor of Harriet Beecher Stowe, to sound the tocsin against a supposed Catholic plot to subvert the liberties of native (i.e., white Protestant) Americans.

All this was prelude to the transformation that the Irish Famine brought. The Famine represented the greatest concentration of civilian suffering and death in Western Europe between the Thirty Years' War and World War II. It rearranged the physical and mental landscape of Ireland, sweeping away a language and a way of life.

Between 1845 and 1855, in an unprecedented movement of people, often less an organized migration than a panic, a mass unraveling, more than two million people left, for England and Australia and the great majority for North America. Part of the continuum of the transatlantic movement of people, the Famine migration was also different and extraordinary. Particularly in the densely populated townlands of the south and west of Ireland, where the bonds of culture and community went deep, the Famine broke the traditional ties of Irish society. More people left Ireland in a single decade than had in the previous 250 years. The exodus from Cork, Tipperary, Kerry, Galway, Clare, Mayo, and Donegal became a self-perpetuating process of removal. It swept aside all the old reluctance of the people to let go of their one hope for survival—the land—and made emigration an expectation rather than an exception.

Just as the mass flight of the Famine years dissolved the under-pinnings of the Irish countryside, its impact on America was profound. From independence to 1845, the republic had absorbed about 1.6 million immigrants, the great majority Protestants looking to settle on the land. The annual number of Irish arriving in the United States tripled between 1843 and 1846, from 23,000 to 70,000. By 1851 it had reached a peak of 219,000, almost ten times what it had been less than a decade before.

In the decade from 1845 to 1855, Irish-Catholic immigration approached that of all groups over the previous seventy years, and the condition of these Irish sometimes bore more resemblance to modern-day "boat people" than to the immigrants arriving from Germany and Scandinavia. In an 1855 address to the Massachusetts legislature, Governor Henry J. Gardner went back to classical history to find a comparable event. The scale of Irish immigration and the inmates it had deposited in the commonwealth's prisons and asylums called to mind, the governor said, the "horde of foreign barbarians" that had overthrown the Roman Empire.

The cause of this influx was the blight that attacked the potatoes of Ireland in the late summer of 1845. It is estimated that the potato crop represented about sixty percent of Ireland's annual food supply. Almost three and a half million people relied on it for the largest part of their diet. The dreadful implications of a sudden and universal threat to the potato, which were instantaneously clear to Irish laborers and government officials alike, threw into dramatic relief the precarious condition of large parts of the population even in the best of times.

A decade earlier, in 1835, four years after his journey to America, Alexis de Tocqueville made a visit to Ireland. "You cannot imagine," he wrote his father soon after landing, "what a complexity of miseries five centuries of oppression, civil disorder, and religious hostility have piled on this poor people." The poverty he subsequently witnessed was, he recorded, "such as I did not imagine existed in this world. It is a frightening thing, I assure you, to see a whole population reduced to fasting like Trappists, and not being sure of surviving to the next harvest, which is still not expected for another ten days." The same year as Tocqueville's visit, a German traveler in Kilkenny, in the relatively prosperous eastern part of the country, watched as a mother collected the skins of gooseberries that had been spit on the ground and fed them to her child.

Asenath Nicholson, the American temperance crusader and evangelist who landed in Ireland as the Famine began, told of giving a "sweet biscuit" to an obviously famished child, who held it in her hand and stared at it. "How is it," Mrs. Nicholson asked the child's mother, "she cannot be hungry?" The mother replied that the child had never seen such a delicacy before and "cannot think of parting with it." Mrs. Nicholson marveled that "such self-denial in a child was quite beyond my comprehension, but so inured are these people to want, that their endurance and self-control are almost beyond belief."

The anecdotes of visitors were confirmed by a commission of inquiry formed to study the extent of Irish poverty. Reporting in 1835, the commission noted that two-fifths of the population lived in "fourth-class accommodations"—one-room windowless mud cabins—and at least two and a half million people annually required some assistance in order to avoid starvation.

Although central to Irish life, the potato was a relatively recent ecological interloper. It is said to have been introduced in Cork in the 1580s by Sir Walter Raleigh, a principal in the plantation of both Ireland and the New World. Until the potato arrived, cattle and oats were the Irish mainstays. The land itself was divided among an amalgam of Gaelic and Norman-Gaelic lords, who were often feuding with one another. In the East a wedge of English-controlled territory—the Pale—had variously expanded and contracted since its conquest by the Normans.

The Atlantic explorations, the contest for overseas empire, and the bitter ideological divisions that accompanied the Reformation conferred on Ireland a new strategic importance. Beginning in the 1540s and extending through a long series of bloody wars and rebellions that ended in the defeat of the Catholic forces in 1691, Ireland was brought under the control of the English crown. Political power and ownership of the land were relentlessly concentrated in the hands of a Protestant ascendancy. The widespread dislocation caused by the long struggle for mastery of Ireland opened the way for the spread of the hardy, reliable, nutritionally rich potato, which not only thrived in the cool, damp climate but yielded, per acre, three times the calories of grain.

Between 1700 and 1845, thanks in large part to the potato, a populace of less than three million grew to almost eight and a half million, to the point where Disraeli pronounced Ireland the most thickly peopled country in Europe. However, the population distribution was uneven. In pre-Famine Ireland the general rule was: The worse the land, the more people on it. The greatest growth was in reclaimed bogs and on mountainsides. The number of small tenant farmers and laborers soared, particularly in the West, where the scramble for land drove an intense process of reclamation and subdivision.

Like the potato, the fungus that destroyed it came from the Americas. In 1843 potato crops in the eastern United States were largely ruined by a mysterious blight. In June of 1845 the blight was reported in the Low Countries. In mid-September an English journal announced "with very great regret" that the blight had "unequivocally declared itself" in Ireland, then posed the question that anyone even passingly acquainted with the country knew must be faced: "Where will *Ireland* be, in the event of a universal potato rot?" The speed of the blight bewildered observers. Over and over they expressed amazement at how fields lush with potato plants could the next day be putrid wastelands. It was a generation before the agent of destruction was fingered as a spore-spreading fungus, *Phytophthora infestans*, and before an antidote was devised.

Without the prospect of a cure, Sir Robert Peel, the Tory prime minister, faced a crisis in Ireland. The appearance of the blight in late summer meant two-thirds of the potatoes had already been harvested, yet the near-total reliance of a sizable part of the population on a single crop left no doubt that extraordinary measures would have to be taken. Peel was an able administrator, knowledgeable about Ireland and its discontents. Responding quickly to the impending food crisis, he ordered the secret purchase of a hundred thousand pounds' worth of American corn to be held in reserve and released into the market when demand threatened to drive food prices out of control.

This same supply was to be available for purchase, at cost, by local relief committees. Landlord-directed committees were set up to cooperate with the Board of Works in funding work schemes. The aim was to provide tenants and laborers with the chance to earn the money they needed to buy imported food and avoid direct government hand-outs that would encourage what was seen as the congenital laziness of the Irish.

In December 1845, in order to lower grain prices, Peel proposed repeal of the Corn Laws, import duties that protected British agriculture from foreign competition. He was convinced that increased competition would result in lowering the price of food for the British working classes, which it did. Cheap imports would not only lessen the immediate threat of mass hunger but help wean the poor from reliance on the potato and transform small tenants into landless, wage-earning laborers. As a result of Peel's relief measures, Ireland averted the worst consequences of the blight through the winter of 1845–46. The weather was unusually cold. The poorhouses began to fill up. The poor exhausted whatever reserves they may have had. But starvation was held at bay.

The repeal of the Corn Laws in June 1846 quickly precipitated the fall of Peel's government. Lord Russell, the new Whig prime minister, faced a more daunting challenge than had Peel. The return of the blight for a second year, and the devastation of three-quarters of the potato crop, drove thousands more onto the public works. In August 1846 the works were temporarily halted and overhauled along lines set down by Charles Trevelyan, the head permanent civil servant in the Treasury. The rules of employment were made stricter, and more of the cost was put on local landlords.

By October the public works employed 114,000; three months later, in January 1847, more than 500,000; by March, 750,000. Reports of extreme suffering and death began to pour in from different parts of the country. In Skibbereen, County Cork, an artist sent by the *Illustrated London News* testified that neither pictures nor words could capture the horror of "the dying, the living, and the dead, lying indiscriminately upon the same floor, without anything between them."

The American Nicholson got her first view of the worsening condition of Ireland in the outskirts of Dublin. In December 1846 a servant in a house where she was staying implored her to see a man nearby, the father of seven, who, though sick with fever and "in an actual state of starvation," had "staggered with his spade" to the public works. The servant brought in a human skeleton "emaciated to the last degree." Horrified as she was, Mrs. Nicholson would remember this as only "the *first* and the beginning of . . . dreadful days yet in reserve."

Daunted by the expense of the public works, the government decided to switch to soup kitchens, a form of relief introduced by the Quakers. The public works began to close in March. By midsummer of 1847 three million men, women, and children were being fed with soup. An indication of the government's capacity to restrain the ravages of hunger, the soup kitchens were the apogee of the relief effort—and its effective end.

Writing in *Blackwood's Magazine* in April 1847, a commentator complained of the expense being incurred to help the Irish. Their hunger was not an English problem, he wrote, and there was no need for wasting another shilling on a disaster "which the heedlessness and indolence of the Irish had brought upon themselves." A month earlier the London *Times* had expressed a similar sense of the widespread frustration with the Irish, again connecting Ireland's agony to the allegedly innate defects of its people: "The Celt is less energetic, less independent, less industrious than the Saxon. This is the archaic condition of his race. . . . [England] can, therefore, afford to look with contemptuous pity on the Celtic cottier suckled in poverty which he is too callous to feel, and too supine to mend."

Since the abolition of the Dublin parliament in 1801, Ireland had theoretically been an integral part of the United Kingdom, its people entitled to the same protections and considerations as those of English shires. But as the Famine made inexorably clear, Ireland remained a colony, one usually viewed as a turbulent, perplexing, intractable anomaly.

During the period immediately preceding the Famine, Daniel O'Connell, who had led the agitation in the 1820s that won Catholics the right to sit in Parliament, had headed a movement to repeal the union with Britain and return a measure of self-rule to Dublin. The union was maintained, but now, in the face of Ireland's continuing distress, a tired, broken O'Connell told the House of Commons: "Ireland is in your hands. If you do not save her, she cannot save herself." His plea went unheeded. As framed by Sir Charles Wood, the Chancellor of the Exchequer, the challenge was no longer to help feed the Irish but "to force them into self-government . . . our song . . . must be—'It is your concern, not ours.'"

The potato didn't fail in the summer of 1847, yet the distress of the past two seasons had seriously curtailed the scale of plantings. Trevelyan, however, convinced that Ireland's problem wasn't inadequate food supplies but "the selfish, perverse and turbulent character of the people," pronounced the Famine over. There would be no more extraordinary measures by the Treasury, not even when the potato failed again in 1848, 1849, and into the early 1850s. Irish needs would be met with Irish resources.

The government's change of direction went beyond the withdrawal of desperately needed assistance. The passage in June 1847 of the Irish Poor Law Extension Act married racial contempt and providentialism—the prevalent conviction among the British elite of God's judgment having been delivered on the Irish—with political economy. According to the theorists of the iron laws of economics, the great deficiencies of Ireland were a want of capital accumulation—the result of the maze of small tenancies—and the incurable lethargy of a people inured to indolent reliance on an inferior food. The Famine provided an opportunity to sweep away the root causes of Ireland's economic backwardness.

The amendment of the Irish Poor Law made landlords responsible for the rates (taxes collected to support the workhouses) on all holdings valued under four pounds per year. Another provision—the Gregory Clause—denied relief to anyone holding more than a quarter-acre of land. This left many tenants with the choice of abandoning their holdings or condemning their families to starvation. Together these clauses were a mandate to clear the land of the poorest and most vulnerable. Entire villages were "tumbled." In one instance, a newspaper reported that some of the evicted were found dead along the roadsides, "emitting green froth from their mouths, as if masticating soft grass."

On the Mullet Peninsula in Mayo, James Hack Tuke, a Quaker involved in the intensive relief effort undertaken by the Society of Friends, witnessed an entire settlement being razed: "Six or seven hundred people were evicted; young and old, mother and babe, were alike cast forth, without shelter and without means of subsistence! A fountain of ink (as one of them said) would not write half our misfortunes."

Asenath Nicholson traveled some of the same territory as Tuke and was horrified by the sheer scale of what she witnessed: "Village upon village, and company after company, have I seen; and one magistrate who was travelling informed me that at nightfall the preceding day, he found a company who had gathered a few sticks and fastened them into a ditch, and spread over what miserable rags they could collect . . . under these more than two hundred men, women, and children, were to crawl for the night . . . and not *one* pound of any kind of food was in the whole encampment."

Across much of Ireland the purgatory of the first two years of Famine became a living hell. The workhouses, which the people had once done their best to avoid, were besieged by mobs clamoring to get in. The dead were buried, coffinless, in mass graves. The Reverend Francis Webb, a Church of Ireland rector in West Cork, published an account of dead children being left unburied and asked in anger and disbelief, "Are we living in a portion of the United Kingdom?"

Emigration from Ireland became a torrent, no longer a quest for new opportunities, but a question of life or death. The ports filled with people. Most sought passage to Liverpool, the former capital of the slave trade and now the entrepôt of emigration. From there they hoped to find a cheap fare to America. Jammed in the holds of coal barges and on the decks of cattle boats, 300,000 Irish sailed to Liverpool in 1847 alone.

The government made a pretense of enforcing regulations that prescribed medical inspection of all passengers and minimum space and rations for each. In reality, emigrants, having scrambled however they could to put together the four pounds that passage to America typically cost, were at the mercy of a laissez-faire system that treated them more like ballast than like human beings.

Dr. J. Custis, who served as a ship's surgeon on half a dozen emigrant vessels, published a series of articles that described their sailings: "I have been engaged during the worst years of Famine in Ireland; I have witnessed the deaths of hundreds from want; I have seen the inmates of a workhouse carried by the hundreds weekly through its gates to be thrown unshrouded and coffinless into a pit with quicklime . . . and revolting to the feelings as all this was, it was not half so shocking as what I subsequently witnessed on board the very first emigrant ship I ever sailed on."

During a journey in steerage of anywhere from three to seven weeks, disease, seasickness, spoiled rations, hostile crews, and a lack of space and air—an experience one observer compared to "entering a crowded jail"— eroded whatever differences of region or accent or status that had once divided the emigrants. By the time they landed, it was easy for nativists to lump them together as a race of feckless Paddies destined to be a permanent drain on American resources.

The reaction to the arrival of growing numbers of impoverished, famished immigrants wasn't long in coming. Congress tightened the regulations that governed passenger ships entering American ports and raised the fines on violators. Massachusetts began to enforce a law requiring that before any pauper or sick person was landed on its shores, the ship's master had to post a bond for every passenger. New York also required a bond and leveled a per-person tax to cover the cost of those who became public charges. The net effect was that in the spring of 1847 a significant portion of the first wave of Famine migrants left not for the United States, but for British North America.

The demand for passage resulted in a hodgepodge of vessels being pressed into service. Poorly provisioned, devoid of medicines or sanitary facilities, crowded with hungry, fever-ridden passengers, they quickly developed a well-earned reputation as "coffin ships." In May 1847 the first of them arrived at a quarantine station, with a small hospital that had been set up on Grosse Île, in the St. Lawrence, thirty miles below Quebec. Out of a company of 240 passengers, eighty were down with typhus, and nine already dead. By June nearly forty vessels were backed up for miles along the river, and 14,000 people awaited quarantine. The dead were buried in mass graves. By the end of the sailing season, the British government's conservative estimate was that, of the 107,000 who had left for Canada from British ports, 17,500—one out of every six—had died.

Despite the barriers raised by American ports, the overwhelming majority of Famine emigrants sought passage to the United States, for few wished to remain under British dominion. Even in 1847, as many as 25,000 immigrants arrived in Boston from British ports, and at least another 5,000 managed to find their way down from Canada. New York received by far the greatest number; a million Irish landed on the wharves and piers around Manhattan during the Famine decade.

The voyage to the United States wasn't characterized by the same catalogue of horrors as the emigration to Canada in 1847, but it was ordeal enough. Stephen de Vere, an Anglo-Irish gentleman with an interest in emigration, sailed to New York aboard the *Washington*, a well-built ship, in 1847. He watched the passengers in steerage being physically abused and denied the rations they were supposedly due. When he protested, the first mate knocked him to the deck. Taking his complaint to the captain, de Vere was threatened with the brig. Dysentery was rampant on the ship; a dozen children died from it. On landing, de Vere collected accounts of similar abuse aboard other ships and wrote a complaint to the emigration commissioners in London. In the end nothing was done.

One of the most compelling renderings of the emigrant trade in the Famine era was by an American whose introduction to the sea was aboard a packet ship between Liverpool and New York. Herman Melville was nineteen when he made the voyage out and back in 1839. Ten years later, in 1849, he published *Redburn*, an account of his journey that is part fiction, part memoir, and part meditation on the changes that the mass descent of strangers was bringing to America. Though a novel, the book is alive with a real sense of the grandeur and misery of Liverpool and of the unromantic business of hauling five hundred emigrants across the Atlantic in a creaking, swaying, wind-driven ship.

The emigrants aboard Melville's fictional ship, the *Highlander*, were mostly Irish, and like many real emigrant ships, the *Highlander* wasn't built for passengers but had been converted to that purpose. Triple tiers of bunks jerry-built along the ship's sides "looked more like dog-kennels than anything else" and soon smelled little different.

"We had not been at sea one week," the protagonist, Wellingborough Redburn, observed, "when to hold your head down the fore hatchway was like holding it down a suddenly opened cesspool." Driven by hunger, some of the passengers stole a small pig, and "*him* they devoured raw, not venturing to make an incognito of his carcass." Fever struck. Emigrants began to die. Venturing down into steerage, Redburn encountered "rows of rude bunks, hundreds of meager, begrimed faces were turned upon us . . . the native air of the place . . . was foetid in the extreme."

Docked at last on South Street, crew and passengers dispersed. As they left, young Redburn wondered at the fate of those who had survived the gauntlet of hunger and emigration but now seemed exhausted and broken: "How, then, with these emigrants, who, three thousand miles from home, suddenly found themselves, deprived of brothers and husbands, with but a few pounds, or perhaps but a few shillings, to buy food in a strange land?"

Other Americans shared such doubts, and for many the answer was that the Catholic Irish were a threat to the country's prosperity and liberty. Nativists focused on Irish poverty as a function of Irish character, a result of their addiction to "rum and Romanism." When the Irish banded together to form religious, fraternal, and labor organizations aimed at improving their lot, this was taken as proof of their conspiratorial clannishness. Near the end of the Famine decade, in 1854, the American Party, which was formed to halt the incursion of foreigners and Catholics, controlled the legislatures of most New England states as well as those of Maryland, Delaware, Kentucky, New Jersey, Pennsylvania, and California. For a time, it was the most successful third-party movement in American history.

The poverty of the Irish, while only a part of the Famine story, was not merely a figment of the nativist imagination. The cities of the Northeast faced problems of public order that wouldn't be repeated until the 1960s. The newcomers didn't invent street gangs or rioting or machine politics—all pre-dated the arrival of the Famine Irish—but the deluge of masses of disoriented, disorganized, unskilled alien labor raised an unprecedented sense of alarm. In 1851 it was estimated that one out of every six New Yorkers was a pauper. Of the 113,000 people residing in jails, workhouses, hospitals, or asylums or receiving public or private charity, three quarters were foreign-born, the bulk of them Irish.

New York State formally opened its first immigrant depot in 1855 at Castle Garden, its purpose to bring order to the process of arrival. Three decades later, under federal control, the depot was moved to Ellis Island. Golden or not, the door America erected at its entryway was a legacy of the Famine.

By the autumn of 1849, when Melville wrote of the travails of his fictional company of tired and poor Irish immigrants, two real-life immigrants reached American shores, who for all their differences— one was an ex-policeman fleeing arrest, the other a young woman seeking work—embodied much of the pain and the promise of the Famine years.

Michael Corcoran was the son of an Irishman who had made a career in the Royal Army. In 1845, at the age of eighteen, Corcoran joined the Revenue Police, which, along with the Irish Constabulary, was organized along military lines. He was posted to Donegal to help suppress the trade in illicit liquor. The advent of famine heightened the role of the constabulary and the army in Ireland, already the most policed and garrisoned part of the British Isles. By 1848 their combined total was at an all-time high of 40,000—almost twice the size of the expeditionary force that the British government would soon send to the Crimea at a cost nine times what it spent on famine relief in Ireland.

Whether Corcoran, as a member of the Revenue Police, was called to the support of the army or constabulary is unknown. Both forces were active during the Famine, especially in areas like Donegal. They helped distribute relief as well as guarantee the all-important rights of property. In the latter capacity they not only assisted in mass clearances but guarded the convoys that carried grain and beef to England. The image of those convoys became a touchstone of Irish bitterness in later years, alleged proof of the charge leveled by the Irish nationalist John Mitchel that "the Almighty indeed sent the potato blight, but the English created the Famine."

Over the course of the Famine, more grain may have entered Ireland than left. But the imports often didn't reach the most distressed parts of the country, or were spoiled by the time they did. Unfamiliar with processing or cooking the yellow corn imported from America, people were made sick by it. The memory of soldiers and police guarding precious stores of food from the starving wasn't an invention. Mrs. Nicholson testified to the sight of well-fed, well-armed soldiers and "haggard, meagre, squalid skeletons . . . grouped in starving multitudes around them." In 1847—"Black '47," the Irish called it—2,000 people were transported to Australia for cattle stealing. On Spike Island, in Cork Harbor, 300 adolescents were imprisoned for "taking bread while starving."

Whatever Corcoran witnessed or took part in as a policeman may have been part of what led him to break his oath to the Crown. In August 1849 he was "relinquished" from his duties on suspicion of belonging to one of the secret agrarian societies that were violently resisting evictions. Before he could be arrested, he slipped aboard an emigrant ship and escaped to New York. There was little to distinguish him from his fellow immigrants when he landed in October 1849. But he quickly made a name for himself. He got work in a tavern and became a district leader for Tammany Hall, which was just awakening to the potential of the Irish vote, and he was an early member of the Fenian Brotherhood, the secret Irish revolutionary society fueled by the burning intent to revenge the Famine and overthrow British rule in Ireland.

Five years after he arrived, Corcoran was elected a captain in a heavily Irish militia unit, the 69th New York. Not long after, he was commended for helping defend the quarantine station on Staten Island, which a mob had attempted to burn. In 1860 when the Prince of Wales visited New York, the militia was ordered to parade in his honor. Corcoran, now the colonel of the 69th, refused to march. He

was court-martialed for what, in many eyes, confirmed the worst suspicions of Irish-Catholic disloyalty to American institutions. The outbreak of the Civil War saved him from being cashiered. He returned to
his regiment, which he commanded at Bull Run, where he was badly
wounded and captured.

Freed a year later in a prisoner exchange, Corcoran returned to
service as head of his own "Irish Legion." He again fell under an official cloud when he shot and killed an officer who had not only assaulted
him, Corcoran said, but had called him "a damned Irish son of a
bitch." Before any official judgment could be reached, Corcoran
died—partly as the result of his wounds—and was given a hero's
funeral in New York.

As with generations of immigrants to come, Irish and otherwise,
Corcoran was eager for the opportunities that America had to offer and
grateful when they proved real. He readily took on American citizenship and showed no hesitation about defending the Union. Yet he was
equally unwilling to turn his back on the culture and people that had
formed him. Fiercely loyal to his new homeland, he had no intention
of abandoning his religion, disguising his ancestry, or detaching himself
from the struggles of his native land. No one who observed Michael
Corcoran could doubt that a powerful new element had been added to
the American mix.

The month Michael Corcoran landed in New York, October 1849,
Henry David Thoreau traveled to Cohasset, Massachusetts, to see
the wreck of the St. John, a Boston-bound brig that had set sail from
Ireland "laden with emigrants." It was one of sixty emigrant ships lost
between 1847 and 1853. Thoreau walked the beach and inspected
the bodies collected there: "I saw many marble feet and matted heads
as the cloths were raised, and one livid, swollen and mangled body of
a drowned girl—who probably had intended to go out to service in
some American family . . . Sometimes there were two or more children, or a parent and child, in the same box, and on the lid would
perhaps be written with red chalk, 'Bridget such-a-one, and sister's
child.'"

Besides what Thoreau tells us of the drowned girl, we know only that she sailed from Galway, part of a legion of Bridget such-a-ones. It's possible that coming from the West, she was an Irish speaker; more than a third of the Famine emigrants were. Perhaps she had relatives waiting for her. Perhaps not. Yet her corpse points to a larger story than the perils of the Atlantic crossing or the travails of a single season of immigrants. The dissolution of Irish rural life resulted in a bleak, narrow society of late marriage and of dowries carefully passed to single heirs, encouraging the young, especially girls, to emigrate.

Encouraged, even expected, to make a contribution to the welfare of the parents and siblings they had left behind, Irishwomen worked in factories and mills. Irish maids became a fixture of bourgeois American life. Domestic service became so associated with the Irish that maids were often referred to generically as "Kathleens" or "Bridgets." The work could be demeaning as well as demanding. In 1845 the anti-slavery crusader Abby Kelley visited fellow abolitionists in Pennsylvania. Her hosts' Irish servant girl came to her in private and catalogued the work she had to perform for a dollar a week. "When I tried to console her and told her that we were trying to bring about a better state of things," Kelley wrote, "a state in which she would be regarded as an equal, she wept like a child."

Female employment was a source of independence and adaptation to American life, but above all, it was a wellspring of the money that poured back into Ireland, rescuing families from starvation and financing a self-perpetuating chain of emigration that would stretch across generations. At the height of the Famine, Mrs. Nicholson marveled that "the Irish in America, and in all other countries where they are scattered, were sending one continued train of remittances, to the utter astonishment of the Postmasters." In the Famine decade more than £8.4 million was remitted for passage out of the British Isles. The British colonial secretary was delighted that the outflow of Irish was being funded at no expense to the government and surprised to discover that "such feelings of family affection, and such fidelity and firmness of purpose, should exist so generally among the lower classes."

In Massachusetts, Edward Everett Hale was struck by the generosity of the Irish but worried that their "clannish" spirit of sharing might drag them down together. "For example," he wrote, "it is within my own observation, that in the winter of 1850 to 1851, fourteen persons, fresh from Ireland, came in on the cabin hospitality of a woman in Worcester, because she was the cousin of one of the party."

The strains of adjustment to America were enormous. The itinerant work of railroad building, in which many took part, and high rates of disease, accidental death, and alcohol abuse put tremendous pressure on families. Irishwomen were more likely to be widowed or deserted than their American counterparts. But amid the epic transformation of potato-growing tenants into urban laborers, moving from the tightly woven fabric of Irish townlands to the freewheeling environment of American cities, what was most remarkable of all was the speed and scope with which the Irish reorganized themselves.

Within little more than a generation they translated their numbers into control of the Democratic Party in the major cities and turned municipal patronage into an immediate and pragmatic method for softening the ravages of boom-and-bust capitalism. Barred from the privileged circle of high finance, equipped with few entrepreneurial skills, suspicious through experience of theories that made capital accumulation a supreme good, the Irish spearheaded the rise of organized labor.

The greatest manifestation of their effort to regroup was the Catholic Church, which was elevated from an ingredient in Irish life to its center, the bulwark of a culture that had lost its language and almost disintegrated beneath the catastrophe of the Famine. In America as well as Ireland, vocations to the priesthood and sisterhood soared. Catholic parishes became the defining institution of Irish neighborhoods. Catholic schools, hospitals, and asylums created a vast social welfare network. Catholic nuns founded protectories and orphanages that countered the placing-out system, which took hundreds of thousands of immigrant children and shipped them west to "Christian" (Protestant) homes. Eventually these institutions were influential in establishing the obligation of the state to the support of dependent children.

The Catholic Church was the strongest institutional link in the exodus from Ireland and adjustment to America. It was *the* enduring monument to the effects of the Famine: to the sexual repression and religious devotionalism that followed it; to the quest for respectability amid jarring dislocation and pervasive discrimination; and to the discipline, cohesion, and solidarity that allowed the Irish to survive, progress, and eventually reach undreamed-of levels of success. Only after a century and a half, when the Irish had erased almost every trace of their once seemingly ineradicable status as outsiders, would the power of the Church begin to wane.

For Irish Catholics in America, the Famine was the forge of their identity, fire and anvil, the scattering time of flight and dissolution, and the moment of regathering that would one day make them an influential part of the world's most powerful democracy. The Famine was rarely recalled in its specifics. There was no record made of its horrors or complexities. The blistering humiliations it inflicted and the divisions it exacerbated—the way it fell hardest on the landless Irish-speaking poor—were subsumed in a bitter and near-universal detestation of British rule in Ireland. Yet, unspoken, unexamined, largely lost to conscious memory, the Famine was threaded into Irish-America's attitudes, expectations, and institutions. The Irish-American film director John Ford said that he was drawn to making the movie version of *The Grapes of Wrath* because, in the Depression-era saga of Okies evicted from the land and left to wander and starve, he recognized the story of his own ancestors.

The Famine was a time of testing for the United States as well as its newest immigrants. As Herman Melville saw it, the immigrants arriving unchecked on the docks of New York were a sign that America had the capacity to become "not a nation, so much as a world." The greatness and genius of America wasn't in reproducing the ethnic sameness of Britain or France, he wrote. The world had no need of more pure-blooded tribes or xenophobic nationalities. Bereft of wealth or education or Anglo-Saxon pedigree, what Bridget such-a-one and all the other nameless, tired, hope-filled immigrants carried with them was the opportunity for America to affirm its destiny: "We are the heirs of all time", Melville wrote, "and with all nations we divide our inheritance. On this Western Hemisphere all tribes and people are forming into federated whole; and there is a future which shall see the estranged children of Adam restored as to the old hearth-stone in Eden."

(This chapter was originally published in *American Heritage* [December 1997] under the title "The Tragedy of Bridget Such-a-One." The more I thought about it, the more I came to feel that the title turned the thesis of the article on its head. Though it contained a multitude of tragedies, the Famine immigration to America eventually ended in triumph for the generations that followed.)

An Interpretation
of Silences

We're Micks, we're non-assimilable, we Micks.
—JOHN O'HARA, *BUtterfield 8*

I N THE MIDST OF JOHN O'HARA'S underrated novel *BUtterfield 8*, with its finely drawn portrait of speakeasy New York as it tottered from the golden twenties into the leaden thirties, there is a short exchange between Jim Malloy, an Irish Catholic from the coal country of Pennsylvania, and his WASP girlfriend. A generation before, such a cross-class, cross-ethnic pairing would have been highly improbable. But in the tumultuous cocktail-shaker mix of post-World War I New York, all sorts of new combinations were being served up.

Malloy, however, isn't simply a self-willed cultural amnesiac imbibing the bootlegged possibilities for passing as a true son of Yale and Brooks Brothers. Malloy has a deeper, older, intractable sense of who he is, a blend of pride and grievance that the lubricants of alcohol and ambition have failed to smooth away. Riled by his companion's disdain for the unglamorous denizens of the speakeasy he has taken her to, Malloy lets fly:

I want to tell you something about myself that will help to explain a lot of things about me. You might as well hear it now. First of all, I am a Mick. I wear Brooks clothes and I don't eat salad with a spoon and I probably could play five-goal polo in two years, but I am a Mick. Still a Mick. Now it's taken me a little time to find this out, but I have at last discovered that there are not two kinds of Irishman. There's only one kind . . . We're Micks, we're non-assimilable, we Micks.

I'm unsure of John O'Hara's connections to the Great Famine. The biography by Matthew Bruccoli, *The O'Hara Concern*, is short on the writer's forebears. It says only that his paternal grandfather arrived in the coal region during the Civil War. Grandfather O'Hara married into a Protestant-Irish family that had converted to Catholicism and was able to join that thin strata of so-called "respectable Irish" who weren't consigned to the lung-destroying work of wresting anthracite from the earth.

The silence about when and how the O'Haras arrived in America may or may not be significant. It has been my experience that the less the members of an Irish-American family know about their Irish antecedents—who came when, from what county or village, the minimal facts that most immigrants preserve—the more likely it is they arrived during the Famine years. Especially when it comes to learning anything of the lives of those who experienced the Famine, the process often seems more archaeology than history—a reconstruction of mute and fragmentary remains that will always be incomplete. Silence is among the greatest legacies of the Great Famine.

The Spring 1997 issue of *Éire-Ireland*, published on the sesquicentennial of "Black '47," confronts that silence. Each of its articles represents a step in piecing together a coherent narrative of what occurred and why; each work seeks to advance our collective knowledge of the Great Famine. It is, I suppose, a cause both for reflection and regret that at this late date we are still trying to fill in the blanks so that we might grasp the enormity of the event. But, as Joan Vincent made clear in her talk on the Famine's impact in County Fermanagh, which she presented at the May 1997 Great Famine Commemoration at Dublin Castle, there is no other way:

I can't help feeling, as an anthropologist, that a great deal of my perception of that Great Irish Famine of one hundred fifty years ago has to be based on the interpretation of silences, on what did not happen, and on what one does not know, but needs to know.

In John O'Hara's case, whatever his personal link to the Famine—a legacy that was common enough among the Catholic Irish of nineteenth-century America—the area he grew up in was intimately and inescapably connected to its consequences. Even lace curtains, washed and rewashed to banish the invidious grime that stained the skin of those toiling in the mines, couldn't adequately shield the O'Haras. "That the O'Haras were indisputably Irish and Catholic," Matthew Bruccoli writes, "could not have been ignored by the 'better element' for whom the Micks were drunken miners or homicidal Mollies or Democrats under orders from the Pope."

In *BUtterfield 8*, Jim Malloy spells out these indisputable associations during the barroom harangue he directs at his Anglo-Saxon consort, making such associations sound almost like a boast:

> America, being a non-Irish, anti-Catholic country, has its own idea of what a real gangster looks like, and along comes a young Mick [Malloy is referring here to Jimmy Cagney] who looks like my brother, and he fills the bill. He is the typical gangster . . . At least it's you American Americans' idea of a perfect gangster type, and I suppose you're right. Yes, I guess you are. The first real gangsters in this country were Irish. The Molly Maguires. Anyway do you see what I mean by all this non-assimilable stuff?

When Malloy cites the Molly Maguires, he reveals his (and his creator's) roots in the anthracite country, and so points to a local dimension of the Famine's legacy in America. Yet contained within the scandalous shadow that the Mollies threw across Irish America—a shadow furiously resisted by the Catholic Church and upwardly mobile families like the O'Haras—is a broader intimation of the pain, rage, confusion, dislocation, and struggle of a rural tenantry suddenly plunked down amid an industrializing nation with little regard (and sometimes outright contempt) for their values, traditions, and, to no small measure, their lives.

Historian Kevin Kenny has laid bare as never before the particular tragedy that befell the twenty men hanged as Molly Maguires in the 1870s. *Making Sense of the Molly Maguires* serves as both title of Kenny's book and as summary of its achievement in rescuing from silence—and from myth—another chapter in the Famine saga. In the Famine context, what is especially interesting is the geographic origin of most of those executed as murderers and terrorists. They came from Donegal, in some cases from Gweedore, a parish known for the pre-Famine efforts of its landlord, Lord George Hill, to break up the traditional system of communal landholding. Hill sought to replace this communal arrangement of shared fields with the pattern of individual tenancies that prevailed throughout most of the British Isles.

Thanks to the American traveler, Mrs. Asenath Nicholson, we are able to supplement the information Kenny provides and learn firsthand what happened in Gweedore during those years. In her account of her travels, *Lights and Shades of Ireland*, Mrs. Nicholson has the highest praise for the innovations Lord Hill imposed on his tenantry—"*savage* [the emphasis is Mrs. Nicholson's] as they were." She reports that, in 1850, Lord Hill wrote to her and stated "that no person died of famine at Gweedore, though many of the aged and infants, from being scantily fed, died earlier than otherwise they would . . ."

The difference between dying from starvation and perishing prematurely "from being scantily fed" cannot always have been easy to determine. As Mrs. Nicholson tells us, she had previously been an eyewitness to actual starvation in Gweedore. Amid her work to relieve the distress in Donegal, she writes:

> [I] went to Gweedore, to meet Mrs. Hewitson, who was to accompany me to Belfast, and we prepared for the journey. She had distributed her grants, and her unceasing labours, often for twenty hours in twenty-four, called for relaxation. We left the pretty spot in sadness, for the starving were crowding about and pressing her for food, following the

carriage—begging and thanking—blessing and weeping. We were obliged to shake them off, and hurried in agony away. "Many of these poor creatures," she observed, "will be dead on my return."

We will never know the identity of those trailing behind Mrs. Nicholson's coach. Like most of the poor—then and now—they are lost to history. But possibly (maybe even probably) some of the children would surface twenty or thirty years later among the Molly Maguires in Pennsylvania. Perhaps the family of Patrick O'Donnell was among those following the coach. A native of Gweedore, Patrick was not only a cousin of some of the Mollies hanged in America in the 1870s but was himself hanged for his involvement in the infamous 1882 Phoenix Park assassination of Lord Frederick Cavendish and T.H. Burke.

What we do know for certain is that the presence of famished, ragged beggars was commonplace throughout Ireland well before the Famine. Every traveler encountered these "poor creatures," who, if not always successful in their quest for alms, usually received a measure of pity. But as Margaret Kelleher reminds us in her article on Maria Edgeworth, they inspired other emotions as well—dread and fear among them—which were heightened by the Great Famine's unprecedented levels of suffering and want. These feelings are explicit in Miss Edgeworth's reaction to the account of a neighbor who had seen a woman on the outskirts of Edgeworthstown "too much stupefied by hunger and despair" to notice that the child she was carrying on her back was already dead. Scenes such as this, Miss Edgeworth writes, are "almost too dreadful to repeat." The only way to avoid them was to stay at home, pull the drapes, and press a perfumed handkerchief to one's nose.

The silent, nameless woman hauling her dead baby had no such options. She is utterly overwhelmed, utterly at the mercy of forces beyond her control—the ascendancy, the government in London, God in heaven. Where is she headed: the workhouse? Liverpool? America? Where will she end up: the Five Points in New York? An English madhouse? A common grave alongside her child? She cannot be romanticized. She will never reappear as a young girl with the walk of a queen.

There are no magic transformations ahead. She is real—so real as to be a fixture of Famine Ireland—and the sheer inescapability of such a spectacle (even in the relatively prosperous precincts of Longford) made it difficult, in Miss Edgeworth's words, "to keep any judgement or powers of calculation and belief cool and sane while such facts are brought daily and hourly before the senses."

If the reality of the Famine threatened the sanity of those who observed it, what precisely did it do to the masses who suffered and survived it? Should any of what she witnessed in Ireland be thought an exaggeration, wrote Mrs. Nicholson, "let it be said that no language is adequate to give the true, the real picture; one look of the eye into the daily scenes there witnessed, would overpower what any pen, however graphic, or tongue, however eloquent, could portray." At a bare minimum, from the remove of 150 years, we can say this: Just as the Holocaust permanently altered Jewish history, forever imprinting itself on the consciousness of Jews, the Great Famine has had a lasting and transformative effect on every aspect of Irish life, throughout Ireland and the diaspora.

Chris Morash writes that the truest parallel between the Great Famine and the Holocaust is in their effects, rather than their causes. In Morash's formulation, "[i]t is with the body, therefore—or, more precisely, with images of the body in fragments—that we find the unconscious relationship between the Famine and the Holocaust, not in the larger narratives of intentionality, culpability, or persecution."

His point is well taken. The necessity of avoiding false equivalencies is particularly important at a time when the fashion of multiculturalism holds sway. At its best, multiculturalism can deepen our understanding, moving us away from a version of history that involves little more than the lives of the rich and famous to a better grasp of the variety and density of human experience. At its worst, multiculturalism raises victimhood into a shibboleth of historical authenticity. The more oppression a group lays claim to, the more attention it feels that it deserves.

Multiculturalism is, of course, the obverse of the old tradition of cultural triumphalism that once pervaded American schools. Under the old dispensation, the norm of American identity was contained and defined by the power and glory of its Anglo-Saxon progenitors. Sharing a common "germ plasm" of blood and culture, Britain and America had a lock on historical greatness. Few others could measure up.

In the 1850s, undoubtedly reacting in part to the flood of Famine immigrants into Massachusetts, Ralph Waldo Emerson sketched this theme succinctly:

> I think it cannot be maintained by any candid person that the African races have ever occupied or do promise to occupy any very high place in the human family. Their present condition is the strongest proof that they cannot. The Irish cannot; the American Indian cannot; the Chinese cannot. Before the energy of the Caucasian race, all other races have quailed and done obeisance.

Today, the Anglo-Saxon historical canon is in hopeless disrepute. Whether fairly or unfairly, its pantheon of rugged individualists now serves as a rogue's gallery of marauders, slave drivers, and bloodthirsty colonialists. The Hall of Fame (Emerson included) is dismissed by some as nothing more than a necropolis of Dead White Males. The recurring temptation is to substitute one collection of legendary heroes and villains with another—one that for all its differences of emphasis replicates the notion of goodness and worthiness residing in certain groups and escaping others. Honest historians cannot help but be vividly aware of this perennial danger. They will recognize their fundamental responsibility to tackle the inherent complexity of history and not hide behind convenient and fashionable simplifications.

This responsibility cuts both ways. A refusal to be intimidated by the excesses of multiculturalism should be accompanied by an equal resistance to the claim that any attempt to explore the culpability of British policy-makers during the Famine is neo-romantic nonsense or, worse, provides a justification for terrorists. The notion of a bungled benevolence—tinged perhaps by imperial arrogance and/or ignorance of the real conditions in Ireland—persists. But can this reading of the Famine stand as truth? Can it withstand the scrutiny of scholarship? The question needs to be answered: that woman and her dead baby in Longford, the pleading crowd Mrs. Nicholson was obliged to shake off in Donegal, the thousands laid in mass graves in Ireland and Grosse Île—were they victims of a human decision-making process that regarded their "removal" as not only acceptable but eminently desirable?

It's impossible to read the articles gathered in *Éire-Ireland* or study the scholarly investigations of the Great Famine and its consequences by Robert Scally, James Donnelly, Christine Kinealy, Kevin Kenny, Kevin Whelan, et al., without a heightened sense of the brutal dimensions of what occurred in Ireland. Nor can we ignore the role of British public opinion and government officials in endorsing and actively abetting what took place.

The Great Famine was not a nineteenth-century version of the factory-style extermination of the Jews carried out by the Nazis. Yet the Victorians were anything but shy in anticipating the extinction of "primitive peoples" and "inferior races." In his *Descent of Man* (1871), Darwin echoed a widely held opinion when he wrote that "At some future period and not very distant measured by centuries, the civilized races of man will almost certainly exterminate and replace the savage races throughout the world." He accounted famine as a prime check on primitive populations, citing an example in distant Australia instead of recent events across the Irish Sea:

> With savages the difficulty of obtaining subsistence occasionally limits their number in more direct manner than with civilized people, for all tribes periodically suffer from severe famines. At such times savages are forced to devour much bad food . . . They are also compelled to wander much, and, as I was assured in Australia, their infants perish in large numbers.

In America, Anglo-Saxons and immigrants alike believed their manifest destiny—a term invented by a journalist named O'Sullivan—was to push the native peoples to the farthest periphery, where the remnants would either perish or be absorbed by the settler population. But as casually callous as their language often was, the Victorians had neither the technological capacity nor the ideological motivation for an industrialized genocide aimed at the systematic murder of an entire ethnic group. (They did not even have the word "genocide," which was not coined until 1944.)

This, however, is not automatically to chalk up the Great Famine's immense toll to fate, or to bad luck, or to administrative incompetence. Nor is it to say that the Famine isn't eminently worthy of study, or that we know all we need to know of it. Nor is it to deny the racist underpinnings of what took place, or to ignore the Famine's place in the evolution of economic—as well as, in time, eugenic— rationales for the modern nation-state to pursue its own brutal ends.

The epic of the Great Famine belongs to the histories of Britain, Ireland, and the United States. To one degree or another, it has affect- ed the destinies of all three nations. The need to distinguish it from the Holocaust does not require accommodating the polite and politically acceptable premise that, oh well, tragic as the whole affair was, the worst anyone can be accused of is bad judgment.

Having witnessed what took place, Mrs. Nicholson echoes John Mitchel's judgment on the cause. "Was there then a 'God's famine' in Ireland, in 1846, '47, '48, '49, and so on?" she asks. "No! It is all mock- ery to call it so, and mockery which the Almighty will expose, before man will believe, and be humbled as he ought to be." The prolonged period of punishing want and deprivation that decimated Ireland was not merely the result of some unavoidable accident, the agricultural equivalent of a ten-car pileup on the highway of history with no one at fault except the weather and a slick road. Ireland was ruled by a glob- al empire that, whenever it judged necessary, asserted its sovereignty by armed force. In 1801, with the Act of Union, the empire removed final authority from Dublin to Westminster, claiming that in the newly "unit- ed kingdom," the Irish people would have the same status as the citi- zens of Somerset and Lancashire. The Great Famine exposed this promise as a lie.

Michael de Nie's examination of Britain's desire to use the hunger in Ireland as an instrument of moral and social transformation is a reminder that the vaunted notion of laissez-faire was an economic rather than a political principle. Though Ireland would be required to feed herself, a heavy contingent of police and troops would guarantee that the starving behave in an orderly fashion, maintaining a proper respect for the rights of property. With the revision of the Irish Poor Law in 1847, Britain's guiding policy was to use famine as a tool to eliminate resistance to a large-scale reordering of the Irish economy. Thus was fulfilled the goal that, as de Nie tells us, the London *Times* had announced the previous year: "an island, a social state, a race is to be changed."

What emerges as most remarkable about the Famine is its modernity, the way in which it seems to anticipate a brand of social engineering that the twentieth century would take to new heights (or depths). The thinking going on among the shapers of British policy and public opinion reflected concepts that would become increasingly influential: the relative superiority/inferiority of ethnic groups, the overriding requirement for economic rationalization and modernization, and the extension or curtailment of government involvement to achieve sweeping social change.

Tribalism is pushed aside. The gods of logic and rationality are invoked. A diagnosis is made. Ireland needs to be cured. Providence and economics are mashed together in the mortar of politics. The medical metaphor is extended. The fever will not break until Ireland is dosed and the body purged of its poisons. "I think I see a bright light shining in the distance through the dark cloud which at present hangs over Ireland," wrote Charles Trevelyan in October 1846:

> The deep and inveterate root of Social evil remain[s], and I hope I am not guilty of irreverence in thinking that, this being altogether beyond the power of man, the cure has been applied by an all wise Providence in a manner as unexpected and unthought of as it is likely to be effectual. God grant that we may rightly perform our part and not turn into a curse what was intended for a blessing.

Others besides Trevelyan came to see this light. The direction of government policy would embody that enlightenment. Policy decisions were not based on an inadequate understanding of Ireland's true condition. Writing to Prime Minister Russell in March 1849, the Lord Lieutenant offered the following explanation for the resignation of

Edward Twistleton, Chief Poor Law Commissioner: "He thinks the destitution here is so horrible, the indifference of the House of Commons to it so manifest, that he is unfit to be an agent of a policy that must be one of extermination." The decision to use hunger as an opportunity to clear the land—"extermination" as it was then called— was more than absent-mindedness or stupidity. Indifference was endorsement, involving method, not madness.

The grinding process of mass depopulation was wrapped within immutable principles of human progress. Ireland's problems were of Irish making. Unbridled population growth and the endless subdivision of the land were both a cause of Irish poverty and prima facie evidence of Irish racial backwardness. The hordes of tenants and laborers clinging to their pathetic plots of potatoes were a blockage that must be removed. The country's moral miasma spared almost no one. The landlords were as lazy and feckless as their tenants. They, too, would have to go. Thus in April 1849, the *Times*, espousing a view prevalent among the British public, accurately catalogued the workings of the revised poor law and celebrated the result:

> The rigorous administration of the Poor Law is destroying small holdings, reducing needy proprietors to utter insolvency, compelling them to surrender their estates into better hands, instigating an emigration far beyond any which government could undertake, and leaving the soil of Ireland open to industrial enterprise and the introduction of new capital. We see Ireland depopulated, her villages razed to the ground, her landlords bankrupt—in a word, we see the hideous chasm prepared for the foundation of a future prosperity.

In this context, as Michael O'Malley's inquiry into the situation in Mayo underscores, though we can be horrified by the account of conditions in places like the Ballinrobe Poor Law Union, we shouldn't be surprised. Ballinrobe was the rule rather than the exception. In Naas, on the outskirts of Dublin, the workhouse, intended for a few hundred at most, held nearly 1,200 individuals. In Skibbereen, a town of just over 3,800 people, 1,300 inmates inhabited the workhouse. In Castlerea, in Roscommon, the workhouse was so crammed with the dead and dying that a jerry-built slide was used to deliver the corpses directly into a pit beside the building.

Mrs. Nicholson visited several workhouses before and during the Famine. She witnessed the mass descent that took place when the soup kitchens were closed and "when funds decreased, when the doors were besieged by imploring applicants, who wanted a place to die, that they might be buried in a coffin." The workhouses, she tells us, became "little more than charnel houses, while the living skeletons that squatted upon the floor, or stood with arms folded against the wall, half-clad with hair uncombed, hands and face unwashed, added a horror, if not TERROR to the sight."

Ubiquitous squalor and degradation were not unintended consequences of an overwhelmed administration, but the desired outcome of a policy of evictions and land clearances. From the government's point of view, this is what the poor deserved, what the Irish poor required—hard labor, three to a bed, inadequate rations, contempt, mistreatment, miseries and indignities sufficient to overcome the incorrigible lassitude of a guileful, superstitious people addicted to the easy cultivation of potato beds.

Here was the answer to Maria Edgeworth's apprehension that the indiscriminate ladling of soup might lead the hungry to assume that the government and landlords had a permanent obligation to feed them. "The character of Paddy," she observed, "knows well how to take advantage of his own misfortunes and of all fears and blunders." The workhouses would help disabuse Paddy of that notion. More than 900,000 souls passed through the system in 1849, learning firsthand what they were owed.

Those outside the workhouse would learn as well. In the short run, by petitioning Parliament about large numbers of the local population who would be "ultimately swept away," the well-meaning Protestant and Catholic clergy of Castlebar may well have helped bring about the establishment of government soup kitchens. In the long run, they missed entirely the unfolding resolve behind Whig policy. This sweeping away was required. To succor the starving any longer would forego the opportunity to render a decisive answer to the Irish Question. Charity would summon the black clouds once again, spurning the blessing and embracing the curse. For their part, the parliamentarians who read countless reports of the country's growing hordes of starving and desperate wanderers—and responded by passing a vagrancy act to punish begging—were not oblivious to what they were doing.

The degree of intent that came to characterize British policy in Ireland is clear in Peter Gray's study of the responses undertaken in other countries across Europe to the failure of the potato. Finding no contemporary parallels to the British treatment of Ireland "as a separate moral entity which required unique treatment and forced Anglicization," Gray writes that

> . . . Ireland differed from other famine-stricken European regions in being interpreted through the lens of colonialism (albeit in this case one that gave greatest priority to the integration of the colony into the imperial centre) . . . What made the Irish experience unique in terms of state response was the British perception of the potato failure as an opportunity rather than an obstacle, and a denial of the benefits of common nationality until Irish society had been remolded according to British norms.

The controversy surrounding the Great Famine will not go away with the passing of the 150th anniversary of "Black '47." Impressive new scholarship has advanced our knowledge and sparked new controversies. We are all revisers (if not revisionists) now. The debate will continue to rage.

As always, the past belongs to the living. It is ours to understand or to ignore. In her account of the survival of Irish music, Sally Sommers Smith offers a poignant reminder that this tradition was preserved and passed down because there were those who refused to let it die. Only a conscious determination to labor for "the salvation of the music from certain extinction" saved this crucial part of Irish culture and identity from the enveloping silence.

More than music has survived as a result of the sometimes heroic, often lonely efforts of individual women and men. Michael Quigley's moving account of the Famine deaths on Grosse Île is a first-class piece of historical investigation, as well as a testament to his own long and persistent—and now successful—effort to preserve and honor "the sanctity of the site."

The more we discover about the Great Famine, the more obvious become the wounds it inflicted. Time didn't heal them. It only made them easier to hide. The carapace of secretiveness accreted through the long and confused trauma of conquest and colonization transformed itself, took on new life, in new forms. The physical trappings of hidden Ireland were swept away by the Famine. The clacháns and cabins became faint outlines upon the pastures. The children of the Famine scattered. The mass graves went unvisited. Memories of the Ballinrobe Poor Law Union, evictions, fever, tattered clothing, abandoned children, and rapacious neighbors gave way to the myth of a rooted peasantry, innocent and simple, steeped in a folk culture unchanged over centuries.

The Famine occurred in the twilight between the final passing of the decrepit, ramshackle remnants of the feudal order and the emergence of the modern, centralized state, with responsibility for the social and economic well-being of its people. To read the debates and newspapers of the time is to be struck by how contemporary they often sound. Though he paid little attention to the Famine, Marx was among the first to recognize *homo economicus* as he emerged upright out of the forest. The Great Famine was a marker in that evolution. Experts were at work. Statistics were compiled, analyzed. Reports were undertaken, disseminated, studied. The sheer amount of paperwork was a sign of the new power of governments and societies, by their actions and/or inactions to decide the shape of things to come.

The Great Famine is embedded in the nineteenth century; it cannot be properly understood if removed from that context. But the eventual outcome was far more than a provincial mishap, an imperial oversight, a case of muddling through. The record bears witness to the official certainty that mastering the future required the removal of the congenitally backward masses whose presence blocked the hope of progress for the strong and healthy. Not merely an Irish event, the Famine was a prelude. It offered a preview of the future.

The verdict is still out on whether Jim Malloy was right— whether the "Micks are non-assimilable." (Perhaps no one ever tried harder to disprove that theory than John O'Hara, Malloy's creator.)

What is certain, however, is that if Irish Americans are to have a role in the ethnic dialectic that is at the heart of our nation's cultural life, if they are to assert the intrinsic importance of the their story as part of any legitimate historical narrative, they must speak up. Silence brings only oblivion.

Closets Full of Bones

> Our own ancestors
> Are hungry ghosts
> Closets so full of bones
> They won't close.
> —TRACY CHAPMAN, "Material World"

A SPECTER IS HAUNTING THE WEST: immigration. From the rising chorus of America's neo-nativists to the growing anti-immigrant movements in Europe, there is a widespread call for economically advanced societies to seal themselves off from the masses in the less-developed and under-developed world. Whether presented in terms of border security or economic prosperity, the imagery most often used to describe these immigrants is the same: Immigrants are to hordes what sheep are to flocks, or fish to schools. They swarm rather than arrive, their faceless uniformity evoking the insect world and its ceaseless, relentless capacity to infest, erode, subvert.

There is no better description of the passions and fears that immigration engenders than the hysterical vision of approaching apocalypse contained in Jean Raspail's novel *The Camp of the Saints*. First published in 1973, *The Camp of the Saints* tells what happens when a million diseased, crippled, impoverished inhabitants of the Indian subcontinent board an armada of decrepit ships and descend on the South of France. In Raspail's story, a weak and effete France, awash in liberal guilt and gushing Christian sentimentalism, finds it doesn't have the power to resist.

Neglected for decades, Raspail's book gained belated attention in Europe and was trumpeted in a cover article ("Must It Be the Rest Against the West?") in the December 1994 issue of *The Atlantic Monthly*. Co-authors Matthew Connelly, a graduate student of history at Yale, and Paul Kennedy, the author of *The Rise and Fall of the Great Powers*, offered a qualified endorsement of the Malthusian and Spenglerian fatalism at the heart of Raspail's novel:

> Readers may well find Raspail's vision uncomfortable and his language vicious and repulsive, but the central message is clear: we are heading into the twenty-first century in a world consisting for the most part of a relatively small number of rich, satiated, demographically stagnant societies and a large number of poverty-stricken, resource-depleted nations whose populations are doubling every twenty-five years or less.

On the face of it, Raspail's notion of a conscience-stricken West being overwhelmed by an army of disheveled immigrants is less discomforting than laughable. The West has shown itself perfectly capable of using sufficient force whenever its vital interests are at stake— or perceived as being so. Indeed, for all the hand-wringing over immigration and a "clash of civilizations," there seems little appreciation that, for the last 500 years at least, it has been the major powers of the West that have been at the head of the clash, threatening and battering the rest of the world, colonizing entire continents and waging war to secure the resources they need.

The pessimism evinced by Connelly and Kennedy is mitigated somewhat by their call for international cooperation to deal with the underlying causes of the present population crisis. But as with so many descriptions of the threat posed by the Third World, the authors' underlying sense of the West's vulnerability before the procreative puissance of the world's huddled masses is far more vivid and forceful than any formulaic list of possible solutions. The threat is from below, from Raspail's "kinky-haired, swarthy-skinned, long-despised phantoms," from the teeming races that Rudyard Kipling once described as "lesser breeds without the law."

In the United States, the question of intelligence as a distinguishing characteristic between greater and lesser breeds was brought center stage with the best-selling *The Bell Curve*, by Charles Murray and the late Richard J. Herrnstein. Unlike *The Camp of the Saints*, this sedate and statistics-laden book wasn't directly concerned with immigration, and its central thesis—that I.Q. is a function of race—was more subtle and complex than the horrific vision evoked by Raspail.

Despite their differences, however, there were similarities. At the heart of *The Bell Curve* and *The Camp of the Saints*, as well as of Connelly's and Kennedy's article, lies a world in which the central divisions are racial and in which, when all is said and done, the white race is endangered. In fairness to Murray and Herrnstein, they credit Asians with higher I.Q.'s than white Americans. Yet, here again, the Caucasian community is challenged by another race, one that has been traditionally credited with being shrewder and craftier—in its own "inscrutable" way, smarter—than Westerners.

The fear that white civilization is growing steadily weaker and is at risk of being overwhelmed by barbarians from within and without marks a new life for an old and ugly tradition. In the United States, the most infamous manifestation of that tradition is the Ku Klux Klan and the host of so-called "Aryan resistance groups" that continue to spring up on the periphery of American political life. The tradition, however, is far older than that, and its powerful and enduring manifestations haven't been limited to cross burnings or rabble-rousing.

The respectable, educated version of this tradition clothed itself in the language of science and not only won a place in the academy, but helped shape our laws on immigration, interracial marriage, and compulsory sterilization of the mentally ill and retarded. The movement derived its authority from the work of an Englishman, Francis Galton—Darwin's first cousin—whose 1869 book *Hereditary Genius* laid down an iron law of hereditary determinism as well as coined a name for it: eugenics. In Galton's view, which was shared by many of his Victorian contemporaries and buttressed by a wealth of pseudo-scientific skull measuring and brain weighing, the races were totally distinct. Eugenics, he believed, would give "the more suitable races or strains of blood a better chance of prevailing speedily over the less suitable."

At the turn of the twentieth century, the United States was ripe for the gospel of eugenics. The country's original immigrant stock—made up of Anglo-Saxon and Scots-Irish Protestants—was feeling battered and besieged by the waves of newcomers from Southern and Eastern Europe (mainly Italians, Slovaks, and Ashkenazi Jews) who were judged so immiscible in appearance and conduct that they would undermine the country's character and identity. According to the eugenicists, the racial "germ plasm" of these groups was riddled with hereditary proclivities to feeblemindedness, criminality, and pauperism. These suspicions were given scientific justification by studies that purported to trace deviancy across several generations and discern in families a clear pattern of inherited behavior.

By the eve of World War I, eugenics was taught in many colleges. Its research arm was generously funded by some of America's wealthiest families, including the Harrimans, Rockefellers, and Carnegies. Alfred Plötz, the German apostle of "racial hygiene," hailed the United States as a "bold leader in the realm of eugenics," a leadership that consisted of the widespread ban on interracial marriage and the growing emphasis on compulsory sterilization.

In the wake of the First World War, the eugenicists helped direct the campaign to halt the "degeneration" of the country's racial stock by changing its immigration laws. As framed by Henry Fairfield Osborn, the president of the American Museum of Natural History (at that time a center of eugenic fervor), America would either stop the influx from Southern and Eastern Europe or it would perish: "Apart from the spiritual, moral and political invasion of alienism the practical question of day-by-day competition between the original American and the alien element turns upon the struggle for existence between the Americans and aliens whose actions are controlled by entirely different standards of living and morals."

The eugenicists played the pivotal role in achieving the Immigration

Restriction Act of 1924, a victory noted and approved of by Adolf Hitler in his book of the same year, *Mein Kampf.* In fact, nine years later, when the Nazis took power in Germany, they would hail U.S. laws on immigration, intermarriage, and sterilization as models for their own legislation.

Eugenics was part of the United States's second large-scale anti-immigrant movement. The country's first great immigrant trauma (that is, aside from the forced importation of African slaves) began in the mid-nineteenth century, with the arrival in large numbers of white Northern-European Christians—a.k.a. Irish Catholics. The flight of the Famine Irish produced an immigrant experience unlike any other in American history. There was no web of private societies or government agencies to encourage or cushion the process of emigration (and, luckily for the Irish, no apparatus in place to keep them out). In effect, traditional Irish society—the life of the townlands and the rudimentary agriculture that supported the mass of the Irish tenantry—dissolved into a chaotic rout. Faced with the choice of flee or starve or, in many cases, leave by eviction with no choice at all, the Irish abandoned the land.

From Liverpool to Boston, contemporary observers remarked on the utter destitution of the Irish who poured into their streets, many of them ill and emaciated and, in the words of one eyewitness, "steeped to all appearances in as hopeless barbarism as the aboriginal inhabitants of Australia."

Today, the sense of the Catholic Irish as wholly alien to white, Christian society seems, perhaps, difficult to credit. But in mid-nineteenth-century America the inalterable otherness of the Irish was, for many, a given. Indeed, the experience of the Famine Irish seems to anticipate the visionary nightmare contained in Jean Raspail's novel. Here in flesh rather than fiction was the descent of a swarming horde of the gaunt and desperate poor on the shores of a comfortable and prosperous West.

Although the formal study of so-called racial biology was yet to be articulated, the theory of Irish racial inferiority was already being discussed. In 1860, Charles Kingsley, English clergyman and Professor of

Modern History at Cambridge University, described the peasants he saw during his travels in Ireland in Darwinian terms: "I am daunted by the human chimpanzees I saw along that hundred miles of horrible country . . . to see white chimpanzees is dreadful; if they were black, one would not feel it so much, but their skins, except where tanned by exposure, are as white as ours."

Three years later, in 1863, Charles Loring Brace, the founder of the Children's Aid Society and a prominent figure in the American social reform movement, published a book entitled *Races of the Old World*. Drawing on the claims of Anglo-Saxon racial superiority found in popular historical works such as Sharon Turner's *History of the Anglo-Saxon* and the pseudo-scientific skull measuring in Samuel George Morton's *Crania Americana*, Brace located the cause of Irish mental deficiency in brain size, a measurement that served for Victorian ethnologists as a sure indication of intelligence, "The Negro skull, though less than the European, is within one inch as large as the Persian and the Armenian," Brace wrote. "The difference between the average English and Irish skull is nine cubic inches, and only four between the average African and Irish."

Among those concurring with Brace's theory of an Irish "race" stigmatized by physical and mental deficiencies was Charles Darwin. In *Descent of Man*, Darwin cites approvingly and at length W.R. Gregg's description of the procreative threat posed by inferior breeds:

> 'The carefree, squalid, unaspiring Irishman multiplies like rabbits [while] the frugal, self-respecting, ambitious Scot, stern in his morality, spiritual in his faith, sagacious and disciplined in his intelligence, passes his best years in struggle and celibacy, marries late, and leaves few behind. Given a land originally peopled by a thousand Saxons and a thousand Celts—and in a dozen generations five-sixths of the population would be Celts, but five-sixths of the property, of the power, of the *intellect* [emphasis added], would belong to the one-sixth of Saxons that remained.'

Irish-Americans, it seems to me, have preferred to focus on the causes of the Famine (i.e., the question of British culpability) than on the consequences, thereby contributing to the romantic haze that obscures much of their immigrant history. They ritually invoke the old slogan of "No Irish Need Apply" and skip over just how bitter and deep the reaction to their arrival was.

Several years ago, while on the final leg of a book tour, I found myself not just a commentator on immigration history but a participant in a present-day controversy. The flap arose when, during a talk at a book venue in Los Angeles, California, I made comparisons between the political reaction and nativist fear-mongering that followed Irish immigration to the East Coast of the United States in the mid-nineteenth century and the burgeoning sense of hysteria and cultural armageddon generated around the current flow of illegal immigrants from Mexico. In the case of authors trying to sell books, controversy is more to be welcomed than avoided. Yet, while I did nothing to discourage the media attention that ensued, I was surprised by it.

The *Los Angeles Times* of March 11, 1995, reported that "Amid the immigration backlash of the last century, the Know-Nothing Party emerged as a potent political force, founded in large part on a revulsion against Irish-Catholic newcomers, Quinn sees a historical continuity to today's immigration . . ." The article also noted: "The roiling, inflamed Lower East Side of the Draft Riots, Quinn says, is in many ways more analogous to contemporary U.S. reality than many might suppose. In his view, the churning urban conflicts so apparent today—embodied in the 1992 riots in Los Angeles—hark back to the earlier tumult in Manhattan."

The response to what I considered fairly innocuous observations was immediate and unsparing. The *Times* article went on to quote Glenn Spencer, founder of the Voice of Citizens Together, a Sherman Oaks-based group: "We're reacting today to an invasion in the United States, and in my judgment, a subversion not only of the culture of the United States, with an inability to assimilate these people, but possibly a subversion of our political system." The comparisons to the earlier waves of immigrants, he said, are "nonsense."

Governor Pete Wilson's office also was quoted by the *Times*: "'It angers us when people try to say the governor's a nativist or comes from a Know-Nothing perspective,' said Sean Walsh, a Wilson spokesman. The governor, Walsh noted, has focused criticism on illegal immigration, not today's lawful flow or the legal, albeit chaotic, process of the nineteenth century."

I've never believed that those who study history automatically inoculate themselves against repeating past errors. Most mistakes—past and present—are rooted in human nature. Pride, cupidity, stupidity, arrogance—take your pick—exist in roughly the same proportions in every era. But at least by knowing what has happened in previous ages and eras, students of history increase the odds of recognizing patterns of behavior and raising awareness of their causes and effects, thus making possible other outcomes. In short we're better off knowing history than not.

In light of this, it is an enduring source of amazement to me how little thought or examination is given to the Irish immigration to the United States that occurred in the mid-nineteenth century, or to the formative effect it had on every aspect of American society. As Robert Dunne points out in his intriguing book, *Antebellum Irish Immigration and Emerging Ideologies of America: A Protestant Backlash*, "Irish immigrants . . . influenced the evolving definition of 'America' and shaped the nation's dominant cultural myth, the American Dream. That they seem so seamless a part of the nation's mainstream today is a reflection not only of their assimilation into 'American' society but also of the contributions they made to redefine that society."

The transfer of the rural Irish to rising urban centers like New York and Boston was an opening chapter in the immense population shift of the late nineteenth and early twentieth centuries, which saw one-seventh of the world's working-age population move from one country to another (including, undoubtedly, the ancestors of some of today's leading anti-immigrant activists). Emigration became, in effect, the organizing principle of Irish society, and Irish America became its partner in the work of collective survival. In families like my own, a human chain of emigration was created, new immigrants sending back the money to would-be ones, a process that continued over half a century until every aunt, uncle, and cousin was in America.

Nowhere in Europe was emigration such a pervasive fact. The Irish were part of the vanguard of rural unskilled poor whose journey to the world's cities—whether to Los Angeles or Rio de Janeiro or Harare—remains a dominant theme in the evolution of urban society across the globe.

As with Muslim immigrants today, the religion of the Irish made them party to, if not a clash of civilizations, then a bitter, long-running civil war. The bugbear of Protestant Anglo-Saxon society (on both sides of the Atlantic), Roman Catholicism was seen both as a symptom of who the Irish were and a cause. Catholicism was, in a sense, the chicken and the egg. The Irish were violent, lazy, ignorant, and disloyal because they were Catholic; and they were Catholic because they were intrinsically lacking the intellectual and moral stamina that put Anglo-Saxon Protestants at the pinnacle of creation.

In Dunne's words, "if one was an immigrant and Roman Catholic, contrary to modern preconceptions, one was deemed, at best, little better than African Americans and women of other marginalized groups in the hierarchy of the have-nots." The numerous tracts and speeches cited by Dunne leave no doubt about the validity of this statement. (It should be noted that while prejudices against European immigrants fluctuated in intensity, anti-Asian sentiment was a constant, reaching its apex in the wartime internment of Japanese Americans before finally going into decline.)

The arguments Dunne puts forth in his book offer a well-documented corrective to the present-day orthodoxy that simplifies and distorts the meaning and significance of ethnic Americans by consigning them all into the dustbin of "white male oppressors." Thus the Molly Maguires and the railroad magistrates who hanged them become one and the same. John D. Rockefeller and the Fenian Brotherhood are joined at the hip. Exploited Irish canal workers, the foot soldiers of the opening phase of America's industrial revolution, join the robber barons as co-conspirators.

Dunne tells a more complicated story. His objective is to recognize the part that the Irish (as well as other immigrants) have played in the history of that most powerful and enduring of our national myths—the American Dream. He argues (quite rightly, I believe) that it is impossible to understand the origins and dimensions of how we as a nation interpret that dream without paying attention to the fractious, bitter, and continuing argument over who owns it. What is needed, he contends (and again, I agree) is a willingness to examine the dialogue between America's insiders and outsiders, which, though often nasty and uncivil, is central to how various groups have been marginalized and to how they have resisted such marginalization.

For me, one of the unexamined ironies of the Irish interactions with mainstream American culture is that John Ford and Eugene O'Neill, two of the twentieth century's master interpreters of the dream—of its possibilities as well as contradictions—were descended from Irish immigrants. No cinematic chronicle of the dream has been more pervasive or powerful than Ford's (born Feeney). The version of this country's history most people have in their heads has less to do with what they were taught in school than with the mental remnants of classic John Ford films such as *Drums Along the Mohawk, She Wore a Yellow Ribbon, The Searchers, Grapes of Wrath, Young Mr. Lincoln,* and *The Man Who Shot Liberty Valance.*

Ford was never the mere idolizer of the American Dream that he has sometimes made out to be. His films confront the American conundrums of race, class, and social injustice. Yet if Ford is often remembered for stressing the more hopeful parts of American history, there has been no more forthright and pioneering investigator of the national subconscious, of the dark recesses of the American id, than Eugene O'Neill. His plays are milestones in the modern exploration of our collective dream and shared nightmare.

The Irish-American experience that formed Ford and O'Neill continues to receive scant attention from current arbiters of American culture and history. (A recent television documentary on O'Neill's life barely mentions his Irishness, despite his assertion that it was central to his work.) Maybe that's part of the reason politicians and media pundits can be so simpleminded and dunderheaded when it comes to the immigration issue. They don't know history.

Now, as always, there are real issues involved in immigration, but they won't be solved or alleviated by the panic-driven paranoia about political, cultural, economic, and genetic subversion that reappears through our history. We need to remind ourselves that immigrants are not a single genus. They come in all shapes and sizes. They are part of a process as old as the human race and as new as the global integration underway on every part of the planet. They have immense strengths and talents as well as weaknesses. If the past is any guide, their long-term potential for enriching and enlivening our society is far greater than the immediate difficulties their presence can create. At the very least, whether they arrived legally or illegally, they are human beings entitled to a modicum of respect and fair treatment.

Today's immigration debate is in danger of being hijacked by the same brand of hysterical alarmists who led the country's two previous anti-immigration movements. Every American has an interest in preventing a third wave of reactionary extremism. But those descended from the Famine Irish have a special responsibility to look past the current evocation of innumerable, anonymous aliens threatening our borders, or the latter-day recycling of theories of ethnic and racial inferiority, and to see in today's immigrants a reminder of our ancestors: those hungry ghosts who, though dispossessed and despised, passed on to us their faith and their hope.

Lost and Found

Among other languages spoken here [Augusta, Maine] must be reckoned the wild Irish. Some of the laborers on the mill-saw can speak nothing else.
—NATHANIEL HAWTHORNE,
The American Notebooks, July 1837

IN 1799, TROOPS WITH NAPOLEON'S ARMY in Egypt unearthed an ancient tablet inscribed with a tribute to the Pharaoh in demotic script as well as Greek and hieroglyphs. As a result of this discovery outside the town of Rashid (Rosetta), the Egyptologist and linguist Jean-François Champollion was eventually able to reveal the meanings of a once-indecipherable language. What had been lost was found, and historians and scholars gained a new understanding of the past. Working with a pen (or more likely, a computer) rather than a spade, and serving both as digger and decoder, Daniel Cassidy presents us with revelations that are, for etymologists in general and Irish-Americans in particular, every bit as momentous as those Champollion extracted from the Rosetta Stone.

The discoveries that Cassidy has gathered into *The Secret Language of the Crossroad: How the Irish Invented Slang* represent a hugely significant breakthrough in our ability to understand the origins of vital parts of the American vernacular. He has solved the mystery of how, after centuries of intense interaction, a people as verbally agile and inventive as the Irish could have made almost no impression on English, a fact that H.L. Mencken, among other students of the language, found baffling. What was missing, it turns out, wasn't a steady penetration of Irish into English, but someone equipped with Cassidy's genius —a unique combination of street smarts and scholarship, of memory, intuition, and intellect—who could discern and decipher the evidence.

Like the Frenchmen who uncovered the Rosetta Stone, Cassidy's discovery began with a serendipitous dig, a solitary stroke of the spade into the fertile earth of his own family's history, at the spot where a piece of the past jutted above the layers of time forgotten or obscured in the form of a single word, "boliver" (*bailbhe*, a mute, silent person), the semi-affectionate, semi-sarcastic nickname used to refer to his taciturn grandfather. Beginning with that key, à la Champollion, Cassidy unlocks the secret of a centuries-long infiltration of Irish into English, exactly where it would be most expected, amid the playfully subversive, syncretic, open-ended olio of slang. "We were not *balbh* in Irish," writes Cassidy:

> The "slang" and accent of five generations and one hundred years in the tenements, working-class neighborhoods, and old *breac-Ghaeltacht* (scattered Irish-speaking district) slums (*'s lom*, is naked, bare, poor) of Brooklyn and New York City held within it the hard-edged spiel (*speal*, cutting words) and vivid cant (*caint*, speech) of a hundred generations and a thousand years in Ireland: *Gaeilge*, the Irish language.

Cassidy's ability to see clearly what others—including myself—had missed entirely, his originality and eagle-eyed insight in locating what was hidden in plain view, brings to mind Edgar Allan Poe's famous short story "The Purloined Letter." At the outset of the story, C. Auguste Dupin is informed by the Prefect of Police that his men are nonplussed because the case they are trying to crack, which seemed simple at the outset, has proven unsolvable. "Perhaps it is the very simplicity of the thing which puts you at fault," replies Dupin. Later, he explains to his companion the underlying reason the police, equipped with microscopes and following the rules of evidentiary logic, overlooked what was right before their eyes:

> [H]ad the purloined letter been hidden anywhere within the limits of the Prefect's examination—in other words, had the principle of its concealment been comprehended within the principles of the Prefect—its discovery would have been a matter altogether beyond question.

Dupin's axiom—that while the obvious is often found in obvious places, locating it can require abandoning the safe harbor of theory for the open waters of reality and experience—underlies Cassidy's work. Take, for example, his explication of the word "crony," which *Merriam-Webster's Collegiate Dictionary* (Tenth Edition) speculates is perhaps from the Greek *chronios* (long-lasting) and was first recorded in English usage in 1663. The dating to 1663, the early days of the Restoration, with returning Irish exiles and refugees from the Cromwellian settlement abounding in English cities and towns, is a clue to the true origin of crony. More direct and, it seems to me, altogether beyond question, is the unadorned fact that the Irish word *comh-roghna*, pronounced cuh-roney, means, Cassidy tells us, "choice selection, the thing chosen, figuratively, a 'chosen one,' a sweetheart, a pal."

The story of the Irish language's survival and its transatlantic impact is inseparable from the course of Irish history. Beginning with the dissolution of the Irish monasteries under Henry VIII through the Elizabethan conquest, the Flight of the Earls, and the aftermath of the Williamite victory, the old Gaelic order was gradually toppled and destroyed. Educated Irish-speaking monks, poets, musicians, genealogists, scholars, and brehons were driven from the scriptora, schools, castles, and courts where they had enjoyed the patronage of chieftans and, in some cases, of the Irish-Norman ("old English") nobility outside the Pale.

By the beginning of the eighteenth century, Irish, the first literate vernacular in Europe, had become, almost exclusively, the language of vagabond storytellers and musicians, hedge-school teachers, peasants, and spalpeens, its purview the cabins, cláchans, and crossroads of the countryside, the vast half-hidden world beneath the new Anglo-Irish colonial order, the territory of the 's lom, or slum. With the great scattering driven by the Famine, the insular, self-referential confines in which most Irish speakers existed was broken open. The language was carried by immigrants, navvies, miners, travelers, laborers, and domestics to the New World. (There was an earlier influx of largely Scots-Gaelic speakers whose settlements reached from Cape Breton and Newfoundland to the Carolinas. Their impact on regional dialects and slang was profound and, as Cassidy is the first to point out, deserves the full attention of linguistic scholars.)

Just as important as the sheer number of those who left during the Famine decade is where they went. A sizeable chunk descended on the burgeoning cities of one of the world's most rapidly industrializing societies at the very moment when railroads and telegraphs were revolutionizing the speed and impact of communications. Almost overnight, port cities such as New York, Boston, and New Orleans became home to large Irish communities, and newly emerging metropolises such as Chicago, San Francisco, and Kansas City weren't far behind.

The exact proportion of Famine immigrants monolingual in Irish or bilingual in Irish and English will never be known. Estimates of primary Irish speakers vary, running as high as thirty-five percent. In his masterfully written, deeply researched history of a single village's fate during the Famine, *The End of Hidden Ireland*, Robert Scally relates how large numbers of arrivees in Liverpool tried to pass as English speakers, knowing that "speaking Irish above a whisper outside the Irish wards instantly marked the emigrant to both the authorities and the swarms of predators." Though the precise numbers of Irish speakers will remain, at best, an educated guess, there's no doubt that the *breac Ghaeltacht*, or scattered Irish-speaking district, seeded itself in American cities, towns, and rural areas.

Sometimes these settlements were in mill towns such as Augusta, Maine, where Nathaniel Hawthorne recorded in his *Notebooks* sighting improvised cláchans, "the board-built and turf-buttressed hovels of these wild Irish, scattered about as if they had sprung up like mushrooms in the dells and gorges, and along the banks of the river"; or near Walden Pond, outside Salem, Massachusetts, where he came upon "a little hamlet of huts or shanties inhabited by Irish people who work upon the railroad . . . habitations, the very rudest, I should imagine, that civilized men ever made for themselves . . ." Other times, the language was embedded among the tenement dwellers of the Five Points, in New York City, and in dockside communities along the East and Hudson rivers. Wherever Irish was found, it had an effect, spicing people's everyday speech and percolating through mongrel networks of saloons, theaters, political clubhouses, union halls, and precinct houses, its spiel full of "pizzazz" (*píosa theas*—pronounced peesa hass—a bit of heat, excitement, passion).

The concentration of the Irish in the hub cities of America's industrial coming of age made the Irish prime participants in the often intertwined professions of politics, entertainment, sports (along with its less reputable sister, gambling), as well as a major part of the local criminal underworld (which was not infrequently an ally of the local political machine). Cut off from the main avenues of social advancement and power—the elite universities, Wall Street, the familial and fraternal networks of the Protestant upper classes—the Irish traveled the back streets and alleyways, becoming a formative ingredient in the swirling mix of a still inchoate national identity.

Irish was an everyday part of the immigrants' journey from mud-splattered outsiders to smooth-talking prototypes of urban cool, from the hard-fisted slugger (*slacaire*) of the Five Points to the streetwise ward heeler (*éilitheoir*) of the ubiquitous political clubhouses to the quintessential American con game, the scam (*'s cam*). The language was woven into the fabric of how they lived, labored, and relaxed. It melded into the musical productions of the prolific Edward Harrigan (whose plays were so popular that he had his own theater in which to house them), into the lingo of street gangs and the police forces created to control them, into hobo camps and circus trains, into folk songs of East and West, into "Paddy Works on the Erie" and the cowboy anthem "Woopie Ti Ti Yo," into the speakeasy shtick of Texas Guinan and the groundbreaking dramas of Eugene O'Neill.

As Ann Douglas points out in *Terrible Honesty*, her intriguing, often brilliant study of New York City in the 1920s, there was—and is—an underlying subversive dynamic to the American vernacular:

> The American language gained its distinctive character by its aware-
> ness of, and opposition to, correct British Standard English; white slang
> was played against conventional middle-class speak, and the Negro
> version of the language worked self-consciously against the white one.
> In both cases, the surprise came from the awareness of conventions
> being flouted.

The Irish-American vernacular was a ready-made alternative to "conventional middle-class Anglo-American speak." It provided a vocabulary that wasn't used in the classrooms or drawing rooms of the "respectable classes" but that reeked of the lower classes (or "the dangerous classes," as nineteenth-century social reformer Charles Loring Brace referred to slum dwellers in general and the Irish in particular).

The infusion of Irish-American vernacular into popular usage involved, as well, the usefulness of words, their quotidian and demotic ability to get a point across, to lubricate the conversation of the streets, which has always—and will always—value "snazz" (*snas*, polish, gloss) and speed over technological precision or highfalutin' airs. It's not an accident, I think, that slang words such as "lulu," "pizzazz," "bally-hoo"—Cassidy's list of Irish derivatives is long and enlightening—have an onomatopoeic resonance similar to that of Yiddish, which explains in part why the two together probably account for so much of American slang.

The evolution of Irish into American vernacular was a gradual vanishing act. The words became such familiar parts of everyday speech that many seemed simply to belong to the way Americans talked, natural ingredients of popular speech. Most were entered into dictionaries as "origin unknown," or received farfetched etymologies. In some measure, this reflected a growing paucity of native Irish speakers—a process accelerated by assimilation, economic mobility, and access to higher education. (Few, if any, of the Catholic universities or colleges in the U.S., the great majority founded in the wake of the Famine, had Irish-studies or Irish-language courses until very recently.)

Ignorance of Irish wasn't the sole culprit, however. There was also the active and aggressive "racial pride" of an immensely influential pan-Atlantic "Anglo-Saxonist" movement that fueled U.S. imperial expansion at the end of the nineteenth century, found widespread expression in the nativist-populist activities of the Klu Klux Klan, and helped drive the highbrow bio-racist paranoia of the eugenics movement. As seen by Anglo-Saxon supremacists, Irish was the tongue of grooms and hod carriers, a provincial vestige of a failed culture, a primitive artifact, and to credit it as influencing the language of America's predominantly Anglo-Saxon civilization was as preposterous as it was insulting.

Time and again, whether the oversight was caused by passive neglect or active disdain, Professor Cassidy wields Occam's razor (the theory that the simplest of competing explanations is always to be preferred to the most complex) to shred the frail guesses of dictionary makers and reveal a self-evident Irish root. Take, for example, good, solid slang words like "slugger," which Webster first finds in print in 1877 and traces to a Scandinavian root meaning "to walk sluggishly"; or "scam," "fluke," and "nincompoop," which are all listed as "origin unknown." Cassidy will have none of it. "Slugger," he points out, is almost a homonym for the Irish *slacaire*, "a mauler or bruiser." "Scam" fits the same pattern, sounding like a resonant echo of the Irish *'s cam*, "(it) is crooked, dishonest." "Fluke"? How about *fo-luach*, pronounced fu-look, Irish for "rare reward or occurrence." "Nincompoop"? The Irish is *naioidhean ar chuma búb*, pronounced neeyan [ar] cum boob, meaning "baby in the shape of a blubbering booby." Think this is all a lot of baloney? Then consider the Irish *béal ónna*, pronounced bael óna, meaning "foolish talk."

While the substance of Irish's lexical presence was ignored or forgotten, there has never been any question of Irish-Americans' impact on the American vernacular style. The rapid-fire, hardboiled, cynical, wise-guy banter that remains a defining characteristic of slangdom was perfected and popularized by a slew (from the Irish *slua*, a multitude) of great Irish-American character actors such as James Gleason (see his role as a Brooklyn detective in *Arsenic and Old Lace*); William Frawley (as a Tammany boss in *Miracle on 34th Street*); Brian Donlevy and William Demarest (together in Preston Sturges's, who was himself the son of an eccentric Canadian-Irish mother, *The Great McGinty*); Eddy Brophy (fittingly cast in his final film, *The Last Hurrah*, as "Ditto" Boland); and the nonpareil big city Irish-American tough guy sharpster, Jimmy Cagney, whose influence continues right down to today's Gangsta rappers. Like words themselves, the Irish-American vernacular style is in the very bloodstream of who we are as a people.

For me personally, the "secret knowledge" that Professor Cassidy exposes to public view has resolved some of my own ruminations over the argot of turn-of-the-century New York's underworld, which I encountered in researching my novel *Banished Children of Eve*. I suspected there was something going on under the always vivid, if often arcane slang but was at a loss to explain what. Thanks to Cassidy's work, I've come to grasp not just the words beneath the words but also to see more clearly than ever before that I wasn't as far removed from the Irish language as I once imagined.

In my own case, my mother's father had been born in Macroom, in County Cork, in the 1860s, which was an Irish-speaking area until the twentieth century. He said his prayers in Irish throughout his life, my mother informed me—a passing comment I filed away without much thought as to its significance. My father's maternal grandparents came to America during the Famine, in 1847, exactly a century before I was born. The urban *breac-Ghaeltachts* were still within living memory, a penumbra whose presence, even if we felt it, we weren't equipped to understand.

As kids in the Bronx, when we skedaddled or lollygagged or made a racket, we had no idea the descriptives we used were direct echoes of the Irish language. We didn't hear it in our speech. The Irish past was hidden from us. It was there, of course, a determining factor in how we worshipped, socialized, and worked, in the framework of our dreams and expectations. But we didn't know the Irish part of ourselves in any conscious way. As Irish-Americans, we put the stress on the second part of the identity, and while proudly acknowledging our Irish legacy, our eyes were trained on the future. The Irish language, we imagined, belonged exclusively to the old country and, like the place itself, was quaint, irrelevant; useless for making headway in the concrete and competitive precincts of urban America.

We weren't totally dumb, however, to the living elasticity of language, to its porousness and powers of infiltration. In the Bronx of the 1960s, we listened to and sometimes adopted the Spanish of the newly emergent Puerto Rican diaspora, referring to beer as *cerveza* and pretty girls as *muchachas*. Puerto Ricans, in turn, began to blend Spanish and English into a patois known as "Spanglish." Looking back, what's most notable for me isn't the pervasive existence of hybridity—the genetic, cultural, and linguistic mixing that is everywhere, part of the crossroads (and isn't that what America is, after all—a great global crossroads?)—but the widespread obliviousness to the inevitability of such mixing and, sillier and more dangerous, the fanatic's quest for an imaginary "purity" of race and tongue.

Cassidy's ground-shifting thesis should transform and enrich much of the scholarly discourse about multiculturalism and the dialectic that drives and defines American society. Words and concepts like "jazz," "poker," "square," "scam," "sucker," "slum," "brag," "knack," etc., are as central to American culture and history as the language itself. What will people make of Cassidy's strongly convincing argument that an Irish derivative—jazz—now identifies America's most powerful and original art form, a creative achievement rooted in the hearts, history, and souls of black folks? Will it help add to our recognition that, despite our differences, we Americans are hopelessly (and hopefully) entwined with one another, our histories, ancestries, stories, songs, dreams, and lives wrapped around each other like dual strands of DNA?

This revolutionary challenge to long-standing orthodoxies embedded in the dictionaries of Webster and the monumental Oxford English Dictionary of Charles Murray and his followers will undoubtedly lead to Cassidy being dismissed by some as heretic or dreamer. Great reappraisals, as Hubert Butler pointed out, are always threatening, especially to those who've helped build and maintain the status quo. But, as Nietzsche (a professional philologist, let's remember) once put it, what we need most times is not the courage of our convictions but the courage to question our convictions. The willingness to see the world afresh, to throw over old presumptions and consider new possibilities, to abandon routine and renew a sense of wonder, is as important to the scholar as the artist. Like the purloined letter in the short story by Poe (whose paternal ancestors were from County Cavan), the persistence of the Irish language was missed in part because it couldn't be comprehended through the narrow focus of conventional principles.

It is not just historians, I think, who come to grasp the proximity of the past, to pierce the illusion of the present's novelty, and perceive in our midst, in our loves, fears, and expectations, on our very tongues, what has gone before. Whether consciously or unconsciously, the further we move away in time from where we began, the more our journey seems—in the spectacularly inventive, polyglot vernacular of James Joyce—"a commodius vicus of recirculation," until we understand the extent to which today entails yesterday, and how much the future is mortgaged to the past. Eventually, perhaps, whether as individuals or a society, we must inevitably come upon our own purloined letters, truths that we failed to see, or successfully disregarded, but that were always there, at the center of who we are.

The explorations that Cassidy undertakes in *The Secret Language of the Crossroad* have a distinctly personal element, about which he is forthright and upfront. He starts with his Irish-American family and New York-Irish upbringing. But in good American fashion, and following in the footsteps of Walt Whitman, who lived not too far from Cassidy's ancestors in Brooklyn's dockside Irishtown, Cassidy celebrates more than the self or a single family and embraces an experience far wider than Irish or Irish-American, penetrating to the dynamic of language-making itself, the most uniquely human of all our species' endeavors.

What Cassidy has done is nothing short of the miraculous: he has brought back to life that which was considered dead and settled. Rollover, Webster and Murray! In place of time-worn proprieties and stale assumptions, Cassidy gives us heat, passion, and excitement of a past rediscovered and made new. And ain't that the real jazz!

A Famine Remembrance

(Written as a prose introduction to composer Patrick Cassidy's "A Famine Remembrance Symphony," and performed at St. Patrick's Cathedral in March 1997, this piece was read by Angelica Huston. In 1999, it was read by Aidan Quinn at the White House St. Patrick's Day Celebration, at which Senator George Mitchell was presented with the Presidential Medal of Freedom. A verse from it is now inscribed on Philadelphia's Famine Memorial Statue.)

Pest, parasite, potato destroyer, invisible, and invincible,
    the fungus arrived in Ireland in the late summer of 1845.
It struck across Europe, the same sudden, unstoppable invasion
    everywhere . . .
    Infection, corruption, devastation.
But Ireland was a special case . . .
    a place where the potato was neither staple nor supplement, but
    sustenance: *Life.*
Women in the fields, amid the blasted, ruined crops, covered their heads,
    cried, mingled anguish with their pleas, beseeched of God, the
    government, the landlord . . .
    Words from the ancient Hebrew psalms were prayed in Irish, English,
    Latin: *O Lord God of Hosts, hear our prayer. O God of Jacob, deliver us*
    from famine.

The lords temporal in London heard.

Her Majesty's government took up once again the perpetual nuisance of Ireland, a province united by conquest and law to the kingdom.

In theory, Ireland was an integral part of Great Britain . . .

In theory, its counties and their subjects were as precious to the Crown as the souls in English shires.

Measures were taken.

American corn . . . Public works . . . Soup . . .

A variety of attempts in the face of spreading, insistent starvation, until fatigue and frustration set in, until the servants of the iron laws of economics laid bare the logic of market forces: *Let nature take its course, we cannot interfere.*

The poor, they said, are the cause of their own misery, let them bear the consequences and learn to be ambitious.

The fault is not in the stars, or in the laws, but in the people's wild, wastrel ways, in the guile and indolence of Irish beggardom.

The government turned away, but not before it ensured that the grinding of the wheel wouldn't go unoiled, that as well as starvation, eviction would help rid Ireland of its wretched burden of subtenants whose very existence, it was said, blocked the path to progress.

These things happened.

Let history judge the simplicity or complexity of those events, the complicity of those responsible.

The rest is indescribable.

There is no lone word, or marriage of them, to capture the totality of what occurred, of those who perished, some from hunger, most from the slow withering it inflicted: fever, diarrhea, exhaustion.

The famine was an end . . .

To lives . . . to families . . . to entire villages . . . to young and old alike . . . their suffering and death made bearable for us in the sanitation of numbers, in one statistic, faceless, nameless, unsexed: *at least a million dead.*

The famine was an exodus . . .

A wound that would not clot.

For everyone who could beg or borrow the fare, for those assisted by their landlords, there was emigration, escape, the descent into Liverpool, the crossing in the crammed, slop-ridden holds of coffin ships, death at sea,

on land, in fever hospitals and quarantine stations. Two million people,
a quarter of the Irish people, left in the space of ten years.

The famine was an arrival.

The hordes of fleeing exiles set the watchdogs to barking. The reception the
newly landed found was often much the same as offered tribes of
strangers before and since . . . *There are too many of them . . . They are
loyal to another sovereign . . . They worship foreign gods . . .*

In a phrase, *No Irish Need Apply.*

The hunger ended.

But it never went away.

It was there in the Fenian war cry, *Remember Skibbereen!*

There in silent memories; a shadow, unnamed but unforgotten, intact from
one generation to the next, a sadness, a longing, an intimation of shame,
a passion for respectability, a hunger for security, for the assurances of
church and state that such a fate would never come again.

The time to take away the silence has come, in ceremony, ritual, art, music,
scholarship, to honor the dead, to recount, to commemorate, to mourn
what was lost—openly . . . to celebrate what survives—without apology
or fear.

We have it in our power not only to remember what took place, but to relive it . . .

To find in the immigrants, in the poor, in the hungry and the lost, not a different race . . .

but the starving, desperate Irish . . . the faces and voices of our ancestors . . .
An image of ourselves.

CONCLUSION

Irish America at the Millennium: How the Irish Stayed Irish

ⓢⓖ

> We cannot help living in history. We can only fail to
> be aware of it. If we are to meet, endure and tran-
> scend the trials and defeats of the future for trials
> and defeats there are certain to be—it can only be
> from a point of view which, seeing the future as part
> of the sweep of history, enables us to establish our
> place in that immense procession in which is incor-
> porated whatever hope humankind may have.
>
> —ROBERT HEILBRONER, *The Future of History*

THE UNIQUE AMERICAN SUBCULTURE that the Irish created in
the wake of the Famine—a culture deeply skeptical about
WASP institutions and pretensions, and suspicious and
resentful of the mainline tradition of Protestant moral reform and economic self-interest—is dead and gone. It lingers in pockets, for sure,
and survives in the formative experiences of pre-Vatican II Irish-
Catholic fossils like myself. But it's doomed as the dodo and no amount
of humpty-dumpty yearning for the way things were—or the way some
like to imagine they were—will bring it back.

274

Today, it's almost impossible to recapture how distinct and apart that world was, how foreign Anglo-Protestant America seemed, how certain we were of our distinct identity and special destiny. We were a parochial people, literally and figuratively. As Alice McDermott has capured so artfully and accurately in her novels, though dispersed across an immense, often bewildering cityscape, the Irish were tied together by the Church, which made the urban world seem "small, parish-sized, and logical." Our basic compass was the parish we were from. That's how we identified ourselves: *I'm from St. Raymond's* or *St. Helena's* or *Sacred Heart* or *St. Nicholas of Tolentine.* And we were parochial in the sense of being intellectually narrow-minded and constricted.

That narrow-mindedness has often been commented on, and often, I think, in a wrongheaded way. The adults I knew were avid devourers of books. They enjoyed the theater. They reveled in the pace and variety of urban life, a pace and variety that the Irish had in fact helped to create. They held high educational ambitions for their children. Almost everyone I knew was wildly addicted to movies, and many of us availed ourselves of the Legion of Decency's rating system, where the C, or "condemned," list conveniently underlined what was *really* worth seeing.

The fundamental narrow-mindedness we suffered from wasn't so much in our attitude to the world as to ourselves. We wanted—we demanded—to be seen in one light and one light only. I remember seeing *The Bells of St. Mary's* (or was it *Going My Way?* The two are impossibly blended in my head into a single story.) on television around the same time my aunt took me to one of those periodic theatrical re-releases of *The Wizard of Oz.* Although I sensed it at that moment, it would be some time before I could articulate the feeling that the relationship between the parish presided over by Monsignor Barry Fitzgerald and his crooning curate Father Bing Crosby and the real-life parish I lived in was the *reverse* of what existed between the Emerald City and Dorothy's Kansas.

The ecclesiastical Oz of the Reverends Fitzgerald and Crosby was populated with characters who bore some resemblance to people I knew firsthand. But on screen, the ironic, tough-minded, combative, argumentative, believing, suspicious, hard-drinking, backbiting, funny, obnoxiously profane, relentlessly sceptical, gloriously complicated people I knew—people as contradictory as any Cowardly Lion and as manipulative as the Wizard himself—became as tame and predictable as Auntie Em's Kansas farmhands.

This, of course, was the *nihil-obstat* version that everyone in the parish applauded. All the adults I knew loved *The Bells of St. Mary's,* even the ones who never stopped bad-mouthing the clergy and couldn't say enough bad things about the licking they'd taken in parochial schools. This was how we wanted the world to see us, America's best-behaved ethnic group, a big-screen refutation of the lies once spread by nativists. The stage Irishman was okay as long as he looked and acted like Bing Crosby and, hell, if the stage Irishwoman wasn't only a nun, but a nun played by Ingrid Bergman with a Swedish accent, well, *Hooray for Hollywood.*

The Irish in America—at least the Irish I grew up with—were still in the defensive crouch they'd arrived in during the Famine, still sensitive to the distrust and dislike of *real* America, to the suspicions about our loyalty and supposed proclivity to raucous misbehavior. We were forever reminding ourselves—and the rest of America—of how many Irish fought with Washington, how many died at Antietam, and how many won the Congressional Medal of Honor, a litany of self-justification that implicitly accepted that it wasn't enough we'd been here for over a century.

Even J.F.K.'s election as president didn't entirely settle the matter. Writing in 1965, in his one-volume *Oxford History of the American People,* Samuel Eliot Morison could dismiss the Famine Irish as having added, quote, "surprisingly little to American economic life, and almost nothing to American intellectual life." The good news, I suppose, is that Morison used the word "surprisingly." The bad news: As far as he was concerned, the arrival of the Catholic Irish was pretty much the high point of the their role in America. From there, it was backward and downward to Tammany Hall and the corruption of American urban politics.

It is in this light that I was particularly intrigued to read Noel Ignatiev's *How the Irish Became White.* Ignatiev's bipolar interpretation of American history turns the long journey of the Irish from rural servitude and poverty into a tragic betrayal of their true selves. Like the versions of history it is meant to replace—both the left-wing mythologizing of working-class solidarity and the old-style canonization of an America free of ethnic differences—this version of history ignores the particularity of the Irish experience, the ways in which the Irish struggled to adopt a new identity while holding fast to the old. Yes, the Irish still fail. In the eyes of some the Irish will *always* fail. But now they fail upwards. It's not that they weren't American enough, as the nativists alleged, but too American, immigrant Esaus who traded their birthright of Irish resistance to oppression for the American stew of material success.

If the question of Irish acceptance were simply a passage from one color to another, the Christian, English-speaking, white Irish should have rapidly blended into America's Anglo-Saxon woodwork. That they didn't is a testament to both the external prejudices they faced and the internal dynamics of their own history. To suppose, for example, as Ignatiev seems to, that there was a moment when the Irish might have chosen to join with the Republican Abolitionists to create an egalitarian America is to imagine that the Republicans both sought such a result and offered a political program for achieving it.

In fact, not only did a significant segment of the Abolitionist community harbor a dislike for Catholics in general and the Irish in particular, but the whole theory of "free labor," which was central to the Republican Party, was an attack on the ability of the working class to organize and make collective demands on factory owners and industrialists. An Abolitionist, such as Thaddeus Stevens, noble and far-seeing in his vision for freed slaves, was an ally of the coal mine owners in Pennsylvania and an opponent of Irish mine workers. For the Irish, the bulk of whom had arrived as a result of the Great Famine—the defining event in modern Irish history on both sides of the Atlantic, and one which Ignatiev barely mentions—the Republican theory of free labor could only have reeked of the free-market orthodoxies that had allowed the British government to abandon relief efforts while the Irish starved.

The widespread distrust of Irish Catholics as intractable foreigners, unable or unwilling to give their full loyalties to America, remained strong for a very long time. It was a significant factor in the post-World War I revival of the Ku Klux Klan—a revival fueled by anti-Catholicism—and was heralded by the burning crosses that greeted Al Smith during the 1928 presidential campaign. In part, along with good old-fashioned anti-Catholicism, it also derived from Irish involvement in the politics of their own homeland. President Wilson was hardly alone in seeing the Irish as afflicted with a "hyphenated" loyalty that detracted from their "Americanness."

Ignatiev has no sense of the post-Famine condition of the Irish in Ireland or America—a defensiveness forged and sharpened in their struggle to avoid the disintegration that had almost overwhelmed them. Their interest was in collective survival, not in self-annihilation through assimilation. He either doesn't see or chooses to disregard the continuities between the Irish at home and those in America. For instance, he characterizes the infamous New York City Draft Riots of 1863 as:

> . . . an insurrection against the government that was waging the war, at a moment when the forces of the enemy were a hundred-odd miles from the City. The number of Irish who took part in the riots was not less than the number who wore the blue uniform. . . . The Irish had two aims in the war: to establish their claim to citizenship, and to define the sort of republic they would be citizens of. Whether in the Army or on the barricades, they took up arms for the White Republic, and their place in it.

Putting aside the highly questionable assertion that the number of Irish rioters equaled the number in the Union army (as well as the implied equivalency between a week's frenzy and four years of service in some of the bloodiest battles of the war), Ignatiev misses what to many Irish was the greatest war aim of all: not defending the White Republic, but seeing to it that the Fenians succeeded in establishing an Irish Republic.

The generation of Irish immigrants that fought in the Civil War was by and large made up of those who had come during or immediately after the Famine, and this colored much of their conduct.

Thousands of them enrolled in the Fenian movement. After the war, many would travel back to Ireland to participate in a planned uprising. Two thousand veterans made their way to Canada for an attempt at seizing that British possession. Though both efforts were unsuccessful, they were indicative of a passion and commitment widespread in Irish communities.

Peter Welsh, a color sergeant with the Irish Brigade who died of wounds incurred at the battle of Spotsylvania, expressed a widely held hope among his immigrant comrades when he wrote to his wife, "When we are fighting for America we are fighting in the interests of Irland [sic], striking a double blow, cutting with a two edged sword . . . striking a blow at Irland's enemy and oppressor . . ."

The Draft Riots themselves began not as Ignatiev has it—"at a moment when the military forces of the enemy were a hundred-odd miles from the City"—but a full ten days after Gettysburg, when Lee was well on his way to making his escape to Virginia. Surely, part of the significance of the Riots' start on July 13, 1863 is the Irish context of that date, which Ignatiev as well as other historians ignore. The draft began on Saturday, July 11, and the next day Sunday July, 12, was Orangemen's Day, which remains to this day a volatile celebration of Catholic subjection to Protestant rule. After a day of allowing the masses to stew in the heat and tribal memories of July 12, the authorities resumed the draft on July 13.

The missing significance of July 12 is indicative, I think, of the ways in which Ignatiev's thesis ignores the ambivalent status of the Irish and their position in a nation every bit as self-consciously Protestant as white. July 12 would be the flashpoint for two more bloody riots on the streets of New York, in 1870 and 1871. On the latter occasion, a panicked militia unit escorting an Orange parade through a Catholic neighborhood opened fire, killing and wounding scores in the single bloodiest incident in the city's history until September 11, 2001.

The overriding interest of the Irish was in their own survival. There is no arguing that. But to read their struggle as a smooth, self-propelled passage into whiteness is to simplify to the point of distortion, substituting a morality tale for the nitty-gritty of real history. If the Irish were entitled to "the wages of whiteness," then often they were underpaid. Irish workers were forced to struggle hard against industrialists and bosses, their putative white brothers, to make enough to survive. In the case of the Molly Maguires, the penalty for their militancy constituted a judicial lynching at the hands of their white employers.

Frank McCourt has written, half in jest (but not wholly), that when the Irish came to America, they fought with two groups: blacks and whites. The truth is, the Irish stayed on that middle ground for some time, antagonistic to black workers—whom they suspected white bosses and employers would use to undercut the wages of Irish workers—but regarded by white Protestants with disdain and distrust. Given the general dislike of Irish Catholics throughout large parts of America, north and south, it's an interesting but unanswerable question whether African Americans were at all interested in joining forces with the Irish. They might well have perceived such an association would do them more harm than good.

As I see it, if there is any central theme in the story of the Irish in America, it is not how they became white, but how they stayed Irish: how an immigrant group already under punishing cultural and economic pressures, reeling in the wake of the worst catastrophe in Western Europe in the nineteenth century, and plunged into the fastest industrializing society in the world, regrouped as quickly as it did; built its own far-flung network of charitable and educational institutions; preserved its own identity; and had a profound influence on the future of both the country it left and the one it came to. It was done imperfectly, for sure, and was marred by sins and stupidity, by mistakes and missed opportunities, but the wonder is that it was done at all.

In general, I'm always suspicious about the search for single themes and unified theories that provide easy explanations for human behavior. As the historian Barbara Fields has written in an essay entitled "Ideology and Race in American History:"

> Each new stage in the unfolding of the historical process offers a new
> vantage point from which to seek out those moments of decision in the

past that have prepared the way for the latest (provisional) outcome. It is the circumstances under which men and women made those decisions that ought to concern historians, not the quest for a central theme that will permit us to deduce the decisions without troubling ourselves over the circumstances.

In the specific case of Irish-Americans, the notion of definitively deciphering their history through the lone perspective of race at least provides the basis for a polar-opposite interpretation to the one enshrined in *The Bells of St. Mary's*. Next door to the idyllic Never Never Land of cinematic fantasy, there is now the mirror-image community of uniformly abusive nuns, ogrelike priests, parish after parish of solidly united bigots determined to get what they can for themselves by becoming active collaborators and supporters of the American system of racial exclusion and exploitation.

What's mostly lacking, I feel, is the saving grace that art can bring to the saga of any family or ethnic group or country, to unearthing the rich contradictions of Irish America, to delineating the bewildering, destructive, exhilarating journey between what were once not so much different cultures as different universes, to exposing the levels of struggle and failure, self-doubt and self-hatred, penetrating wit and indelible grievance, paralyzing depression, and deep, resonant laughter.

I don't want to sound as though I'm entirely dismissing the role of history in this process of self-examination and reclamation. At its best, history can penetrate generalities and statistics to touch the lives of those now dead, to give us a sense of the density and intensity of every human life, and even to allow the poor and powerless a dignity that they were denied in their own lifetimes.

Recently, I stumbled across a small jewel of historical detective work that recounts the history of a case tried in the New York Surrogate's Court in 1932. *The Recluse of Herald Square*, written by Joseph Cox, presents the story of Mrs. Ida Mayfield Wood who, along with her sister, spent a quarter of a century hiding in a hotel room. When her sister died and the police were called, they discovered that amid the clutter and debris of her room, Mrs. Wood had nearly a million dollars in cash and bonds. This was at the bottom of the worst depression in

American history. As well as her hidden treasure, Mrs. Wood had another secret, one that would take dozens of lawyers, investigators, and would-be heirs to unravel. Without entirely ruining the mystery for those who might want to read the book, I'll simply point out that Mrs. Wood's secret casts a good deal of light on the status of the Irish in mid-nineteenth-century America and on a desire for "passing" that wasn't restricted to racial disguise.

As a lapsed historian, however, I don't feel qualified to stand in public and pass judgment on the practices of a priesthood of which I'm no longer part. Instead, I continue to enjoy the happy, carefree life of the apostate, unburdened of a historian's scrupulosity, willingly giving in to every temptation to speculate and invent, to avoid the virtuous work of analysis and indulge in the pleasures of anecdote. For instance, I remember my father—a remarkable, difficult, usually inaccessible man—on the triumphal night John Kennedy was elected president, the same night my father was elected to the State Supreme Court, the fourteenth and last time he ran for office. This grandson of Famine emigrants, well-oiled and declaiming to the swaying crowd in our Bronx living room, "Well, now, Mr. Nixon, you can kiss our royal Irish ass!"

"Beautiful lofty things," in Yeats's words, *"a thing never known again."*

In fiction Elizabeth Cullinan has captured that world, I think, as have Alice McDermott and William Kennedy. Mostly, it remains enshrouded and unrevealed, pretty much a peripheral concern (at best) in the dominant form of American cultural self-examination—the movies. A story central to the making of the American identity, it has yet to be explicated and celebrated as fully as it should be. Perhaps it will never be.

Yes, then, Irish America is rich, successful, influential—fat and happy with its lists of successful entrepreneurs and zillionaires. We're headed somewhere, that's for sure. The momentum of the journey is increasingly weighted toward the American part of the Irish-American equation, which is why we came here in the first place. Anyone who has the courage to predict where it will end has more courage than I do—or less fear of being exposed as an idiot. But to paraphrase

Captain Kirk, "as we boldly go where no Irishman or woman has ever gone before," I hope, as Sydney Carton hoped, "it is a far, far better place than we have ever gone before."

Let me suggest one possibility.

A while ago, the *New York Times Sunday Magazine* ran a double page of photographs of American girls and boys whose multi-ethnic, multi-racial background defied easy characterization—a level of mongrelization that is continuing to gather steam, to the consternation of racial purists of various persuasions. The most common identity shared in this depiction of ethnic fusion, which may one day rise to the level of a racial meltdown, was Irish. Perhaps, then, the history of Irish-Americans that will be written at the end of the twenty-first century will be entitled *How the Irish Became Brown*. What a wonderful prospect! What a welcomed fate! The Irish as the common denominator of a new American construct, the Irish as gravediggers for that last and most enduring of all nineteenth-century superstitions—scientific racism.

Whatever the future may hold, wherever it may take us, we can bring along only what we possess, and if we don't possess our past, if instead of a true history and a significant literature, we bring along only trivia, empty myths and a handful of stories, or—worst of all—the latest intellectually fashionable versions of ourselves, we will offer those to come after us nothing of lasting consequence.

A long time ago, in a bar called The Bells of Hell, while I was in the embryonic phase of thinking about writing a novel about the Famine Irish in New York and was unsure whether there was a story worth telling—and where better to worry over an unborn novel than in a place named The Bells of Hell?—I heard the late Kevin Sullivan— ex-Jesuit, scholar of Irish literature, and raconteur—recite Paddy Kavanagh's poem "Epic."

It stayed with me across the years. It sustained me then, and still does. I've always found in it the anti-toxin to the Irish-American original sin of self-doubt. The poem goes like this:

> I have lived in important places, times
> When great events were decided, who owned
> That half a rood of rock, a no-man's land

Surrounded by our pitchfork-armed claims.
I heard the Duffeys shouting "Damn your soul"
And old McCabe stripped to the waist, seen
Step the plot defying blue cast-steel—
"Here is the march along these iron stones."
That was the year of the Munich bother. Which
Was more important? I inclined
To lose my faith in Ballyrush and Gortin
Till Homer's ghost came home whispering to my mind.
He said: I made the Iliad from such
A local row. Gods make their own importance.

Today, Irish America is powerful enough and wealthy enough to decide for itself where it's headed and what it will take on the journey. Wherever we may end up, suburbs or city, the south end of Jersey or the outer end of the galaxy, it is we the living who will choose what will be recorded, remembered, and redeemed from silence and oblivion by scholarship and art.

Gods make their own importance.